THE CHURCH YEAR IN PRAYER

THE CHURCH YEAR IN PRAYER

Rev. Jerome M. Neufelder

Our Sunday Visitor, Inc.
Huntington, Indiana 46750

Nihil Obstat:
Rev. Msgr. Charles J. Koch, S.T.L., J.C.L.
Censor Deputatus

Imprimatur:
✝Francis R. Shea, D.D.
Bishop of Evansville
November 5, 1984

The Nihil Obstat and Imprimatur are official declarations that a book or pamphlet is free of doctrinal or moral error. No implication is contained therein that those who have granted the Nihil Obstat or Imprimatur agree with the contents, opinions or statements expressed.

Library of Congress Catalogue No.: 84-62162
ISBN: 0-87973-729-8

Cover design by James E. McIlrath

Printed in the United States of America

729

Dedicated to my large and loving family,
and to Sister M. Acquin Verkamp, O.S.B.,
whose assistance made this book possible.

ACKNOWLEDGMENTS

The editor wishes to acknowledge his debt to the following original publishers or their successors, book or periodical, and/or copyright holders, for brief excerpts quoted from the works and authors cited below: especially to the Division of Christian Education of the National Council of Churches of Christ in the U.S.A. for excerpts from the Revised Standard Version of the Bible (Catholic Edition), used throughout this book; then to AMS Press, Inc., New York, for *The Book of the Spiritual Life* by Lady Emilia Dilke; Abingdon Press, Nashville, for *Instruction on Prayer* by Wilhelm Bossuet, *Prayer* by George A. Buttrick, *The Meaning of Prayer* by Harry Emerson Fosdick and *Growing in the Life of Prayer* by Harold Wiley Freer; Abingdon-Cokesbury Books for *Prayer and the Common Life* by Georgia Harkness and *Making Prayer Real* by Lynn James Radcliffe; Alba Books, Canfield, O., for *The Rediscovery of Prayer* by Bernard Bro; Alba House, Div. of the Society of St. Paul, Staten Island, N.Y., for *Response in Christ* by Edward Carter and *Loving Awareness of God's Presence* by Fabio Giardini; F. Alcan, Paris, for *The Problem of Prayer* by Fernand Menagoz; Associated Newspapers Ltd., London, for writings of Monica Furlong in the *London Daily Mail*; Association Press, New York, for *Spiritual Renewal Through Personal Groups* by John L. Casteel; Augsburg Publishing House, Minneapolis, for *The Christian Life* by Ole Hallesby; Ave Maria Press, Notre Dame, Ind., for *The Gospel Without Compromise* and *Poustinia* by Catherine de Hueck Doherty, *Opening to God* by Thomas H. Green, *Prayer of the Heart* by George A. Maloney and *Out of Solitude* by Henri J.M. Nouwen; Ayer Press, New York, for *The Religious Way* by Gregory Vlastos; Verlag C.H. Beck, Munich, for *Twelve Addresses on the Christian Religion* by Karl Girgensohn; William Blackwood & Sons Ltd., London, for *The Expositor* by James Morrison; Burns, Oates, Washbourne & Co. Ltd., London, for *The Craft of Prayer* by Vincent McNabb, *Spiritual Life and Prayer* by Madame Cécile J. Bruyère, *World Intangible* by Robert H.J. Steuart and *The Soul and the Spiritual Life* by Anscar Vonier; Carmel Monastery, Bettendorf, Iowa, for *The Gift of Oneself* by Joseph Schryvers; Carter Publisher, New York, for *Mount of Olives* by James Hamilton; *Chicago Studies,* Chicago, for "Forms of Prayer in Christian Spirituality" by Agnes Cunningham; Christian Literature Crusade, Port Washington, Pa., for *Knocking at God's Door* by Oswald Chambers; James Clarke & Co. Ltd., Cambridge-London, for *Creative Prayer* by Emily Herman; and *Intelligent Prayer* by Lewis Maclachlan; William Collins Sons & Co. Ltd., Glasgow-London, for *The Practice of Prayer* by George Appleton, *Making Prayer Real* by Nels Ferre and *Christianity Close to Life* by Rita Snowdon; Costello Publishing Co. Inc.,, Northport, N.Y., for *Vatican Council II: The Conciliar and Post Concilar Documents,* edited by Rev. Austin Flannery, O.P.; Crossroad / Continuum Books, New York, for *Christian Prayer* by Ladislaus Boros, *Prayer for Pilgrims* by Sheila Cassidy, *The Holy and the Good* by Bernard Häring and *Our Faith* by Max Thurian; Dacre Press, London, for *Straight Course to God* by Augustine Morris; Darton, Longman & Todd Ltd., London, for *An Experience of Prayer* by Kevin Maguire; Dell Publishing Co., New York, for *Systematic Theology* by Paul Tillich; Editions Desclée et Cie., Paris, for *The Spiritual Life* by Adolphe Tanquerey, S.S; Dimension Books, Denville, N.J., for *Guidelines for Mystical Prayer* by Ruth Burrows, *Prayer Is a Hunger* by Edward Farrell, *The Journey Homeward* by Susan Muto and *The Prayer of the Presence of God* by Dom Augustin Guillerand; Doubleday & Co., New York, for *Contemplation in a World of Action* (Image) and *Thoughts in Solitude* (Image) by Thomas Merton, *Centering Prayer* by Basil Pennington and *The Christ Is Alive* (Image) by Michel Quoist; E.P. Dutton & Co., Inc., New York, for *The Life of Prayer* by Friederich von Hügel and *Concerning the Inner Life* by Evelyn Underhill; Editions du Temps Présents, Paris, for

Joy of the Cross by Madeleine Delbrel; Folcroft Library Editions, Folcroft, Pa., for *Prayer and Poetry* by Henri Brémond and *On the Philosophy of Religion* by Auguste Sabatier; Fortress Press, Philadelphia, for *On Prayer* by Gerhard Ebeling, *The Community of the Christian With God* by Wilhelm Herrmann and *Prayer* by Olive Wyon; Franciscan Herald Press, Chicago, for *Teach Us to Pray* by André Louf; Franciscan Printery for *Prayer Without Headaches* by Florence Wedge; M.H. Gill & Son, Dublin, for *The Ways of Mental Prayer* by Vitalis Lehodey; Michael Glazier, Inc., Wilmington, Del., for *Challenges in Prayer* by Basil Pennington; Guild Press, New York, for *Approach to Prayer* by Hubert Van Zeller; Harcourt Brace Jovanovich, Inc., New York, for *Letters to Malcolm* and *The World's Last Night* by C.S. Lewis and *Deep Is the Hunger* by Howard Thurman; Harper & Row Publishers, Inc., New York, for *The Realm of the Spirit* by Nicholas Berdyaev, *The Practice of Prayer* by Albert D. Belden, *The Struggle of Prayer* by Donald G. Bloesch, *Way of the Ascetics* by Tito Coliander, *A Preface to Prayer* by Gerald Heard, *Understanding Prayer* by Gerald N. Jackson, *Strength to Love* by Martin Luther King, *True Prayer* by Kenneth Leech, *Paths in Spirituality* by John MacQuarrie, *Dimensions of Prayer* by Douglas Steere, *The Divine Milieu* by Pierre Teilhard de Chardin, *Dynamics of Faith* by Paul Tillich and *Waiting on God* by Simone Weil; Hawthorn Books, Inc., New York, for *Prayer* by Jean Daujat; Helicon Press, Baltimore, for *Prayer: An Adventure in Living* by B.C. Butler, *Spiritual Letters* by Dom Columba Marmion, *Theological Investigations* by Karl Rahner, *Living Today for God* by Roger Schutz and *Letters to the Little Brothers* by René Voillaume; B. Herder Book Co., St. Louis, Mo., for *Stages in Prayer* by Juan Arintero, *Christian Perfection and Contemplation* by Reginald Garrigou-Lagrange, *Christian Prayer* by Franz N. Moschner, *The Crown of Life* by Conrad Pepler and *More Joy* by Paul Wilhelm von Keppler; Herder and Herder, New York, for *The Prayer of All Things* by Pierre Charles and *Psychological Dynamics and Religious Living* by Charles A. Curran; Hodder & Stoughton Ltd., London, for *Prayer: A New Encounter* by Martin

Thornton and *The Reality of the Religious Life* by Henry Bett; Holt, Rinehart & Winston Co., New York, for *Psychology: Briefer Course* by William James; Houghton Mifflin Co., Boston, for *The Essence of Religion* by Borden Parker Bowne; Independent Press, London, for *The Soul of Prayer* by P.T. Forsythe; P.J. Kenedy & Sons, New York, for *The Golden String* by Bede Griffiths, *Notes on the Lord's Prayer* by Raïssa Maritain and *The Practice of Mental Prayer* by René de Maumigny, S.J.; Lindsey Press, London, for *Prayer and Experience* by S.J. Mellone; The Liturgical Press, Collegeville, Minn., for *The Pilgrim Contemplative* by Herbert F. Smith; Longmans, Green & Co., New York, for *Lord, Teach Us to Pray* by Paul Claudel, *The Nature of Belief* by Martin C. D'Arcy, *In Defense of Prayer* by E.J. Bicknell, *The Catechism Today* by G. Ashton Oldham and *Letters* by Janet Erskine Stuart; Lutheran Publishing Society, Philadelphia, for *The Throne of Grace* by Mosheim Rhodes; Macmillan Publishing Co., Inc., New York, for *The Cost of Discipleship* by Dietrich Bonhoeffer, *The Elements of the Spiritual Life* by F.P. Harton, *Pathways to the Reality of God* by Rufus Jones and *The Issues of Life* by Henry N. Wiemann; José Morales, New York, for *Spiritual Writings* by Mother Mary St. Peter; Morehouse-Gorham Co., New York, for *Recipes for Happiness* by William Purcell and *Prayer* by Dr. Alexis Carrel; A.R. Mowbray & Co., Ltd., Oxford-London, for *Spiritual Writings* by Archimandrite Sophroney; New Directions Publishing Corp., New York, for *New Seeds of Contemplation* by Thomas Merton; Newman Bookshop, Westminster, Md., for *Conferences* by Desiré Joseph Mercier; Orbis Books, Maryknoll, N.Y., for *Letters from the Desert* by Carlo Carretto, *Prayer at the Heart of Life* by Pierre-Yves Emery and *Letters* by Charles de Foucauld; Oxford University Press, Oxford-London, for *Prayer* by Friedrich Heiler and *The Use of Praying* by J. Neville Ward; Pantheon Books, New York, for *Prayer in Practice* by Romano Guardini; Paulist Press, New York-Ramsey, N.J., for *Courage to Pray* by Anthony Bloom, *Teach Us How to Pray* by Louis Evely, *Solitude and Sacrament* by Katherine M. Dyckman and L. Patrick Carroll, *The Experience of Praying* by Sean Caulfield,

Spiritual Letters by Mother Maria Gysi, *Searching for God* by Basil Cardinal Hume, *The Other Side of Silence* by Morton Kelsey, *A Primer of Prayer* by Joseph McSorley, and *On Prayer* by Karl Rahner; Penguin Publishing Co. Ltd., London, for *Prayer and Meditation* by F.C. Happold; George A. Pflaum, Publisher, Inc., Dayton, O., for *Prayer from Where You Are* by James Carroll; Pilgrim Press, New York, for *Teach Us to Pray* by Charles F. Whiston; Prentice-Hall, Inc., Englewood Cliffs, N.J., for *Hidden Power for Human Problems* by Frederick W. Bailes; Fleming H. Revell Co., Old Tappan, N.J., for *The Essentials of Prayer* by E.M. Bounds and *Practicing His Presence* by Frank C. Laubach; S.P.C.K., London, for *Life and Fire of Love* by Herbert M. Waddams and *The Venture of Prayer* by Hubert Northcott; St. Bede's Publications, Los Angeles, for *The Life of Prayer* by Mary Clare Vincent; Sands & Co., New York, for *Christ the Life of the Soul* by Dom Columba Marmion; Verlag Ferdinand Schöningh, Paderborn, for *Christian Asceticism* by Francis X. Mutz; Charles Scribner's Sons, New York, for *A Diary of Private Prayer* by John Baillie and *Doctrine of Christian Prayer* by James Hastings; Servant Publications, Ann Arbor, Mich., for *Prayer: Our Journey Home* by Sister Maria Boulding; Sheed & Ward Ltd., London, for *Spiritual Letters* by John Chapman, *Spiritual Writings* by Léonce de Grandmaison, *Personal Letters* by Caryll Houselander, *Progress Through Mental Prayer* by Edward Leen, *Prayer and Intelligence* by Jacques Maritain, *God's Encounter with Man* by Maurice Nedoncelle, S.J., *The Roads of Prayer* by Kornelis H. Miskotte, *Spiritual Letters* by Albert Peyriguère, *A Map of Life* by Frank Sheed, *Diversity in Holiness* by Robert H.J. Steuart, *The Mass and the Life of Prayer* by Anthony Thorold and *Prayer* by Hans Urs von Balthasar; Sunday School Times Co., Philadelphia, for *Effective Praying* by Henry W. Frost; Unity Books, Lee's Summit, Mo., for *Prayer: The Master Key* by James D. Freeman; Upper Room, Nashville, Tenn., for *An Autobiography of Prayer* by Albert Edward Day and *Taste and See* by William O. Paulsell; Westminster Press, Philadelphia, for *Prayer According to the Catechism of the Reformation* by Karl Barth, *Man the Choicemaker* by Elizabeth B. Howes, *Prayer* by Henry Le Saux, O.S.B., and *Honest to God* by John A.T. Robinson; Winston-Seabury Press, Minneapolis, for *The Wonder of Prayer* by Shelton H. Bishop, *Hidden in Plain Sight* by Avery Brooke, *Prayer and Modern Man* by Jacques Ellul, *History of Christian Spirituality* by Urban T. Holmes, *The Concept of Prayer* by D.Z. Phillips, *Rediscovering Prayer* by John Yungblut, *Way of a Pilgrim* (anonymous) and *Praying* by Robert Faricy; and Yale University Press, New Haven, Conn., for *The Meaning of God in Human Experience* by W. E. Hocking. We have been unable to locate or verify some of the original publishers and/or their addresses. Anyone with information on publishers not included or incorrectly attributed is asked to contact the publisher of this book so that correct credit can be made in the next printing.

Contents

PREFACE

The simple purpose of this modest book is to assist Christians today in their daily effort to seek God in personal prayer. Christians from every age of the Church, women and men, Anglican, Protestant, Roman Catholic, and Orthodox, are included as models for prayer.

The method used is practical. Each page for every day of the year is arranged as follows. First is given a personal description of prayer from a fellow Christian; the descriptions begin with the earliest centuries and go up to 1980. Secondly, there is a brief quotation from the Word of God for each day's prayer. There is no obvious connection intended between the description of prayer and the Scripture quotation. The Scripture quotations are chosen to reflect the particular season of the Church Year. The purpose of this is to direct a person's prayerful reflection according to the spirit of each season of the Church Year.

The book is divided into six sections to reflect the main seasons of the Church Year: Advent, Christmas and Epiphany, Lent, Easter through Pentecost, and the Ordinary Time of the Year. Since the number of days in Ordinary Time varies from year to year, some additional days are added for the time after Epiphany and the time after Pentecost.

The choice of daily readings from the Word of God was made with the particular season of the Church Year in mind. The Advent selections are from Isaiah, Christmas from Luke's and Matthew's Infancy Narratives, Lent from Jeremiah, Easter from John's Gospel, Pentecost from The Acts of the Apostles, and Ordinary Time from the Gospel of Matthew, the Letters, and the Book of Revelation.

These Scripture Readings are taken from the *Revised Standard Version* of 1973.

CALENDAR

Year	Advent Season	Christmas Season	Season of Lent	Easter Season	Pentecost (Ord. Time)	Ordinary Time Before Lent	Ordinary Time After Pentecost
1985	Dec. 1	Dec. 25	Feb. 20	Apr. 7	May 26	1/7-2/19	5/27-11/30
1986	Nov. 30	Dec. 25	Feb. 12	Mar. 30	May 18	1/6-2/11	5/19-11/29
1987	Nov. 29	Dec. 25	Mar. 4	Apr. 19	June 7	1/5-3/3	6/8-11/28
1988	Nov. 27	Dec. 25	Feb. 17	Apr. 3	May 22	1/4-2/16	5/23-11/26
1989	Dec. 3	Dec. 25	Feb. 8	Mar. 26	May 14	1/9-2/7	5/15-12/2
1990	Dec. 2	Dec. 25	Feb. 28	Apr. 15	June 3	1/8-2/27	6/4-12/1
1991	Dec. 1	Dec. 25	Feb. 13	Mar. 31	May 19	1/7-2/12	5/20-11/30
1992	Nov. 29	Dec. 25	Mar. 4	Apr. 19	June 7	1/6-3/3	6/8-11/28
1993	Nov. 28	Dec. 25	Feb. 24	Apr. 11	May 30	1/4-2/23	5/31-11/27
1994	Nov. 27	Dec. 25	Feb. 16	Apr. 3	May 22	1/3-3/15	5/23-11/26
1995	Dec. 3	Dec. 25	Mar. 1	Apr. 16	June 4	1/9-2/28	6/5-12/2
1996	Dec. 1	Dec. 25	Feb. 21	Apr. 7	May 26	1/8-2/20	5/27-11/30
1997	Nov. 30	Dec. 25	Feb. 12	Mar. 30	May 18	1/6-2/12	5/19-11/29
1998	Nov. 29	Dec. 25	Feb. 25	Apr. 12	May 31	1/5-2/24	6/1-11/28
1999	Nov. 28	Dec. 25	Feb. 17	Apr. 4	May 23	1/4-2/16	5/24-11/27
2000	Dec. 3	Dec. 25	Mar. 8	Apr. 23	June 11	1/3-3/7	6/12-12/2
2001	Dec. 2	Dec. 25	Feb. 28	Apr. 15	June 3	1/8-2/27	6/4-12/1
2002	Dec. 1	Dec. 25	Feb. 13	Mar. 31	May 19	1/7-2/12	5/20-11/30
2003	Nov. 30	Dec. 25	Mar. 5	Apr. 20	June 8	1/6-3/4	6/9-11/29
2004	Nov. 28	Dec. 25	Feb. 25	Apr. 11	May 30	1/5-2/24	5/31-11/27
2005	Nov. 27	Dec. 25	Feb. 9	Mar. 27	May 15	1/4-2/8	5/16-11/26
2006	Dec. 3	Dec. 25	Mar. 1	Apr. 16	June 4	1/9-2/28	6/5-12/2
2007	Dec. 2	Dec. 25	Feb. 21	Apr. 8	May 27	1/8-2/20	5/28-12/1
2008	Dec. 1	Dec. 25	Feb. 6	Mar. 23	May 11	1/7-2/5	5/12-11/30

INTRODUCTION

"When you pray, go into your room and shut the door and pray to your Father who is in secret; and your Father who sees in secret will reward you." (Matt. 6:6)

Recently we have not heard very much about the practice of personal or private prayer. But the introductory quotation from the Sermon on the Mount reminds us that Christ did consider solitary prayer an indispensable Christian duty. He also showed us by example His own commitment to private prayer every time He sought solitude on a hill or in the desert to pray to His Father in secret.

What is intended here is a personal statement concerning the relative primacy of private prayer, not its absolute primacy in the Christian life. Community prayer, Liturgy, the Prayer of the Church must always be absolutely first in one's priority of prayer. But personal prayer, alone and in private, has a relative importance because it definitely is a necessary condition for all meaningful community prayer. If one cannot pray alone in solitude, alone with one's God, it is unlikely that liturgical prayer in common will have genuine meaning and value.

"The spiritual life . . . is not limited solely to participation in the liturgy. The Christian is indeed called to pray with others, but he must also enter into his bedroom to pray to his Father in secret; furthermore, according to the teaching of the apostle, he must pray without ceasing." (*Constitution on Sacred Liturgy* No. 12)

Common prayer and solitary prayer are interdependent, one with the other. One's private prayer prepares and leads one to common prayer. It also gives common prayer its spirit and its life. One will not survive long without the other.

My limited purpose here is to focus on private prayer. I want to promote a return to daily personal prayer in our Christian living. To do this I want to offer a few practical pointers.

The heart of private prayer is certainly not words, nor our empty speaking to God. Prayer is rather the overflow from our daily life, lived in God's presence. Prayer flows out of a life lived in our daily waiting for and patient expectation of the coming of the Lord.

If daily private prayer is anything, it is a daily struggle for us, a struggle for meaning, a struggle to find a time and a place, and a struggle to persevere. We will not stay long with the struggle without faith. Only our faith will keep before us the reminder that to be a Christian, we must also be a pray-er. Praying daily is a command for a Christian.

Without a sense of the value of prayer for us we will not long persevere in our commitment to it. To sharpen this sense, to keep it alive in us daily, we need to pay attention to God's presence within us and within our lives. We also need the support of the Word of God, spiritual reading, spiritual direction, and the support of our praying family and friends.

Finding time and a place for prayer can also be a struggle. It was for Jesus in His busy ministry. Frequently He went off to a quiet place to be alone to pray. He felt a need to do this regularly.

If my own personal experience has taught me anything, it is that we need a precise time and place to pray. Daily prayer demands a discipline of the spirit. And the discipline of prayer requires an exact time and a precise place for meeting the Lord. Only then can we find the quiet, the atmosphere, the space, the silent hospitality to meet God.

In personal prayer we do indeed meet God in silent hospitality. He has made us for himself and delights in the close and intimate relation which finds expression in our personal prayer, our time alone in quiet silence with God.

Besides personal prayer there is also the common prayer of the Sacred Liturgy. While personal prayer is offered in silence by our mind, our heart, even our lips, the Sacred Liturgy is grander; it is a prayer of action, a prayer of the community of believers in song and in refrain. Personal prayer and the Liturgy are the two great interdependent moments in our spiritual life. Each has its own character and importance for us. Both together mutually sustain each other and nourish us as individuals and as members of the family of God.

May the following 365 offerings aid and support us all in our struggle to grow as persons of prayer.

ADVENT

Advent is simultaneously a beginning and an end in the Church's year of grace. This multifaceted and rich celebration is observed annually to prepare all Christians for the Parousia, the final *Adventus* or Coming of the Lord. Advent is the season of patient expectation for the Coming of the Lord, His daily coming now in mystery, His coming at the hour of death, His final coming in glory.

The season of Advent calls us to once again share in the longing for the coming of our God. It calls us to conversion of life, a personal moving from darkness to light. Isaiah and John the Baptist are our Advent teachers and challengers in this spiritual struggle.

The Advent season calls us to celebrate every coming of Christ Jesus into our world. His first coming into the world at Bethlehem is again celebrated. His continuing coming here and now into our personal and communal lives is also celebrated. And finally His coming in glory at the end of time is celebrated.

Our Advent prayer, then, should be a prayer of hope, patient expectation, quiet joy, conversion of life, and heartfelt faith. The ancient prophet Isaiah is a good guide for our Advent prayer.

DAY OF ADVENT 1

Prayer is conversation with God. Although whispering and not opening the lips, we speak in silence, still we cry inwardly. God continually hears all this inner conversation. So also we raise the head and lift the hands to heaven, and set the feet in motion at the closing utterance of the prayer.
— *Stromata,* Bk. 2, 7, Clement of Alexandria (150-215)

It shall come to pass in the latter days, that the mountain of the house of the Lord shall be established as the highest of the mountains, and shall be raised above the hills: and all the nations shall flow to it, and many peoples shall come, and say: "Come, let us go to the mountain of the Lord, to the house of the God of Jacob; that he may teach us his ways and that we may walk in his paths." (Isaiah 2:2-3)

Create in me, O God, an obedient heart, so that I may walk in Your path this Advent.

DAY OF ADVENT 2

When the faithful wake in the morning, the first thing they should all do, both men and women, is to wash their hands and pray to God. Only then should they go about their daily occupations.
— *The Apostolic Tradition,* St. Hippolytus (3rd century)

Again the Lord spoke to Ahaz, "Ask a sign of the Lord your God; let it be deep as Sheol or high as heaven." But Ahaz said, I will not ask, and I will not put the Lord to the test." And he said, "Hear then, O house of David! Is it too little for you to weary men, that you weary my God also? Therefore the Lord himself will give you a sign. Behold, a young woman shall conceive and bear a son, and shall call his name Immanuel." (Isaiah 7:10-14)

God, You who dwell within me, may I look for no sign but to know Your will for me.

DAY OF ADVENT 3

Prayer alone overcomes God. . . . Prayer is the wall of faith, our shield and weapon against the enemy who studies us from all sides. Hence, let us never go out unarmed. Let us be mindful of our duty to be on guard by day and on vigil by night.
— *On Prayer,* Tertullian (c. 160-c. 240)

Bind up the testimony, seal the teaching among my disciples. I will wait for the Lord, who is hiding his face from the house of Jacob, and I will hope in him. Behold, I and the children whom the Lord has given me are signs and portents in Israel from the Lord of hosts, who dwells on Mount Zion. (Isaiah 8:16-18)

You are the God who does wonderful things for Your people. Help me today.

DAY OF ADVENT 4

The person who links together his prayer with deeds of duty and performs actions in conformity with his prayer is the person who prays without ceasing, for his virtuous deeds or the commandments he has fulfilled, are taken up as part of his prayer.
— *On Prayer,* Origen (185-253)

18

The people who walked in darkness have seen a great light; those who dwelt in a land of deep darkness, on them has light shined. Thou hast multiplied the nation, thou hast increased its joy; they rejoice before thee as with joy at the harvest, as men rejoice when they divide the spoil. (Isaiah 9:2-3)

May the Spirit of Light flood the hearts of all during this Advent season.

DAY OF ADVENT 5

Let those who pray have words and petitions ruled by discipline and possessing a quiet modesty. Let us bear in mind that we stand in the presence of God. We must be pleasing in the sight of God both with the action of the body and the tone of the voice.
— *On the Lord's Prayer,* St. Cyprian (d. 258)

For to us a child is born, to us a son is given; and the government will be upon his shoulder, and his name will be called "Wonderful Counselor, Mighty God, Everlasting Father, Prince of Peace." Of the increase of his government and of peace there will be no end, upon the throne of David, and over his kingdom, to establish it, and to uphold it with justice and with righteousness from this time forth and for evermore. The zeal of the Lord of hosts will do this. (Isaiah 9:6-7)

Mighty God, come to me in my need and make me one with You.

DAY OF ADVENT 6

In prayer we should simply direct our mind to wait for the Lord, so that when He comes He may enter into the soul through all her entrances and paths and the sense organs. One should sometimes be silent and at other times pray with tears. Only the mind should always be firmly focused on God.
— *Homily on Prayer,* Macarius of Egypt (c. 300-389)

There shall come forth a shoot from the stump of Jesse, and a branch shall grow out of his roots. And the Spirit of the Lord shall rest upon him, the spirit of wisdom and understanding, the spirit of counsel and might, the spirit of knowledge and the fear of the Lord. And his delight shall be in the fear of the Lord. (Isaiah 11:1-3)

Lord, my God, give me Your gift of Advent hope, so that I may receive Your Son.

DAY OF ADVENT 7

Prayer to God bears fruit. Let us not neglect it, and lose its fruits. He who offers up sincere and earnest prayer, reaps and gathers in its fruits. He who is lazy in prayer will be a stranger to its fruits. Let us see then that our mouth does not pray in a negligent manner. It greatly profits us to pray, and to know also what kind of prayer we are offering: for there is power in the prayer of a just person.
— *Sermon on Prayer,* St. Ephrem the Syrian (c. 306-373)

The wolf shall dwell with the lamb, and the leopard shall lie down with the kid, and the calf and the lion and the fatling together, and a little child shall lead them. . . . The sucking child shall play over the hole of the asp, and the weaned child shall put his hand on the adder's den. They shall not hurt or destroy in all my holy mountain; for the earth shall be full of the knowledge of the Lord as the waters cover the sea. (Isaiah 11:6, 8-9)

O God of Peace, may I know Your will for me this day.

DAY OF ADVENT 8

Prayer is a duty which is appropriate to our human weakness in relation to God.
— *Treatise on Ps. 118,* St. Hilary of Poitiers (315-367)

You will say in that day: "I will give thanks to thee, O Lord, for though thou wast angry with me, thy anger turned away, and thou didst comfort me. Behold, God is my salvation; I will trust, and will not be afraid; for the Lord God is my strength and my song, and he has become my salvation." (Isaiah 12:1-2)

Make me walk this day in holiness, and live the day for You, O my Savior.

DAY OF ADVENT 9

Prayer is an appeal for good things made to God by devout people. . . .
Prayer is to be encouraged, for it creates in the soul a clear notion of God. And the indwelling of God is this — to hold God ever in mind, His dwelling place resting within us.
— *Homily on Martyr Julitta,* St. Basil (329-379)

And you will say in that day; "Give thanks to the Lord, call upon his name; make known his deeds among the nations, proclaim that his name is exalted. Sing praises to the Lord, for he has done gloriously; let this be known in all the earth. Shout, and sing for joy, O inhabitant of Zion, for great in your midst is the Holy One of Israel." (Isaiah 12:4-6)

May we spend this day in Your praise, O Lord, our God.

DAY OF ADVENT 10

Prayer is conversation with God. When you read, God speaks to you; but when you pray, you speak to God. . . . Prayer is the begging for good things, which is offered to God with heartfelt cries. . . . Prayer is conversation and exchange with God, which defeats evil and heals sin.
— *On the Lord's Prayer,* St. Gregory of Nyssa (332-394)

O Lord, thou art my God; I will exalt thee, I will praise thy name; for thou hast done wonderful things, plans formed of old, faithful and sure. For thou hast made the city a heap, the fortified city a ruin; the palace of aliens is a city no more, it will never be rebuilt. Therefore strong peoples will glorify thee; cities of ruthless nations will fear thee. For thou hast been a stronghold to the poor, a stronghold to the needy in his distress, a shelter from the storm and a shade from the heat. (Isaiah 25:1-4)

Sanctify us in mind and body, Lord, and preserve us from all evil.

DAY OF ADVENT 11

Prayer is discourse with the Divine Majesty. . . . Prayer is the act whereby mortal and passing creatures are taken up to the immortal life of God through the most familiar and personal interaction with Him.
— *Homily on Prayer,* St. John Chrysostom (344-407)

On this mountain the Lord of hosts will make for all peoples a feast of fat things, a feast of wine on the lees, of fat things full of marrow, of wine on the lees well refined. . . . He will swallow up death for ever, and the Lord God will wipe away tears from all faces, and the reproach of his people he will take away from all the earth; for the Lord has spoken. (Isaiah 25:6, 8)

Lord God, never permit me to doubt Your fidelity. Strengthen Your Advent faith in us.

21

DAY OF ADVENT 12

To pray is to call out with your whole heart. Our heart calls out not with the voice of our body, but from the intensity of our thoughts and the balance of good living. It is a magnificent cry of faith.
— *Book Concerning the Sacraments,* St. Ambrose (c. 334-397)

It will be said on that day, "Lo, this is our God; we have waited for him, that he might save us. This is the Lord; we have waited for him; let us be glad and rejoice in his salvation." For the hand of the Lord will rest on this mountain, and Moab shall be trodden down in his place, as straw is trodden down in a dung-pit. And he will spread out his hands in the midst of it as a swimmer spreads his hands out to swim; but the Lord will lay low his pride together with the skill of his hands. . . . (Isaiah 25:9-11)

Lord, God of our Advent, speak Your saving Word to us.

DAY OF ADVENT 13

Prayer is an ongoing conversation of the spirit with God. . . . Prayer is an ascent of the spirit to God.
— *Chapters on Prayer,* Evagrius of Pontus (346-399)

In that day this song will be sung in the land of Judah: "We have a strong city; he sets up salvation as walls and bulwarks. Open the gates, that the righteous nation which keeps faith may enter in. Thou dost keep him in perfect peace, whose mind is stayed on thee, because he trusts in thee. Trust in the Lord for ever, for the Lord God is an everlasting rock." (Isaiah 26:1-4)

Prince of Peace, speak to Your servant, who is listening in humble prayer.

DAY OF ADVENT 14

Prayer is a small, delicate, little bird which by the wings of faith and virtue flies up over the choirs of Cherubim and Seraphim and stands in the hall of the Great King as a distinguished intercessor for each and every one.
— *Letters,* St. Jerome (c. 347-419)

The way of the righteous is level; thou dost make smooth the path of the righteous. In the path of thy judgments, O Lord, we wait for thee; thy memorial name is the desire of our soul. My soul yearns for thee in the night, my spirit within me earnestly seeks thee. For when thy judgments are in the earth, the inhabitants of the world learn righteousness. (Isaiah 26:7-9)

Make us walk today in Your way of holiness, Lord, so that we may live devoutly in Your sight.

DAY OF ADVENT 15

As a word, prayer refers to every way of speaking. Its etymology may be explained thus: prayer is the reasoning of the voice. In Holy Scripture it is rare to read this meaning for prayer, but that it rather means petitions and appeals made to God.
— *Letters,* St. Jerome (c. 347-420)

Is it not yet a very little while until Lebanon shall be turned into a fruitful field, and the fruitful field shall be regarded as a forest? In that day the deaf shall hear the words of a book, and out of their gloom and darkness the eyes of the blind shall see. The meek shall obtain fresh joy in the Lord, and the poor among men shall exult in the Holy One of Israel. (Isaiah 29:17-19)

Lord, send us Your Holy One so that we may all be born again this Advent.

DAY OF ADVENT 16

Prayer can be diverse. It is one reality to pray to God with undistracted thought, and another for the body to stand at prayer, while the mind is elsewhere. It is one reality to choose one's time and pray when daily conversations and cares are complete, and something else, as far as it is possible, to prefer prayer to all worldly cares and to give it priority in life.
— *Salutary Precepts for the Lord,* St. Mark, Ascetic (4th century)

Therefore thus says the Lord, who redeemed Abraham, concerning the house of Jacob: "Jacob shall no more be ashamed, no more shall his face grow pale. For when he sees his children, the work of my hands, in his midst, they will sanctify my name; they will sanctify the Holy One of Jacob, and will stand in awe of the God of Israel. And those who err in spirit will come to understanding, and those who murmur will accept instruction." (Isaiah 29:22-24)

Help us, O Lord, to live watchful and ready lives, so we may hear Your word.

DAY OF ADVENT 17

What a marvelous reality prayer is! How magnificent are its deeds! Prayer is pleasing when it is joined to good deeds. Prayer is heard when generous service comes from it. Prayer is granted when it is free of all deception. Prayer is powerful when it is filled with divine strength. Beloved, I think that this is the right way to look at things; when a person does the will of God, this is prayer indeed.
— *Demonstrations,* St. Aphraates (4th century)

Though the Lord give you the bread of adversity and the water of affliction, yet your Teacher will not hide himself any more, but your eyes shall see your Teacher. And your ears shall hear a word behind you, saying, ''This is the way, walk in it,'' when you turn to the right or when you turn to the left. (Isaiah 30:20-21)

O Wisdom, holy Word of God, You rule Your creation with care. Come and show us Your way.

DAY OF ADVENT 18

The authentic basis for prayer is this, to truly attend to one's thoughts and in deep peace and calmness to pour forth one's petitions to God.
— *Spiritual Homilies,* Pseudo-Macarius (c. 4th century)

The Lord is exalted, for he dwells on high; he will fill Zion with justice and righteousness; and he will be the stability of your times, abundance of salvation, wisdom, and knowledge; the fear of the Lord is his treasure. (Isaiah 33:5-6)

O holy God of ancient Israel, who appeared to Moses in the burning bush, come now and be our salvation.

DAY OF ADVENT 19

Prayer is our conversation with God.
— *Lives of Desert Fathers,* Desert Fathers (4th-5th centuries)

The wilderness and the dry land shall be glad, the desert shall rejoice and blossom; like the crocus it shall blossom abundantly, and rejoice with joy and singing. The glory of Lebanon shall be given to it, the majesty of Carmel and Sharon. They shall see the glory of the Lord, the majesty of our God. Strengthen the weak hands, and make firm the feeble knees. Say to those who are of a fearful heart, "Be strong, fear not! Behold, your God will come with vengeance, with the recompense of God. He will come and save you." (Isaiah 35:1-4)

O Flower of Jesse, come and let nothing hinder You from our aid.

DAY OF ADVENT 20

Prayer is the raising of the mind from earth to heaven, the searching after the supernatural and invisible.
— *Sermon No. 73 on Scripture,* St. Augustine (354-430)

And a highway shall be there, and it shall be called the Holy Way; the unclean shall not pass over it, and fools shall not err therein. No lion shall be there, nor shall any ravenous beast come up on it; they shall not be found there, but the redeemed shall walk there. And the ransomed of the Lord shall return, and come to Zion with singing; everlasting joy shall be upon their heads; they shall obtain joy and gladness, and sorrow and sighing shall flee away. (Isaiah 35:8-10)

O Key of David, Gate of Heaven, come, and be our way to the Father.

DAY OF ADVENT 21

To use much speaking in prayer is to involve an excessive number of words to ask for a necessary thing. To extend prayer means to have the heart throbbing with reverent devotion toward Him to whom we pray. For in most cases our prayer is made up of deep longing rather than in speaking, in weeping rather than in words.
— *Letter to Proba,* St. Augustine (354-430)

A voice cries: "In the wilderness prepare the way of the Lord, make straight in the desert a highway for our God. Every valley shall be lifted up, and every mountain and hill be made low; the uneven ground shall become level, and the rough places a plain. And the glory of the Lord shall be revealed, and all flesh shall see it together, for the mouth of the Lord has spoken," (Isaiah 40:3-5)

O Dawn of Eternal Light, come and reveal Yourself to us this Advent.

DAY OF ADVENT 22

Prayers are all those acts by which we offer or promise something to God. . . . We pray when we repudiate worldly things and promise that, being dead to all worldly deeds and the life of this world, we will serve the Lord with total determination of heart. . . . We pray when we promise that we will always preserve the most perfect purity of body and constant patience, or when we vow that we will completely weed out of our heart the roots of anger or of sorrow that bring death.
— *Conferences,* John Cassian (c. 360-c. 435)

Get you up to a high mountain, O Zion, herald of good tidings; lift up your voice with strength, O Jerusalem, herald of good tidings, lift it up, fear not; say to the cities of Judah, "Behold your God!" Behold, the Lord God comes with might, and his arm rules for him; behold, his reward is with him, and his recompense before him. He will feed his flock like a shepherd, he will gather the lambs in his arms, he will carry them in his bosom, and gently lead those that are with young. (Isaiah 40:9-11)

O King of all peoples, come, and gently rule and guide us Your people.

DAY OF ADVENT 23

Prayer is a conversation of our spirit with God. . . . Prayer is reasonable discourse with God. . . . Prayer is the lifting of the mind to God. . . . Prayer includes contemplation with reverence, and amendment, and sorrow of soul, made with groans, but without sound.
— *On Prayer,* St. Nilus of Sinai (d. 450)

Who has measured the waters in the hollow of his hand and marked off the heavens with a span, enclosed the dust of the earth in a measure and weighed the mountains in scales and the hills in a balance? Who has directed the Spirit of the Lord, or as his counselor has instructed him? Whom did he consult for his enlightenment, and who taught him the path of justice, and taught him knowledge, and showed him the way of understanding? (Isaiah 40:12-14)

O Emmanuel, God with us, guide us along Your path.

DAY OF ADVENT 24

If, when we wish to bring anything to the notice of persons in high places, we do not presume to do so except with humility and reverence, how much more ought we with all humility and purity of intention to offer our prayer to the Lord God of all things? And let us remember that we shall be heard not because of much speaking, but for our purity of heart and tears of sincere sorrow.
— *Holy Rule,* Rule of St. Benedict (5th century)

"Fear not, for I have redeemed you; I have called you by name, you are mine. When you pass through the waters I will be with you; and through the rivers, they shall not overwhelm you; when you walk through fire you shall not be burned, and the flame shall not consume you. For I am the Lord your God, the Holy One of Israel, your Savior." (Isaiah 43:1-3)

God of this Advent, be with us this day as the God of all Hope.

DAY OF ADVENT 25

True prayer is not to be found in the words of our voice, but in the thoughts of our heart. The sounds that reach the hearing of God are not words but desires. If we seek the eternal life with our lips, without desiring that life with our heart, our beseeching is nothing but silence. But when we desire that life from our heart, though our mouth be silent, in that silence we pray to God.
— *Moralia on Job,* St. Gregory the Great (540-604)

Thus says the Lord, the King of Israel and his Redeemer, the Lord of hosts: "I am the first and I am last; besides me there is no god. Who is like man? Let him proclaim it, let him declare and set it forth before me. Who has announced from of old the things to come? Let them tell us what is yet to be. Fear not, nor be afraid; have I not told you from of old and declared it? And you are my witnesses! Is there a God besides me? There is no Rock; I know not any." (Isaiah 44:6-8)

Lord Jesus, You come with great power; make us worthy of Your gifts.

DAY OF ADVENT 26

Prayer is a beseeching for, a concern for, a longing for something, either freedom from evil things here or in the world to come, or a desire for prom-

ised things, or a request for something by which a person wishes to be brought closer to God.
— *Mystic Treatises,* St. Isaac of Nineveh (6th century)

Shower, O heavens, from above, and let the skies rain down righteousness; let the earth open, that salvation may sprout forth, and let it cause righteousness to spring up also; I the Lord have created it. (Isaiah 45:8-9)

Lord, we long for the grace of Your coming; pour down on us the gift of Your life.

DAY OF ADVENT 27

To pray is to speak. . . . To pray, it is said, is to seek; for to pray is to petition as to entreat is to obtain.
— *Etymologies*, St. Isidore of Seville (c. 560-636)

Arise, shine; for your light has come, and the glory of the Lord has risen upon you. For behold, darkness shall cover the earth, and thick darkness the peoples; but the Lord will arise upon you, and his glory will be seen upon you. And nations shall come to your light, and kings to the brightness of your rising. (Isaiah 60:1-3)

Show Yourself to us, Lord, and let us see Your saving works.

DAY OF ADVENT 28

Prayer is essentially a dialogue and a union of a person with God. Its effect is to hold the world together. It achieves a reconciliation with God.
— *The Ladder of Divine Ascent,* St. John Climacus (579-649)

Behold, the Lord has proclaimed to the end of the earth: Say to the daughter of Zion, "Behold, your salvation comes; behold, his reward is with him, and his recompense before him." And they shall be called The holy people, The redeemed of the Lord; and you shall be called Sought out, a city not forsaken. (Isaiah 62:11-12)

O saving God, be our Savior, and set us free from all evil.

CHRISTMAS and EPIPHANY

At Christmas we celebrate the Christ, who is present in mystery in the Church and in her Christmas worship; we honor the Christ who was born in our world. This birth and His life among us are still a reality for us who believe in His presence.

Christmas is also the season of giving. God gives us the Gift of Life in the person of His Son. This gift, our participation in God's life, can be received only by faith, which is also a gift. In our joy and our gratitude at this holy season we seek to give our gift to God and to others.

The season of Christmas is also the season of Light. Christ is this Light of the world, and He is born to us and in us today as light. We too, then, are born today to a new light. This new light, this life, floods us with the peace and joy of this holy season. In our prayer let us offer our gifts of simplicity, love, faith, hope, and joy, like Joseph, Mary, the shepherds and the magi.

Epiphany means manifestation or showing. The feast of Epiphany is the annual Christian celebration of the manifestation of the dignity and divinity of the Savior of the world. On this feast of Epiphany the Church invites the faithful to recall and relive three mysteries: the adoration of Christ the Lord by the magi, the baptism of Christ in the River Jordan, and the miracle of the marriage at Cana.

In an ancient homily for the season of Epiphany St. Gregory the Great sees the traditional Epiphany gifts of gold, frankincense, and myrrh from the viewpoint of the giver. In the gold he sees wisdom. In incense he sees the power of prayer. In myrrh he sees the value of self-denial.

Epiphany is the climax of the Christmas celebration and the perfect fulfillment of Advent. In our prayer we should bring all our golfrn powers of intellect to our Lord, the incense of our praise to our Great High Priest, and the myrrh of our self-denial and suffering to our God.

DAY OF CHRISTMAS 1

Prayer is petition for the blessings bestowed by God on a person with a view to his salvation and as a reward for the good inner state of those who made the prayer.
— *Century of Texts II,* St. Maximus Confessor (c. 580-662)

Now the birth of Jesus Christ took place in this way. When his mother Mary had been betrothed to Joseph, before they came together she was found to be

29

with child of the Holy Spirit; and her husband Joseph, being a just man and unwilling to put her to shame, resolved to divorce her quietly. But as he considered this, behold, an angel of the Lord appeared to him in a dream, saying, "Joseph, son of David, do not fear to take Mary your wife, for that which is conceived in her is of the Holy Spirit; she will bear a son, and you shall call his name Jesus, for he will save his people from their sins." (Matthew 1:18-21)

Lord Jesus, God with us, come into our lives this Christmas.

DAY OF CHRISTMAS 2

When we call upon God in our prayer we unveil our mind in His presence.
— *The Celestial Hierarchy,* Dionysius the Areopagite (c. 6th century)

And Joseph also went up from Galilee, from the city of Nazareth, to Judea, to the city of David, which is called Bethlehem, because he was of the house and lineage of David, to be enrolled with Mary, his betrothed, who was with child. And while they were there, the time came for her to be delivered. And she gave birth to her first-born son and wrapped him in swaddling cloths, and laid him in a manger, because there was no place for them in the inn. (Luke 2:4-7)

Open our hearts, O Jesus, so that we may receive Your word with joy.

DAY OF CHRISTMAS 3

Prayer is made not only with words, by which we invoke divine mercy, but in everything which we do through faith in the service of our Creator. . . . Prayer results when the mind is raised above bodily concerns by concentration on heavenly goods.
— *Commentary on Mark,* Venerable Bede (673-735)

And in that region there were shepherds out in the field, keeping watch over their flock by night. And an angel of the Lord appeared to them, and the glory of the Lord shone around them, and they were filled with fear. And the angel said to them, "Be not afraid; for behold, I bring you good news of a great joy which will come to all the people; for to you is born this day in the city of David a Savior, who is Christ the Lord. And this will be a sign for you: you will find a babe wrapped in swaddling cloths and lying in a manger. (Luke 2:8-12)

Lord, help me to trust Your word and place all my confidence in You.

DAY OF CHRISTMAS 4

Prayer is the ascent of the mind to God or the asking of appropriate things from him.
— *On Orthodox Faith,* St. John Damascene (c. 650-750)

And suddenly there was with the angel a multitude of the heavenly host praising God and saying, "Glory to God in the highest, and on earth peace among men with whom he is pleased!" When the angels went away from them into heaven, the shepherds said to one another, "Let us go over to Bethlehem and see this thing that has happened, which the Lord has made known to us." And they went with haste, and found Mary and Joseph, and the babe lying in a manger. And when they saw it they made known the saying which had been told them concerning this child; and all who heard it wondered at what the shepherds told them. But Mary kept all these things, pondering them in her heart. (Luke 2:13-19)

Glory and praise to You, O Lord, for You do all things well.

DAY OF CHRISTMAS 5

Prayer is a gentle petition of the mind combined with compunction of heart.
— *Exposition, Ps. 101,* St. Alcuin (735-804)

And at the end of eight days, when he was circumcised, he was called Jesus, the name given by the angel before he was conceived in the womb. And when the time came for their purification according to the law of Moses, they brought him up to Jerusalem to present him to the Lord (as it is written in the law of the Lord, "Every male that opens the womb shall be called holy to the Lord") and to offer a sacrifice according to what is said in the law of the Lord, "a pair of turtledoves, or two young pigeons." (Luke 2:21-24)

Teach me Your holy will, O God, so that I might offer You my whole life.

DAY OF CHRISTMAS 6

To pray in any manner at all, one must strive to be taught how. It is this that the Lord himself taught us in the Our Father, and teaches us to seek nothing

passing, only the kingdom of God and eternal salvation.
— *The Catechesis,* St. Theodore the Studite (759-926)

Now there was a man in Jerusalem, whose name was Simeon, and this man was righteous and devout, looking for the consolation of Israel, and the Holy Spirit was upon him. And it had been revealed to him by the Holy Spirit that he should not see death before he had seen the Lord's Christ. And inspired by the Spirit he came into the temple; and when the parents brought in the child Jesus, to do for him according to the custom of the law, he took him up in his arms and blessed God and said, "Lord, now lettest thou thy servant depart in peace, according to thy word; for mine eyes have seen thy salvation which thou hast prepared in the presence of all peoples, a light for revelation to the Gentiles, and for glory to thy people Israel." (Luke 2:25-32)

Jesus, You are the light of God among us; show us the way to Your peace.

DAY OF CHRISTMAS 7

Prayer is petition; thus, it is the ascent of the mind from earth to heaven. . . . Prayer is said to be petition; for to pray is to ask for, as to exhort is to beseech.
— *On the Nature of Things,* Bl. Rabanus Maurus (776-856)

And his father and his mother marveled at what was said about him; and Simeon blessed them and said to Mary his mother, "Behold, this child is set for the fall and rising of many in Israel, and for a sign that is spoken against (and a sword will pierce through your own soul also), that thoughts out of many hearts may be revealed." (Luke 2:33-35)

Jesus, our Brother, teach us humility; give us wisdom.

DAY OF CHRISTMAS 8

A person who prays with few words can be conscious of what he says in prayer. . . . A person who has learnt to be conscious of what he says in prayer cannot say many things, lest his mind become scattered. There is no need to say much to God, but a person should be intelligently conscious of the little he does say, that is, he should understand it. But to be intelligently conscious in prayer without the work of the Holy Spirit is in no way possible.
— *On Three Modes of Prayer,* St. Simeon the New Theologian (c. 949-1022)

32

And there was a prophetess, Anna, the daughter of Phanuel, of the tribe of Asher; she was of a great age, having lived with her husband seven years from her virginity, and as a widow till she was eighty-four. She did not depart from the temple, worshiping with fasting and prayer night and day. And coming up at that very hour she gave thanks to God, and spoke of him to all who were looking for the redemption of Jerusalem. (Luke 2:36-38)

Lord, make me attentive to Your word and ponder it in my heart.

DAY OF CHRISTMAS 9

Prayer is the reasoning of the lips which prompts us to offer our vows to God.
— *Exposition, Ps. 37,* St. Bruno (d. 1101)

And when they had performed everything according to the law of the Lord, they returned into Galilee, to their own city, Nazareth. And the child grew and became strong, filled with wisdom; and the favor of God was upon him. (Luke 2:39-40)

We thank You, Father, for Your gift of Jesus, and we pray for a deeper faith in Him.

DAY OF CHRISTMAS 10

Come now, free yourself for a while for God, and rest awhile in Him. Enter the room of your soul. Shut out everything but God and that which can assist you in seeking Him.
— *Letters,* St. Anselm (1033-1109)

Now when Jesus was born in Bethlehem of Judea in the days of Herod the king, behold, wise men from the East came to Jerusalem, saying, "Where is he who has been born king of the Jews? For we have seen his star in the East, and have come to worship him." When Herod the king heard this, he was troubled, and all Jerusalem with him; and assembling all the chief priests and scribes of the people, he inquired of them where the Christ was to be born. They told him, "In Bethlehem of Judea; for so it is written by the prophet: 'And you, O Bethlehem, in the land of Judah, are by no means least among the rulers of Judah; for from you shall come a ruler who will govern my people Israel.' " (Matthew 2:1-6)

Holy Spirit of Truth, make us sensitive to Your presence in the little things of our daily world.

DAY OF CHRISTMAS 11

Prayer is the devout inclining of our heart directed to God to remove evil from us and to provide us with good things.
— *The Ladder of Paradise,* Dom Guigo II (d. 1193)

Then Herod summoned the wise men secretly and ascertained from them what time the star appeared; and he sent them to Bethlehem, saying, "Go and search diligently for the child, and when you have found him bring me word, that I too may come and worship him." When they had heard the king they went their way; and lo, the star which they had seen in the East went before them, till it came to rest over the place where the child was. When they saw the star, they rejoiced exceedingly with great joy; and going into the house they saw the child with Mary his mother, and they fell down and worshiped him. Then, opening their treasures, they offered him gifts, gold and frankincense and myrrh. (Matthew 2:7-10)

King of glory, give us a willing spirit of adoration and service.

DAY OF CHRISTMAS 12

Among all those things which fragile humanity can do to please the Creator, or try to please Him, prayer is the most powerful, if it is done with a pure conscience and humility of heart.
— *Treatise on Lord's Prayer,* Peter Abélard (1079-1142)

Now when they had departed, behold, an angel of the Lord appeared to Joseph in a dream and said, "Rise, take the child and his mother, and flee to Egypt, and remain there till I tell you; for Herod is about to search for the child, to destroy him." And he rose and took the child and his mother by night, and departed to Egypt, and remained there until the death of Herod. This was to fulfil what the Lord had spoken by the prophet, "Out of Egypt have I called my son." (Matthew 2:13-15)

Christ Jesus, teach us Your way, so that we may follow You in faith.

DAY OF CHRISTMAS 13

Prayer is the affection of a person holding fast to God, and a certain familiar and devout conversation, and a state where the mind enjoys a certain temporary enlightenment.
— *On the Solitary Life,* William of St. Thièrry (c. 1085-1148)

Then Herod, when he saw that he had been tricked by the wise men, was in a furious rage, and he sent and killed all the male children in Bethlehem and in all that region who were two years old or under, according to the time which he had ascertained from the wise men. Then was fulfilled what was spoken by the prophet Jeremiah: "A voice was heard in Ramah, wailing and loud lamentation, Rachel weeping for her children; she refused to be consoled, because they were no more." (Matthew 2:16-18)

Jesus Lord, help me to find You in the pain and hope of daily life.

DAY OF CHRISTMAS 14

Prayer is a devotion of mind, that is, a turning to God by a holy and humble affection.
— *On the Interior Home,* St. Bernard of Clairvaux (1090-1153)

But when Herod died, behold, an angel of the Lord appeared in a dream to Joseph in Egypt, saying, "Rise, take the child and his mother, and go to the land of Israel, for those who sought the child's life are dead." And he rose and took the child and his mother, and went to the land of Israel. But when he heard that Archelaus reigned over Judea in place of his father Herod, he was afraid to go there, and being warned in a dream he withdrew to the district of Galilee. And he went and dwelt in a city called Nazareth, that what was spoken by the prophets might be fulfilled, "He shall be called a Nazarene." (Matthew 2:19-23)

Jesus, You became like us in all things, sanctifying us through prayer and the word of God.

DAY OF CHRISTMAS 15

Prayer is a certain devotion proceeding from a repentant soul. . . . Prayer asks, and action obtains from God the grace to lay hold on life, to taste and see that the Lord is sweet.

— *On the Manner of Praying,* Hugh of St. Victor (1096-1141)

Now his parents went to Jerusalem every year at the feast of the Passover. And when he was twelve years old, they went up according to custom; and when the feast was ended, as they were returning, the boy Jesus stayed behind in Jerusalem. His parents did not know it, but supposing him to be in the company they went a day's journey, and they sought him among their kinsfolk and acquaintances; and when they did not find him, they returned to Jerusalem, seeking him. After three days they found him in the temple, sitting among the teachers, listening to them and asking them questions; and all who heard him were amazed at his understanding and his answers. And when they saw him they were astonished; and his mother said to him, "Son, why have you treated us so? Behold, your father and I have been looking for you anxiously." And he said to them, "How is it that you sought me? Did you not know that I must be in my Father's house?" (Luke 2:41-49)

Christ Jesus, teach us also to seek first the kingdom of God.

Please note: For the time until Lent begins, the readings are to be found in Ordinary Time beginning on Page 89.

LENT

Lent is an English word, which comes to us from the Old High German word for spring, "Lenz." This word refers to the lengthening of days. Lent and length are related words. In all other languages the name of this season comes from the word "Forty." Lent is forty days of penance and prayer.

Lent is meant to be a positive experience for all of us. We are to fast, to abstain from all sin and practice acts of charity, compassion, and mercy. Our Lenten penance calls us to simplify our bodily needs, for a narrowing of our concerns from physical comforts to spiritual delights in daily prayer and worship. Lent is fasting, prayer, and almsgiving; these three are the basic elements of our Lenten observance. At Lent we are more and more conscious of the solidarity of all people. We are conscious of the guilt we share for the sufferings in the world. We are conscious of the poverty of the many and the wealth of a few. We are conscious of the need to share our spiritual experience and insight with our brothers and sisters. We are conscious of the value of a simple life, of the joy arising from simple things. We are conscious of the value of tuning out the nonessentials and getting down to basics. The observance of Lent is a time for Christians to remind their world that this is the season when we can truly do all of these things in a very Christian way as a public act of solidarity, so that in a calm spirit and a deep interior joy we might be prepared to celebrate the Resurrection of the Lord, who is the liberator of all persons.

The season of Lent is also our annual preparation for the celebration of Easter. It is, therefore, a time for conversion and strengthening of faith in the risen and present Lord. The catechumens remind us of the Lord's call to "reform our lives and believe in the Gospel." The baptized faithful journey toward Easter with the catechumens. Lent is also the normal time for the immediate spiritual preparation of catechumens for their baptism at the Easter Vigil. With them and for them let us grow in a deeper spirit of prayerfulness.

DAY OF LENT 1

Prayer is a matter of the heart, not of the lips. It is better to pray in the silence of the heart than to pray with words only, without the sincere concentration of the mind.
— *The Mirror of Charity,* Aelred of Rievaulx (1109-1167)

Now the word of the Lord came to me saying, "Before I formed you in the womb I knew you, and before you were born I consecrated you; I appointed you a prophet to the nations." Then I said, "Ah, Lord God! Behold, I do not know how to speak, for I am only a youth." But the Lord said to me, "Do not say, 'I am only a youth'; for to all to whom I send you you shall go, and whatever I command you you shall speak. Be not afraid of them, for I am with you to deliver you, says the Lord." (Jer. 1:4-8)

This Lent, Lord, may we be filled and satisfied by the word You will give us.

DAY OF LENT 2

We pray when we petition God by the deep sighs of our prayers for the acquisition of necessary virtues. . . . We pray every time that we beseech God through His mercy to take away all our sins. . . .
— *Sunday Homilies 10,* Godfrey of Admont (d. 1142)

The word of the Lord came to me, saying, "Go and proclaim in the hearing of Jerusalem, Thus says the Lord, I remember the devotion of your youth, your love as a bride, how you followed me in the wilderness, in a land not sown. Israel was holy to the Lord, the first fruits of his harvest. All who ate of it became guilty; evil came upon them, says the Lord." (Jer. 2:1-3)

Teach me to love You, Lord, not just in the big moments, but above all in the ordinariness of each day.

DAY OF LENT 3

Prayer is conversing familiarly with God, speaking with Him face to face; if need be, pressing and urging Him to grant her [the soul's] request.
— *Spiritual Treatises,* Richard of St. Victor (d. 1173)

Hear the word of the Lord, O House of Jacob, and all the families of the house of Israel. Thus says the Lord: "What wrong did your fathers find in me that they went far from me, and went after worthlessness, and became worthless? They did not say, 'Where is the Lord who brought us from the land of Egypt, who led us in the wilderness, in a land of deserts and pits, in a land of drought and deep darkness, in a land that none passes through, where no man dwells?' And I brought you into a plentiful land to enjoy its fruits and its good things. But when you came in you defiled my land, and made my heritage an abomination." (Jer. 2:4-7)

As we begin this Lent, Lord, make our day holy by prayer and fasting.

DAY OF LENT 4

Prayer means to beseech God for good things above all, and to beg Him to remove all evil. . . . Prayer is a devout affection of the mind toward God, by which the wandering mind is exhorted by the voice.
— *Homilies on Epistles,* Rudolfus Ardens (12th century)

"Therefore I still contend with you, says the Lord, and with your children's children I will contend. For cross to the coasts of Cyprus and see, or send to Kedar and examine with care; see if there has been such a thing. Has a nation changed its gods, even though they are no gods? But my people have changed their glory for that which does not profit. Be appalled, O heavens, at this, be shocked, be utterly desolate, says the Lord, for my people committed two evils; they have forsaken me, the fountain of living waters, and hewed out cisterns for themselves, broken cisterns, that can hold no water." (Jer. 2:9-13)

Destroy all my idols, Lord, so that I may serve You alone.

DAY OF LENT 5

Prayer fulfills the function of both myrrh and incense. First it gathers and binds together into yourself your affections when you pray; then it releases them to send them to God. What is more like myrrh, when there is such a flowing towards union with God? What is more like incense, when there is such an outpouring towards some awareness of God?
— *Homilies,* Gilbert of Holland (d. 1172)

"As a thief is shamed when caught, so the house of Israel shall be shamed: they, their kings, their princes, their priests, and their prophets, who say to a tree, 'You are my father,' and to a stone, 'You gave me birth.' For they have turned their back to me, and not their face. But in the time of their trouble they say, 'Arise and save us!' But where are your gods that you made for yourself? Let them arise, if they can save you, in your time of trouble; for as many as your cities are your gods, O Judah." (Jer. 2:26-28)

May my heart thirst for Your Christ, O God, our only true God.

DAY OF LENT 6

If you wish to pray, consider these three things; the way you approach prayer, how to offer yourself to God, at the time of prayer how you act when it is over. The point is: how peaceful and undisturbed you are when you begin it, how pure and undivided you are while it lasts, how somber and sincere you are when it is devoutly completed.
— *The Fourfold Exercise of a Monk in His Cell,* Adam Scotus
     (Dryburgh) (d. c. 1212)

"Why do you complain against me? You have all rebelled against me, says the Lord. In vain have I smitten your children, they took no correction; your own sword devoured your prophets like a ravening lion. And you, O generation, heed the word of the Lord. Have I been a wilderness to Israel, or a land of thick darkness? Why then do my people say, 'We are free, we will come no more to thee'? Can a maiden forget her ornaments, or a bride her attire? Yet my people have forgotten me days without number." (Jer. 2:29-32)

Teach us Your ways, Lord, so that we may be faithful and true.

DAY OF LENT 7

Prayer is a devout calling on God by which a person begs Him for some blessing. . . . Genuine prayer is orderly and is made for the good of the spirit; it is a begging for all those blessings which foster reverence toward God.
— *On Prayer, Bk. 8,* Gunther of Paris (d. 1220)

Return, faithless Israel, says the Lord. I will not look on you in anger, for I am merciful, says the Lord; I will not be angry for ever. Only acknowledge your guilt, that you rebelled against the Lord your God and scattered your favors among strangers under every green tree, and that you have not obeyed my voice, says the Lord. Return, O faithless children, says the Lord; for I am your master; I will take you, one from a city and two from a family, and I will bring you to Zion. (Jer. 3:12-14)

Forgive us our sins, Lord, and help us walk in the way of justice.

DAY OF LENT 8

The holy father Dominic also had another beautiful way of praying, full of devotion and grace. After the Liturgical Hours and the grace which is said in

common after meals, the father would go off quickly by himself to a cell or somewhere, sober and alert and anointed with a spirit of piety which he had received from the divine words which had been sung in choir or during the meal; there he would sit down to read or pray, recollecting himself in himself and placing himself in the presence of God.
— *Nine Ways of Prayer,* St. Dominic (c. 1171-1221)

Run to and from through the streets of Jerusalem, look and take note! Search her squares to see if you can find a man, one who does justice and seeks truth; that I may pardon her. Though they say, "As the Lord lives," yet they swear falsely. O Lord, do not thy eyes look for truth? Thou hast smitten them, but they felt no anguish; thou hast consumed them, but they refused to take correction. They have made their faces harder than rock; they have refused to repent. (Jer. 5:1-3)

Teach me, Lord, to be attentive at the table of Your Word and Body, so that I may live rightly.

DAY OF LENT 9

So, brothers all, let us keep a close guard on ourselves, lest under the pretext of some compensation or of work or advantage we let our mind and heart stray or be withdrawn from the Lord. . . . And always let us make a home and dwelling within us for Him, the Lord God almighty, Father and Son and Holy Ghost, who says: "Watch, therefore, and pray all the time, so that you may be found worthy to escape all the evils which are to come, and to stand before the Son of Man."
— *First Rule of the Friars,* St. Francis of Assisi (1182-1226)

Declare this in the house of Jacob, proclaim it in Judah: "Hear this, O foolish and senseless people, who have eyes, but not see, who have ears, but hear not. Do you not fear me? says the Lord; Do you not tremble before me? I placed the sand as the bound for the sea, a perpetual barrier which it cannot pass; though the waves toss, they cannot prevail, though they roar, they cannot pass over it. But this people has a stubborn and rebellious heart; they have turned aside and gone away." (Jer. 5:20-23)

Open my heart, O God, so that I may welcome You into my life daily.

DAY OF LENT 10

Often, without moving the lips, he would meditate within himself and drawing external things within himself, he would lift his spirit to higher things. All his attention and affection he directed with his whole being to the one thing which he was asking of the Lord. . . .
— *Life of St. Francis,* St. Francis of Assisi (1182-1226)

Thus says the Lord: "Stand by the roads, and look, and ask for the ancient paths, where the good way is; and walk in it, and find rest for your souls. But they said, 'We will not walk in it.' I set watchmen over you, saying, 'Give heed to the sound of the trumpet!' But they said, 'We will not give heed.' Therefore hear, O nations, and know, O congregation, what will happen to them. Hear, O earth; behold I am bringing evil upon this people, the fruit of their devices, because they have not given heed to my words; and as for my law, they have rejected it." (Jer. 6:16-19)

Make me more watchful, Lord, so I'll never miss the sound of Your voice.

DAY OF LENT 11

Prayer is the beginning, the middle, and the end of all good; prayer enlightens the soul, and enables it to discern between good and evil. Every sinner ought to pray daily with fervor of heart; he should pray to God humbly to give him a perfect knowledge of his own miseries and sins, and of the benefits which he has received and still receives from the good God. How can a person know God who does not know how to pray?
— *Golden Sayings,* Bl. Brother Giles of Assisi (d. 1262)

The word that came to Jeremiah from the Lord. . . . "Thus says the Lord of hosts, the God of Israel, Amend your ways and your doings, and I will let you dwell in this place. Do not trust in these deceptive words: 'This is the temple of the Lord, the temple of the Lord, the temple of the Lord.' For if you truly amend your ways and your doings, if you truly execute justice one with another, if you do not oppress the alien, the fatherless or the widow, or shed innocent blood in this place, and if you do not go after other gods to your own hurt, then I will let you dwell in this place, in the land that I gave of old to your fathers for ever." (Jer. 7:1, 3-7)

Make us worthy, Lord, to come into Your holy temple and stand in Your presence.

DAY OF LENT 12

Prayer has great power, when a person prays with all his strength. It makes a bitter heart gentle, a sad heart joyful, a poor heart rich, a dull heart wise, a cynical heart caring, a sick heart healthy, a blind heart able to see, a cold heart enflamed. It draws the Great God into a small heart; it drives the hungry heart to the fullness of God.
— *Revelations,* St. Mechtilde of Magdeburg (c. 1209-1283)

"As for you, do not pray for this people or lift up cry or prayer for them, and do not intercede with me, for I do not hear you. . . . The children gather wood, the fathers kindle fire, and the women knead dough, to make cakes for the queen of heaven; and they pour out drink offerings to other gods, to provoke me to anger. Is it I whom they provoke? says the Lord. Is it not themselves, to their own confusion? Therefore thus says the Lord God: Behold, my anger and my wrath will be poured out on this place, upon man and beast, upon the trees of the field and the fruit of the ground; it will burn and not be quenched." (Jer. 7:16, 18-20)

Do not hold us away from Your love, Lord, but forgive us and heal us.

DAY OF LENT 13

There are three things necessary for prayer to be pleasing and welcome to God. They are: A "making ready" must lead the way to prayer. Attentiveness must accompany prayer. Passionate joy must follow close after prayer. These correspond to the three actions of prayer: scrubbing, brightening, and polishing.
— *Homily on Prayer,* St. Bonaventure (c. 1217-1274)

"But this command I gave them. 'Obey my voice, and I will be your God, and you shall be my people; and walk in all the way that I command you, that it may be well with you.' But they did not obey or incline their ear, but walked in their own counsels and the stubbornness of their evil hearts, and went backward and not forward. From the day that your fathers came out of the land of Egypt to this day, I have persistently sent all my servants the prophets to them, day after day; yet they did not listen to me, or incline their ear, but stiffened their neck. They did worse than their fathers." (Jer. 7:23-26)

During these Lenten days, O God, help us to hear Your word clearly.

DAY OF LENT 14

Pure prayer is made when the lips do not move, but the heart speaks to God.
— *The Soul's Journey Unto God,* St. Bonaventure (1217-1274)

"So you shall speak all these words to them, but they will not listen to you. You shall call to them, but they will not answer you. And you shall say to them, 'This is the nation that did not obey the voice of the Lord their God, and did not accept discipline; truth has perished; it is cut off from their lips. Cut off your hair and cast it away; raise a lamentation on the bare heights, for the Lord has rejected and forsaken the generation of his wrath.' " (Jer. 7:27-29)

On this day of penance, we call to You, O God, with all our heart.

DAY OF LENT 15

True and perfect [prayer] is the gathering of all the affections and powers of the soul to know God with delight and with wonder of mind.
— *Paradise of the Soul,* St. Albert (1200-1280)

My grief is beyond healing, my heart is sick within me. Hark, the cry of the daughter of my people from the length and breadth of the land: "Is the Lord not in Zion? Is her King not in her?" "Why have they provoked me to anger with their graven images, and with their foreign idols?" "The harvest is past, the summer is ended, and we are not saved." For the wound of the daughter of my people is my heart wounded, I mourn, and dismay has taken hold on me. (Jer. 8:18-21)

Keep me sound in body and spirit, Lord, so I may be Your good servant.

DAY OF LENT 16

Prayer is the ascent made by the mind and the heart, by its concentration on God's goodness. . . . Prayer is an act of our reason which joins the desire of our will to Him, who is not under our power, our God. . . . Prayer is a certain unfolding of our own desire to God so that He may satisfy it. . . .
— *Summa Theologica,* St. Thomas Aquinas (c. 1225-1274)

Therefore thus says the Lord of hosts: "Behold, I will refine them and test them, for what else can I do, because of my people? Their tongue is a deadly arrow; it speaks deceitfully; with his mouth each speaks peaceably to his neighbor, but in his heart he plans an ambush for him. Shall I not punish them for these things? says the Lord; and shall I not avenge myself on a nation such as this?" (Jer. 9:7-9)

Watch over us, eternal Savior, and do not let us fail You ever.

DAY OF LENT 17

Prayer draws the great God down into our small heart. It drives the hungry soul up to God in His fullness.
— *The Book of Spiritual Grace,* St. Mechtilde of Hackeborn (c. 1240-1298)

Thus says the Lord: "Let not the wise man glory in his wisdom, let not the mighty man glory in his might, let not the rich man glory in his riches; but let him who glories glory in this, that he understands and knows me, that I am the Lord who practice steadfast love, justice, and righteousness in the earth; for in these things I delight, says the Lord." (Jer. 9:23-24)

God of mercy, make us grow daily in Your wisdom and justice.

DAY OF LENT 18

When we pray we must keep our whole heart fixed on prayer, for if our heart is divided we lose the fruit of true prayer. . . . We must give our heart wholly unto God. . . . It is through prayer and in prayer that we find God.
— *Book of Divine Consolation,* Bl. Angela of Foligno (1249-1309)

The word that came to Jeremiah from the Lord: "Hear the words of this covenant, and speak to the men of Judah and the inhabitants of Jerusalem. You shall say to them, Thus says the Lord, the God of Israel: Cursed be the man who does not heed the words of this covenant which I commanded your fathers when I brought them out of the land of Egypt, from the iron furnace, saying, Listen to my voice, and do all that I command you. So shall you be my people, and I will be your God, that I may perform the oath which I swore to your fathers, to give them a land flowing with milk and honey, as at this day." Then I answered, "So be it, Lord." (Jer. 11:1-5)

Renew the covenant, Lord, You made with me at baptism.

DAY OF LENT 19

No one prays to God properly except the person who prays to God solely for God, without a thought of anything else but God.
— *Sermons,* Meister Eckhart (1260-1327)

"Therefore do not pray for this people, or lift up a cry or prayer on their behalf, for I will not listen when they call to me in the time of their trouble. What right has my beloved in my house, when she has done vile deeds? Can vows and sacrificial flesh avert your doom? Can you then exult? The Lord once called you, 'A green olive tree, fair with goodly fruit'; but with the roar of a great tempest he will set fire to it, and its branches will be consumed. The Lord of hosts, who planted you, has pronounced evil against you, because of the evil which the house of Israel and the house of Judah have done, provoking me to anger by burning incense to Baal." (Jer. 11:14-17)

May we give praise, glory, and thanksgiving to You alone, our God.

DAY OF LENT 20

In prayer we may begin by praising God, and then we can recall His favors; next we lay our needs before Him, and, finally, we make our humble request of Him.
— *Science of Prayer,* Louis of Besse (13th century)

The Lord made it known to me and I knew; then thou didst show me their evil deeds. But I was like a gentle lamb led to the slaughter. I did not know it was against me they devised schemes, saying, "Let us destroy the tree with its fruits, let us cut him off from the land of the living, that his name be remembered no more." But, O Lord of hosts, who judgest righteously, who triest the heart and the mind, let me see thy vengeance upon them, for to thee have I committed my cause. (Jer. 11:18-20)

Keep me humble before You, Lord, so that I may always do Your will.

DAY OF LENT 21

True prayer is nothing other than our simple abandonment to God, with complete faithfulness to trust Him in all that He is.
— *Letters,* Bl. Hadewijch (13th century)

"Hear and give ear; be not proud, for the Lord has spoken. Give glory to the Lord your God before he brings darkness, before your feet stumble on the twilight mountains, and while you look for light he turns it into gloom and makes it deep darkness. But if you will not listen, my soul will weep in secret for your pride; my eyes will weep bitterly and run down with tears, because the Lord's flock has been taken captive." (Jer. 13:15-17)

Spirit of eternal light, flood my heart and mind this Lent with Your word.

DAY OF LENT 22

We really pray well when we think of no other thing, but all our mind is directed heavenwards and our soul is on fire with the fire of the Holy Spirit. Then a wonderful fulness of God's goodness is found in us. Then also from the innermost depths of our hearts shall the love of God rise, and all our prayer shall be made with intensity and purpose. . . .
— *The Amending of Life,* Richard Rolle (c. 1300-1349)

"Though our iniquities testify against us, act, O Lord, for thy name's sake; for our backslidings are many, we have sinned against thee. O thou hope of Israel, its savior in time of trouble, why shouldst thou be like a stranger in the land, like a wayfarer who turns aside to tarry for a night? Why shouldst thou be like a man confused, like a mighty man who cannot save? Yet thou, O Lord, art in the midst of us, and we are called by thy name; leave us not." (Jer. 14:7-9)

Help us to do what is good, right, and just in Your sight and to seek You with one heart.

DAY OF LENT 23

In true prayer the heart and soul of a person must go directly to God, and that is the essential thing. True prayer is this and nothing else: a person's mind is totally subjected to God in loving desire and humble submission to Him. . . .
— *Conferences,* John Tauler, O.P. (c. 1300-1361)

"You shall say to them this word: 'Let my eyes run down with tears night and day, and let them not cease, for the virgin daughter of my people is smitten with a great wound, with a very grievous blow. If I go out into the field, behold, those slain by the sword! And if I enter the city, behold, the diseases

47

of famine! For both prophet and priest ply their trade through the land, and have no knowledge.' " (Jer. 14:17-18)

We confess, Lord, that we have sinned; wash us clean by Your gift of salvation.

DAY OF LENT 24

Prayer is God, doing all things in all persons, for united is the action of the Father, the Son and the Holy Spirit, doing all through Jesus Christ.
— *On the Contemplative Life and Prayer,* St. Gregory of Sinai (d. 1346)

Hast thou utterly rejected Judah? Does thy soul loathe Zion? Why hast thou smitten us so that there is no healing for us? We looked for peace, but no good came; for a time of healing, but behold, terror. We acknowledge our wickedness, O Lord, and the iniquity of our fathers, for we have sinned against thee. Do not spurn us, for thy name's sake; do not dishonor thy glorious throne; remember and do not break thy covenant with us. Are there any among the false gods of the nations that can bring rain? Or can the heavens give showers? Art thou not he, O Lord our God? We set our hope on thee, for thou doest all these things. (Jer. 14:19-22)

Give us a fresh spirit, O God, to receive Your word and bear fruit in patience.

DAY OF LENT 25

Prayer offered within the heart, with attention and sincerity, with no other thought or imagining, by repeating the words "Lord Jesus Christ, Son of God," silently and innerly, leads the mind to our Lord Jesus Christ himself. By the words "have mercy upon me," it turns the prayer back towards him who prays, since he cannot as yet not pray about himself. But when he experiences perfect love, he stretches out completely towards our Lord Jesus Christ alone. . . .
— *Centuries on Prayer and Attention,* Callistus and Ignatius (14th century)

O Lord, thou knowest; remember me and visit me, and take vengeance for me on my persecutors. In thy forbearance take me not away; know that for thy sake I bear reproach. Thy words are found, and I ate them, and thy words became to me a joy and the delight of my heart; for I am called by thy name, O Lord, God of hosts. I did not sit in the company of merrymakers, nor did I rejoice; I sat alone, because thy hand was upon me, for thou hadst filled me with indignation. Why is my pain unceasing, my wound incurable, refusing to be healed? (Jer. 15:15-18)

Lord, feed us at the table of Your word and bread so that we may spend this Lent in Your service.

DAY OF LENT 26

Prayer is the elevation of the mind and heart to God through a devoted and humble love.
— *Works,* John Gerson (1363-1429)

Thus says the Lord: "Cursed is the man who trusts in man and makes flesh his arm, whose heart turns away from the Lord. He is like a shrub in the desert, and shall not see any good come. He shall dwell in the parched places of the wilderness, in an uninhabited salt land. Blessed is the man who trusts in the Lord, whose trust is the Lord. He is like a tree planted by water, that sends out its roots by the stream, and does not fear when heat comes, for its leaves remain green, and is not anxious in the year of drought, for it does not ceast to bear fruit." (Jer. 17:5-8)

Help me to place all my trust in You alone, O my God.

DAY OF LENT 27

Prayer is nothing other than the rising desire of the heart to God, and its detachment from all worldly thought. . . . Prayer is often likened to fire, which of its own nature always flees the earth and jumps into the air. Similarly, prayerful desire, when stroked and enflamed by the spiritual fire of God, faithfully goes up to Him from whom it comes.
— *The Scale of Perfection,* Walter Hilton (d. 1395)

Heal me, O Lord, and I shall be healed; save me, and I shall be saved; for thou art my praise. Behold, they say to me, "Where is the word of the Lord? Let it come!" I have not pressed thee to send evil, nor have I desired the day of disaster, thou knowest; that which came out of my lips was before thy face. Be not a terror to me; thou art my refuge in the day of evil. Let those be put to shame who persecute me, but let me not be put to shame; let them be dismayed, but let me not be dismayed; bring upon them the day of evil; destroy them with double destruction! (Jer. 17:14-18)

Deliver us from all evil, O Lord, which blinds us to Your mercy and love.

DAY OF LENT 28

Prayer is in essence a reverent and deliberate openness to God full of the desire to grow in personal uprightness and to overcome all evil.
— *The Cloud of Unknowing* (14th century)

The word that came to Jeremiah from the Lord: "Arise, and go down to the potter's house, and there I will let you hear my words." So I went down to the potter's house, and there he was working at his wheel. And the vessel he was making of clay was spoiled in the potter's hand, and he reworked it into another vessel, as it seemed good to the potter to do. Then the word of the Lord came to me: "O house of Israel, can I not do with you as this potter has done? says the Lord. Behold, like the clay in the potter's hand, so are you in my hand, O house of Israel. If at any time I declare concerning a nation or a kingdom, that I will pluck up and break down and destroy it, and if that nation, concerning which I have spoken, turns from its evil, I will repent of the evil that I intended to do to it." (Jer. 18:1-8)

O God, come to Your people and make us whole and holy.

DAY OF LENT 29

Prayer makes a person at peace with himself, and makes him tranquil and meek who was in strife and pain before. Prayer unites the person to God. Although a person is always like to God in nature and in substance, it is often unlike God in its state, through sin on the part of a person. Prayer, then, makes the person like to God in its state as it is in nature. God teaches us to pray and to trust greatly that we shall have what we pray for.
— *Revelations,* Julian of Norwich (1342-1416)

Then they said, "Come, let us make plots against Jeremiah, for the law shall not perish from the priest, nor counsel from the wise, nor the word from the prophet. Come, let us smite him with the tongue, and let us not heed any of his words." Give heed to me, O Lord, and hearken to my plea. Is evil a recompense for good? Yet they have dug a pit for my life. Remember how I stood before thee to speak good for them, to turn away thy wrath from them. (Jer. 18:18-20)

Let Your Lenten word be a lamp to guide us, O God, so that we may live in Your truth.

DAY OF LENT 30

Perfect prayer is achieved not with many words but with loving desire, when the soul rises up to me [God] with knowledge of herself. Every action is tempered by the other. In this way the person will have vocal and mental prayer at the same time, for the two go together like the active life and the contemplative life.
— *The Dialogue,* St. Catherine of Siena (1347-1380)

O Lord, thou hast deceived me, and I was deceived; thou art stronger than I, and thou hast prevailed. I have become a laughingstock all the day; every one mocks me. For whenever I speak, I cry out, I shout, "Violence and destruction!" For the word of the Lord has become for me a reproach and derision all day long. If I say, "I will not mention him, or speak any more in his name," there is in my heart as it were a burning fire shut up in my bones; and I am weary with holding it in, and I cannot. For I hear many whispering. Terror is on every side! "Denounce him! Let us denounce him!" say all my familiar friends, watching for my fall. "Perhaps he will be deceived, then we can overcome him, and take our revenge on him." (Jer. 20:7-10)

Good Master, teach us to love You in our neighbors, and in serving them to serve You.

DAY OF LENT 31

In prayer it is proper for us to know by experience that the person looks upon Him Who in one single gaze looks upon all things past, present and to come, and that thus He speaks to the person.
— *Fiery Soliloquy with God,* Gerlac Peters (1378-1411)

But the Lord is with me as a dread warrior; therefore my persecutors will stumble, they will not overcome me. They will be greatly shamed, for they will not succeed. Their eternal dishonor will never be forgotten. O Lord of hosts, who triest the righteous, who seest the heart and the mind, let me see thy vengeance upon them, for to thee have I committed my cause. Sing to the

Lord; praise the Lord! For he has delivered the life of the needy from the hand of evildoers. (Jer. 20:11-13)

Give us Your strength to love our enemies, O God, and to do good to them.

DAY OF LENT 32

Prayer is a faithful messenger, well known to the King of Heaven, and has entrance into His private dwelling. . . . Prayer is a most faithful messenger, known to the King, who is accustomed to enter His dwelling, and by its insistence to influence the compassionate mind of the King, and to obtain aid for us in our toils.
— *Sermons,* St. Bernardine of Siena (1380-1444)

"Woe to him who builds his house by unrighteousness, and his upper rooms by injustice: who makes his neighbor serve him for nothing, and does not give him his wages; who says, 'I will build myself a great house with spacious upper rooms,' and cuts out windows for it, paneling it with cedar, and painting it with vermilion. Do you think you are a king because you compete in cedar? Did not your father eat and drink and do justice and righteousness? Then it was well with him. He judged the cause of the poor and needy; then it was well. Is not this to know me? says the Lord." (Jer. 22:13-16)

Strengthen the weak, console the sorrowful, care for the lonely, and give hope to the dying, O merciful Lord.

DAY OF LENT 33

Prayer is the great art of knowing how to converse with Jesus; and knowing how to keep Jesus with you in great wisdom. Be humble and peaceful, and Jesus will dwell with you. Be devout and quiet, and Jesus will remain with you. . . . If you drive Him away from you and lose Him, to whom will you go, and whom will you then seek as your friend?
— *Imitation of Christ,* Thomas à Kempis (c. 1380-1471)

"Woe to the shepherds who destroy and scatter the sheep of my pasture!" says the Lord. Therefore thus says the Lord, the God of Israel, concerning the shepherds who care for my people: "You have scattered my flock, and have driven them away, and you have not attended to them. Behold, I will attend to you for your evil doings, says the Lord. Then I will gather the remnant of my flock out of all the countries where I have driven them, and I will bring them back to their fold, and they shall be fruitful and multiply. I will set shepherds over them who will care for them, and they shall fear no more, nor be dismayed, neither shall any be missing, says the Lord." (Jer. 23:1-4)

O Good Shepherd, help us to deny ourselves today, and not deny those in need.

DAY OF LENT 34

Prayer is the way to oneness with God. It is like a certain golden rope or chain extended from heaven, by which we try to draw God to us, whereas we are more truly brought up to God.
— *A Treatise on Prayer*, St. John Fisher (1469-1535)

"Am I a God at hand, says the Lord, and not a God afar off? Can a man hide himself in secret places so that I cannot see him? says the Lord. Do I not fill heaven and earth? says the Lord. I have heard what the prophets have said who prophesy lies in my name, saying, 'I have dreamed, I have dreamed! How long shall there be lies in the heart of the prophets who prophesy lies, and who prophesy the deceit of their own heart, who think to make my people forget my name by their dreams which they tell one another. . . . Is not my word like fire, says the Lord, and like a hammer which breaks the rock in pieces? Therefore, behold, I am against the prophets, says the Lord, who steal my words from one another." (Jer. 23:23-30)

Teacher and Guide, teach us Your truth and keep us in Your care.

DAY OF LENT 35

The ancients correctly defined prayer as a climbing up of the heart to God. . . . As a shoemaker makes a shoe, and a tailor makes a jacket, so should a Christian pray. Prayer is the daily business of a Christian.
— *Table Talk*, Martin Luther (1483-1546)

Then the word of the Lord came to me: "Thus says the Lord, the God of Israel: Like these good figs, so I will regard as good the exiles from Judah, whom I have sent away from this place to the land of the Chaldeans. I will set my eyes upon them for good, and I will bring them back to this land. I will build them up, and not tear them down; I will plant them, and not uproot them. I will give them a heart to know that I am the Lord; and they shall be my people and I will be their God, for they shall return to me with their whole heart." (Jer. 24:4-7)

Master our rebellious hearts, O God, and teach us Your gracious kindness.

DAY OF LENT 36

Whatever our bodies may be doing, we should at the same time always elevate our minds to God, which is the most pleasing form of prayer. For no matter where we may walk, as long as our minds are directed to God, we definitely do not turn away from Him who is present everywhere.
— *Treatise on Prayer,* St. Thomas More (1487-1535)

"And it shall come to pass in that day, says the Lord of hosts, that I will break the yoke from off their neck, and I will burst their bonds, and strangers shall no more make servants of them. But they shall serve the Lord their God and David their king, whom I will raise up for them. Then fear not, O Jacob my servant, says the Lord, nor be dismayed, O Israel; for lo, I will save you from afar, and your offspring from the land of their captivity. Jacob shall return and have quiet and ease, and none shall make him afraid. For I am with you to save you, says the Lord; I will make a full end of all the nations among whom I scattered you, but of you I will not make a full end. I will chasten you in just measure, and I will by no means leave you unpunished." (Jer. 30:8-11)

Give Your strength to all in distress, O God, and help us show Your loving concern to others.

DAY OF LENT 37

Prayer consists in this, that with the grace of our Lord, the lights of the mind, the love of the will, persevering union with God (even outside of formal prayer) accompany and guide all our actions, so that we find God in all things and that all our other thoughts may freely be on the Lord. Our prayer should be such that it increases in us the spiritual desire for work . . . and the work should increase our capacity and pleasure in prayer.
— *Spiritual Letters,* St. Ignatius Loyola (1491-1556)

"For thus says the Lord: Your hurt is incurable, and your wound is grievous. There is none to uphold your cause, no medicine for your wound, no healing for you. All your lovers have forgotten you; they care nothing for you; for I have dealt you the blow of an enemy, the punishment of a merciless foe, because your guilt is great, because your sins are flagrant. Why do you cry out over your hurt? Your pain is incurable. Because your guilt is great, because your sins are flagrant, I have done these things to you." (Jer. 30:12-15)

Help us to see Your sacred passion in our daily problems, O Christ, and to use them all for Your glory.

DAY OF LENT 38

Prayer is a service owed to God in that by it we bestow this honor to God, namely that in the midst of so many sorrows He assists all who call upon Him.
— *Treatise on Prayer,* Philip Melanchthon (1497-1560)

"At that time, says the Lord, I will be the God of all the families of Israel, and they shall be my people." Thus says the Lord: "The people who survived the sword found grace in the wilderness; when Israel sought for rest, the Lord appeared to him from afar. I have loved you with an everlasting love; therefore I have continued my faithfulness to you. Again I will build you, and you shall be built, O virgin Israel!" (Jer. 31:1-4)

Pour out Your love into our hearts, O good Jesus, as we share in the mystery of Your cross this Lent.

DAY OF LENT 39

Prayer is our way to go and converse with God familiarly; it is a conversation with God which is pleasing and heavenly.
— *Treatise on Mental Prayer,* St. Peter of Alcantara (1499-1562)

For thus says the Lord: "Sing aloud with gladness for Jacob, and raise shouts for the chief of the nations; proclaim, give praise, and say, The Lord has saved his people, the remnant of Israel. Behold, I will bring them from the north country, and gather them from the farthest parts of the earth, among them the blind and the lame, the woman with child and her who is in travail, together; a great company, they shall return here. With weeping they shall come, and with consolations I will lead them back, I will make them walk by brooks of water, in a straight path in which they shall not stumble; for I am a father to Israel, and Ephraim is my first-born." (Jer. 31:7-9)

God of mercy, may this Lenten day be for us a day rich in good works to our neighbor.

DAY OF LENT 40

By prayer I understand a secret and inner conversation in which a person communicates with God, thinking, asking, giving thanks, contemplating, and in general everything which in such secret conversation goes on between the person and God. . . .
— *The Ascent of Mt. Carmel,* St. John of Avila (1500-1568)

"I have heard Ephraim bemoaning, 'Thou hast chastened me, and I was chastened, like an untrained calf; bring me back that I may be restored, for thou art the Lord my God. For after I had turned away I repented; and after I was instructed, I smote upon my thigh; I was ashamed, and I was confounded, because I bore the disgrace of my youth.' Is Ephraim my dear son? Is he my darling child? For as often as I speak against him, I do remember him still. Therefore my heart yearns for him; I will surely have mercy on him, says the Lord." (Jer. 31:18-20)

God of merciful forgiveness, give us the spirit of prayer and repentance.

DAY OF LENT 41

Prayer is the coming forth of the person to receive God, when He comes in His abundant grace and the person takes Him to itself. Prayer is the remaining of the person in the presence of God, and of God in the presence of the person.
— *Summa of the Christian Life,* Luis de Granada (1504-1588)

"Behold, the days are coming, says the Lord, when I will make a new covenant with the house of Israel and the house of Judah, not like the covenant which I made with their fathers when I took them by the hand to bring them out of the land of Egypt, my covenant which they broke, though I was their husband, says the Lord. But this is the covenant which I will make with the house of Israel after those days, says the Lord: I will put my law within them, and I will write it upon their hearts; and I will be their God, and they shall be my people." (Jer. 31:31-33)

During this Holy Week, O God, help us to renew our covenant of fidelity to You.

DAY OF LENT 42

When we set out to pray there are two things we must seek above all: first, that we may have access to God, and secondly, that we may dwell in Him with full and secure confidence, knowing His fatherly love for us and His limitless kindness.
— *Biblical Commentary,* John Calvin (1509-1564)

"Now therefore thus says the Lord, the God of Israel, concerning this city of which you say, 'It is given into the hand of the king of Babylon by sword, by famine, and by pestilence': Behold, I will gather them from all the countries to which I drove them in my anger and my wrath and in great indignation; I will bring them back to this place, and I will make them dwell in safety. And they shall be my people, and I will be their God. I will give them one heart and one way, that they may fear me for ever, for their own good and the good of their children after them. I will make with them an everlasting covenant, that I will not turn away from doing good to them; and I will put the fear of me in their hearts, that they may not turn from me." (Jer. 32:36-40)

Jesus, You went up to Jerusalem to suffer for us. May we benefit from Your victory over sin for us.

DAY OF LENT 43

Prayer is a crying out and a desire of the spirit Godward for that which the person needs, just like the sick sorrowing in heart and longing for health. In this manner we may enjoy the thing we desire, or have need of.
— *The Pomander of Prayer,* Thomas Becon (1513-1567)

"Thus says the Lord: In this place of which you say, 'It is a waste without man or beast,' in the cities of Judah and the streets of Jerusalem that are desolate, without man or inhabitant or beast, there shall be heard again the voice of mirth and the voice of gladness, the voice of the bridegroom and the voice of the bride, the voices of those who sing, as they bring thank offerings to the house of the Lord: 'Give thanks to the Lord of hosts, for the Lord is good, for his steadfast love endures for ever!' For I will restore the fortunes of the land as a first, says the Lord." (Jer. 33:10-11)

O God, Your Son Jesus humbled himself by death on the cross for us; give us all this week Your continuing care.

DAY OF LENT 44

Prayer is nothing but a simple friendly affair, it seems to me, a conversing frequently and privately with the One who we know loves us.
— *Her Life,* St. Teresa of Avila (1515-1582)

"Behold, the days are coming, says the Lord, when I will fulfill the promise I made to the house of Israel and the house of Judah. In those days and at that time I will cause a righteous Branch to spring forth for David; and he shall execute justice and righteousness in the land. In those days Judah will be saved and Jerusalem will dwell securely. And this is the name by which it will be called: 'The Lord is our righteousness.' " (Jer. 33:14-16)

You made Your cross the tree of life, O Jesus; give us its life-giving fruit today.

DAY OF LENT 45

Prayer is to the supernatural order what speech is to the natural order. A person who does not pray is similar to an animal that does not speak. There is nothing that Satan fears more than prayer, and what he tries most is to destroy this spirit of prayer in persons.
— *Spiritual Conferences,* St. Philip Neri (1515-1595)

All the people from the least to the greatest, came near and said to Jeremiah the prophet, "Let our supplication come before you, and pray to the Lord your God for us, for all this remnant (for we are left but a few of many, as your eyes see us), that the Lord your God may show us the way we should go, and the thing that we should do." Jeremiah the prophet said to them, "I have heard you; behold, I will pray to the Lord your God according to your request, and whatever the Lord answers you I will tell you; I will keep nothing back from you." Then they said to Jeremiah, "May the Lord be a true and faithful witness against us if we do not act according to all the word with which the Lord your God sends you to us." (Jer. 42:1 5)

Redeemer of the world, give us a greater share in Your paschal mystery through the gift of Your word.

DAY OF LENT 46

Prayer is the main and most effective means to bring into harmony and put in order our whole life and to overcome and make smooth all the obstacles that impede the way of virtue.

— *Practice of Perfection and Christian Virtues,* Alphonsus Rodriguez
    (1531-1617)

For thus says the Lord of hosts, the God of Israel. . . . "Know for a certainty that I have warned you this day that you have gone astray at the cost of your lives. For you sent me to the Lord your God, saying, 'Pray for us to the Lord our God, and whatever the Lord our God says declare to us and we will do it.' And I have this day declared it to you, but you have not obeyed the voice of the Lord your God in anything that he sent me to tell you. Now therefore know for a certainty that you shall die by the sword, by famine, and by pestilence in the place where you desire to go to live." (Jer. 42:18-22)

Christ, our salvation, You gave Yourself up for us in death; help us die to self this Good Friday for You.

DAY OF LENT 47

Prayer is the path of all divine grace; by it God is driven, as it were, to grant us the strength of heaven, and to destroy, by our weak strength, the worst of our enemies.

— *The Spiritual Combat,* Lawrence Scupoli (c. 1530-1610)

The elders of the daughter of Zion sit on the ground in silence; they have cast dust on their heads and put on sackcloth; the maidens of Jerusalem have bowed their heads to the ground. My eyes are spent with weeping; my soul is in tumult; my heart is poured out in grief because of the destruction of the daughter of my people, because infants and babes faint in the streets of the city. They cry to their mothers, "Where is bread and wine?" as they faint like wounded men in the streets of the city, as their life is poured out on their mothers' bosom. What can I say for you, to what compare you, O daughter of Jerusalem? What can I liken to you, that I may comfort you, O virgin daughter of Zion? For vast as the sea is your ruin; who can restore you? (Jeremiah, Lamentations 2:10-13)

Christ our Savior, Your sorrowing Mother stood by You at your death and burial; may she intercede for us this day.

EASTER

Easter is the season of peace and joy, two attitudes to daily life which are hard to realize. They demand an inner reality, one that comes from faith in our new Easter life. Without this faith Easter makes no sense, and the peace and joy of Easter are utterly impossible.

The special signs of Resurrection and Easter faith are the ones Jesus himself gave us: His sacred actions and teachings, holy baptism, forgiveness of sin and reconciliation, the Holy Eucharist, and the continuing presence of His Spirit among us. Only by faith can we know the power of his new Easter life.

One special characteristic of this new life of Easter joy is its intimate relationship with the experience of forgiveness and reconciliation. Baptism, or Reconciliation, "our second baptism," has allowed all of us to know Christ's forgiveness intimately. This is the real source of our new peace and joy.

The catechumen's journey of conversion and the Church's own journey of baptism and renewal culminate in this Easter season. The fifty days from the Sunday of the Resurrection to Pentecost are celebrated as one feast day, sometimes called the "Great Sunday," as St. Athanasius called it. The mystery of the Lord's life into which we are baptized is so rich that we take a full fifty days to savor it in prayer and personal reflection.

DAY OF EASTER 1

Prayer is nothing other than the quiet and loving outpouring of God which, if accepted, inflames the person with the spirit of love.
— *The Ascent of Mt. Carmel,* St. John of the Cross (1542-1591)

Now on the first day of the week Mary Magdalene came to the tomb early, while it was still dark, and saw that the stone had been taken away from the tomb. So she ran, and went to Simon Peter and the other disciple, the one whom Jesus loved, and said to them, "They have taken the Lord out of the tomb, and we do not know where they have laid him." . . . Simon Peter came and went into the tomb; he saw the linen cloths lying, and the napkin, which had been on his head, not lying with the linen cloths but rolled up in a place by itself. Then the other disciple, who reached the tomb first, also went in, and saw and believed; for as yet they did not know the scripture, that he must rise from the dead. Then the disciples went back to their homes. (John 20:1-2, 6-10)

Lord Jesus, praise, glory, and thanksgiving be Yours for the new life You have given us.

DAY OF EASTER 2

Prayer is the elevation of our mind to God. . . . Prayer is conversation with God both by speaking to Him and especially by listening to Him.
— *Ascetical Treatises,* St. Robert Bellarmine (1542-1621)

Mary stood weeping outside the tomb, and as she wept she stooped to look into the tomb; and she saw two angels in white, sitting where the body of Jesus had lain, one at the head and one at the feet. They said to her, "Woman, why are you weeping?" She said to them, "Because they have taken away my Lord, and I do not know where they have laid him." Saying this, she turned round and saw Jesus standing, but she did not know that it was Jesus. Jesus said to her, "Woman, why are you weeping? Whom do you seek?" Supposing him to be the gardener, she said to him, "Sir, if you have carried him away, tell me where you have laid him, and I will take him away." Jesus said to her, "Mary." She turned and said to him in Hebrew, "Rabboni!" (which means Teacher). (John 20:11-16)

Lord, help me believe deeply in the power of Your resurrection in my life.

DAY OF EASTER 3

All the different elevations of our spirit to God are included in the meaning of prayer.
— *Laws of Ecclesiastical Polity,* Richard Hooker (1554-1600)

On the evening of that day, the first day of the week, the doors being shut where the disciples were, for fear of the Jews, Jesus came and stood among them and said to them, "Peace be with you." When he said this, he showed them his hands and his side. Then the disciples were glad when they saw the Lord. Jesus said to them again, "Peace be with you. As the Father has sent me, even so I send you." And when he had said this, he breathed on them, and said to them, "Receive the Holy Spirit. If you forgive the sins of any, they are forgiven; if you retain the sins of any, they are retained." (John 20:19-23).

Lord, let us know Your peace, so that we may go to others to share Your gifts with them.

DAY OF EASTER 4

The basis of our prayer is God's grace in Christ. . . . The second basis for prayer is God's gracious presence. This ought to stir us up at all times and places to speak to God. A third basis of prayer is God's truth. . . . A fourth basis of prayer is God's eternal Word.
— *True Christianity,* Johann Arndt (1555-1621)

Now Thomas, one of the twelve, called the Twin, was not with them when Jesus came. So the other disciples told him, "We have seen the Lord." But he said to them, "Unless I see in his hands the print of the nails, and place my finger in the mark of the nails, and place my hand in his side, I will not believe." Eight days later, his disciples were again in the house, and Thomas was with them. The doors were shut, but Jesus came and stood among them, and said, "Peace be with you." Then he said to Thomas, "Put your finger here, and see my hands; and put out your hand, and place it in my side; do not be faithless, but believing." Thomas answered him, "My Lord and my God!" Jesus said to him, "Have you believed because you have seen me? Blessed are those who have not seen and yet believe." (John 20:24-29)

Lord, increase our Easter faith. Give us the faith only You can give.

DAY OF EASTER 5

Prayer is the lifting up of our spirits to God together with a confession of our sins.
— *Pattern of Catechetical Doctrine,* Lancelet Andrewes (1555-1626)

After this Jesus revealed himself again to the disciples by the Sea of Tiberias; and he revealed himself in this way. Simon Peter, Thomas called the Twin, Nathanael of Cana in Galilee, the sons of Zebedee, and two others of his disciples were together. Simon Peter said to them, "I am going fishing." They said to him, "We will go with you." They went out and got into the boat; but that night they caught nothing. Just as day was breaking, Jesus stood on the beach; yet the disciples did not know that it was Jesus. (John 21:1-4)

Lord Jesus, share with us Peter's gift of faith in Your word.

DAY OF EASTER 6

Prayer allows us to place our request before God according to his word from a contrite heart in the name of Christ with the assurance of being heard.
— *Exposition on the Lord's Prayer,* William Perkins (1558-1602)

Jesus said to them, "Children, have you any fish?" They answered him, "No." He said to them, "Cast the net on the right side of the boat, and you will find some." So they cast it, and now they were not able to haul it in, for the quantity of fish. That disciple whom Jesus loved said to Peter, "It is the Lord!" When Simon Peter heard that it was the Lord, he put on his clothes, for he was stripped for work, and sprang into the sea. But the other disciples came in the boat, dragging the net full of fish, for they were not far from the land, but about a hundred yards off. (John 21:5-8)

Lord, may we too recognize You today as You come into our lives.

DAY OF EASTER 7

Even if you have not expressed any desire, yet if your heart is ready to act and is prepared to do good, placing its confidence not in itself but in God, such readiness will be accepted as a prayer, and the grace needed for good living will be given to you.
— *On the Spiritual Life,* Alvarez de Paz (1560-1620)

When they got out on land, they saw a charcoal fire there, with fish lying on it, and bread. Jesus said to them, "Bring some of the fish that you have just caught." So Simon Peter went aboard and hauled the net ashore, full of large fish, a hundred and fifty-three of them; and although there were so many, the net was not torn. Jesus said to them, "Come and have breakfast." Now none of the disciples dared to ask him, "Who are you?" They knew it was the Lord. Jesus came and took the bread and gave it to them, and so with the fish. This was now the third time that Jesus was revealed to the disciples after he was raised from the dead. (John 21:9-14)

Lord, may we continue to know You in the breaking of the bread.

DAY OF EASTER 8

The chief exercise of prayer is to speak to God in the depth of one's

heart. . . . Prayer is a dialogue, a familiar talk or conversation of the person with God; we speaking to God and He to us, we ascending to Him, breathing in Him, and He in return breathing His inspiration upon us.
— *Love of God,* St. Francis de Sales (1567-1622)

When they had finished breakfast, Jesus said to Simon Peter, "Simon, son of John, do you love me more than these?" He said to him, "Yes, Lord; you know that I love you." He said to him, "Feed my lambs." A second time he said to him, "Simon, son of John, do you love me?" He said to him, "Yes, Lord; you know that I love you." He said to him, "Tend my sheep." He said to him the third time, "Simon, son of John, do you love me?" And he said to him, "Lord, you know everything; you know that I love you." Jesus said to him, "Feed my sheep. Truly, truly, I say to you, when you were young, you girded yourself and walked where you would; but when you are old, you will stretch out your hands, and another will gird you and carry you where you do not wish to go." (This he said to show by what death he was to glorify God.) And after this he said to him, "Follow me." (John 21:15-19)

Lord, You accepted Peter as the weak person he was. Accept me too.

DAY OF EASTER 9

Praying is a kind of wrestling and contending with God, a striving with Him.
— *Bruised Reed and Smoking Flax,* Richard Sibbes (1577-1635)

Lifting up his eyes, then, and seeing that a multitude was coming to him, Jesus said to Philip, "How are we to buy bread, so that these people may eat?" This he said to test him, for he himself knew what we would do. Philip answered him, "Two hundred denarii would not buy enough bread for each of them to get a little." One of his disciples, Andrew, Simon Peter's brother, said to him, "There is a lad here who has five barley loaves and two fish; but what are they among so many?" Jesus said, "Make the people sit down." Now there was much grass in the place; so the men sat down, in number about five thousand. Jesus then took the loaves, and when he had given thanks, he distributed them to those who were seated; so also the fish, as much as they wanted. And when they had eaten their fill, he told his disciples, "Gather up the fragments left over, that nothing may be lost." (John 6:5-12)

Thank You, Lord, for the many wonderful ways You help us in our needs.

DAY OF EASTER 10

To pray is to get as close to God as one can. . . . And to make a prayer a right prayer, there are so many essential factors that even the best person may justly suspect his best prayer. Since prayer must be of faith, prayer can only be so perfect, as the faith is perfect.
— *Sermon,* John Donne (1572-1631)

When evening came, his disciples went down to the sea, got into a boat, and started across the sea to Capernaum. It was now dark, and Jesus had not yet come to them. The sea rose because a strong wind was blowing. When they had rowed about three or four miles, they saw Jesus walking on the sea and drawing near to the boat. They were frightened, but he said to them, "It is I; do not be afraid." Then they were glad to take him into the boat, and immediately the boat was at the land to which they were going. (John 6:16-20)

Help us overcome our fears of daily life, Lord. You alone have the power.

DAY OF EASTER 11

The great method of prayer is to have none. If in going to prayer one can form in oneself a simple desire for receiving the spirit of God, that will suffice for all methods. Prayer should proceed from grace and not by artifice.
— *Discourses,* St. Jane Frances de Chantal (1572-1641)

On the next day the people who remained on the other side of the sea saw that there had been only one boat there, and that Jesus had not entered the boat with his disciples, but that his disciples had gone away alone. However, boats from Tiberias came near the place where they ate the bread after the Lord had given thanks. So when the people saw that Jesus was not there, nor his disciples, they themselves got into the boats and went to Capernaum, seeking Jesus. (John 6:22-24)

Through Your words and wonderful signs, Lord, deepen our faith.

DAY OF EASTER 12

Prayer consists not in thinking much but in loving much. . . . The longing of a loving heart for God and its acceptance of undesirable trials is one of the most perfect prayers. . . . When we pray we should be as empty cups before God, into which His blessings may be poured drop by drop if He so wills, and

we should be as ready to go home with our cup empty as if it had been filled to the brim.
— *Discourses,* St. Jane Frances de Chantal (1572-1641)

[Jesus said,] "Do not labor for the food which perishes, but for the food which endures to eternal life, which the Son of man will give to you; for on him has God the Father set his seal." Then they said to him, "What must we do, to be doing the works of God?" Jesus answered them, "This is the word of God, that you believe in him whom he has sent." So they said to him, "Then what sign do you do, that we may see, and believe you? What work do you perform? Our fathers ate the manna in the wilderness; as it is written, 'He gave them bread from heaven to eat.' " Jesus then said to them, "Truly, truly, I say to you, it was not Moses who gave you the bread from heaven; my Father gives you the true bread from heaven. For the bread of God is that which comes down from heaven, and gives life to the world." They said to him, "Lord, give us this bread always." (John 6:27-34)

Jesus, Lord, help me really believe You will save me.

DAY OF EASTER 13

Prayer is our communication with God.
— *The Art of Divine Meditation,* Joseph Hall (1574-1656)

Jesus said to them, "I am the bread of life; he who comes to me shall not hunger, and he who believes in me shall never thirst. But I said to you that you have seen me and yet do not believe. All that the Father gives me will come to me; and him who comes to me I will not cast out. For I have come down from heaven, not to do my own will, but the will of him who sent me; and this is the will of him who sent me, that I should lose nothing of all that he has given me, but raise it up at the last day. For this is the will of my Father, that every one who sees the Son and believes in him should have eternal life; and I will raise him up at the last day." (John 6:35-40)

Lord, You overcame death. In this Easter celebration, may I know Your new life.

DAY OF EASTER 14

In our prayer, then, we adore Jesus in himself, all that He is, and in all that He does, for all His days and moments are to be reverenced because of the

dignity of His Person; the least actions of Jesus are to be prayed over.
— *Discourse on the Grandeur of Jesus,* Cardinal De Berulle (1575-1620)

The Jews then murmured at him, because he said, "I am the bread which came down from heaven." They said, "Is not this Jesus, the son of Joseph, whose father and mother we know? How does he now say, 'I have come down from heaven'?" Jesus answered them, "Do not murmur among yourselves. No one can come to me unless the Father who sent me draws him; and I will raise him up at the last day." (John 6:41-44)

Grant me, Lord, a positive spirit. Help me overcome my tendency to complain.

DAY OF EASTER 15

Prayer is the union with God brought about by the sacrifice of the personal will. It is, therefore, the only "Yoga Exercise" worthy of our serious thought.
— *The Way to Christ,* Jacob Boehme (1575-1624)

"It is written in the prophets, 'And they shall all be taught by God.' Every one who has heard and learned from the Father comes to me. Not that any one has seen the Father except him who is from God; he has seen the Father. Truly, truly, I say to you, he who believes has eternal life. I am the bread of life. Your fathers ate the manna in the wilderness, and they died. This is the bread which comes down from heaven, that a man may eat of it and not die. I am the living bread which came down from heaven; if any one eats of this bread, he will live for ever; and the bread which I shall give for the life of the world is my flesh." (John 6:45-51)

Living Bread of God, nourish my Easter life with Your gifts.

DAY OF EASTER 16

Prayer is nothing else but a devout intention, directed to God for the obtaining of blessings, and the removing of evils.
— *Holy Wisdom,* Augustine Baker (1575-1641)

The Jews then disputed among themselves, saying, "How can this man give us his flesh to eat?" So Jesus said to them, "Truly, truly, I say to you, unless you eat flesh of the Son of man and drink his blood, you have no life in you; he who eats my flesh and drinks my blood has eternal life, and I will raise him up at the last day. For my flesh is food indeed, and my blood is drink indeed. He who eats my flesh and drinks my blood abides in me, and I in him. As the living Father sent me, and I live because of the Father, so he who eats me will live because of me. This is the bread which came down from heaven, not such as the fathers ate and died; he who eats this bread will live for ever." (John 6:52-58)

Hold us close to You, Lord, by the strength of Your Paschal Mystery.

DAY OF EASTER 17

Prayer is a raising up of the mind to God, through which the person is as it were detached from itself and seeks God in himself. It is a conversation of the person with God, a mutual dialogue in which God tells the person inwardly what He wants it to know and do and in which the person says to its God what He himself has told it to request from Him.
— *Conferences,* St. Vincent de Paul (1581-1660)

Many of his disciples, when they heard it, said, "This is a hard saying; who can listen to it?" But Jesus, knowing in himself that his disciples murmured at it, said to them, "Do you take offense at this? Then what if you were to see the Son of man ascending where he was before? It is the spirit that gives life, the flesh is of no avail; the words that I have spoken to you are spirit and life. But there are some of you that do not believe." For Jesus knew from the first who those were that did not believe, and who it was that would betray him. And he said, "This is why I told you that no one can come to me unless it is granted him by the Father." (John 6:60-65)

You alone, Lord, are the Truth. Help us to believe Your words of salvation.

DAY OF EASTER 18

Every inner movement of the soul toward God, either a thought or a desire, is a prayer.
— *Theological Treatise,* Francis Suarez (1584-1617)

After this many of his disciples drew back and no longer went about with him. Jesus said to the twelve, "Do you also wish to go away?" Simon Peter answered him, "Lord, to whom shall we go? You have the words of eternal life; and we have believed, and have come to know, that you are the Holy

69

One of God." Jesus answered them, "Did I not choose you, the twelve, and one of you is a devil?" He spoke of Judas the son of Simon Iscariot, for he, one of the twelve, was to betray him. (John 6:66-69)

Holy One of God, never allow us to part from You.

DAY OF EASTER 19

In prayer our only object ought to be to perfect the will, and not merely to become more enlightened. . . . Prayer presupposes a peaceful and recollected person, who is neither disturbed by violent passions, nor mastered by any inordinate love, nor burdened by too many cares, nor hindered by worries; nor does God ordinarily communicate himself until we have been faithful in the exercise of prayer for some time.
— *Spiritual Teaching,* Louis Lallemant, S.J. (1587-1635)

"Truly, truly, I say to you, he who does not enter the sheepfold by the door but climbs in by another way, that man is a thief and a robber; but he who enters by the door is the shepherd of the sheep. To him the gatekeeper opens; the sheep hear his voice, and he calls his own sheep by name and leads them out. When he has brought out all his own, he goes before them, and the sheep follow him, for they know his voice. A stranger they will not follow, but they will flee from him, for they do not know the voice of strangers." This figure Jesus used with them, but they did not understand what he was saying to them. (John 10:1-6)

Good Shepherd, lead us gently but firmly in Your ways.

DAY OF EASTER 20

To pray is to walk with our eyes fixed only on God. To contemplate Christ is to look on Him alone with the eyes of faith, without asking oneself or imagining anything further, but just continuing to look at Him and love Him.
— *Spiritual Works,* Friar Juan Falconi (1596-1638)

So Jesus again said to them, "Truly, truly, I say to you, I am the door of the sheep. All who came before me are thieves and robbers; but the sheep did not heed them. I am the door; if any one enters by me, he will be saved, and will go in and out and find pasture. The thief comes only to steal and kill and destroy; I came that they may have life, and have it abundantly. I am the good shepherd. The good shepherd lays down his life for the sheep. He who is a hireling and not a shepherd, whose own the sheep are not, sees the wolf coming and leaves the sheep and flees; and the wolf snatches them and scatters them. He flees because he is a hireling and cares nothing for the sheep." (John 10:7-13)

Jesus, our only Shepherd, help us hear Your voice above all others.

DAY OF EASTER 21

Prayer is loving familiarity with God, who by His divine approaches permits the person to converse with Him, and, if I may say so, to be delighted with Him. . . . The clear purpose of prayer is to raise our hearts to God. That is why in prayer the heart should be more at work than the intellect.
— *Autobiography,* St. Marie of the Incarnation (1599-1672)

"I am the good shepherd; I know my own and my own know me, as the Father knows me and I know the Father; and I lay down my life for the sheep. And I have other sheep, that are not of this fold; I must bring them also, and they will heed my voice. So there shall be one flock, one shepherd. For this reason the Father loves me, because I lay down my life, that I may take it again. No one takes it from me, but I lay it down of my own accord. I have power to lay it down, and I have power to take it again; this charge I have received from my Father." (John 10:14-18)

Lord, Jesus, continue to know me as Your own. May You be my only Guide.

DAY OF EASTER 22

In prayer, as in the Holy Eucharist, we adore Jesus Christ present, in such a way that only a curtain must be removed so that we might see Him. In prayer He nourishes and strengthens the soul and unites himself intimately to it. He dwells in it and it in Him, making it like himself.
— *Christian Catechism for Interior Life,* J.J. Olier (1608-1657)

It was the feast of the Dedication at Jerusalem; it was winter, and Jesus was walking in the temple, in the portico of Solomon. So the Jews gathered round him and said to him, "How long will you keep us in suspense? If you are the Christ, tell us plainly." Jesus answered them, "I told you, and you do not believe. The works that I do in my Father's name, they bear witness to me; but you do not believe, because you do not belong to my sheep. My sheep hear my voice, and I know them, and they follow me; and I give them eternal life, and they shall never perish, and no one shall snatch them out of my hand. My Father, who has given them to me, is greater than all, and no one is able to snatch them out of the Father's hand. I and the Father are one." (John 10:22-30)

Gentle Shepherd, give us Your word. Help us follow it boldly.

DAY OF EASTER 23

Prayer is a gift of God which depends much more on grace than on our industry and labor. The Holy Ghost is the author and Master of it. It is He who calls us to it; it is from Him that we may expect success. We can, nevertheless, on our side, dispose ourselves for it by purity of heart, by recollection, by the practice of the virtues which render souls capable of conversing with God.
— *Spiritual Treatises,* Jean Rigoleuc, S.J. (d. 1662)

Now a certain man was ill, Lazarus of Bethany, the village of Mary and her sister Martha. It was Mary who anointed the Lord with ointment and wiped his feet with her hair, whose brother Lazarus was ill. So the sisters sent to him, saying, "Lord, he whom you love is ill." But when Jesus heard it he said, "This illness is not unto death; it is for the glory of God, so that the Son of God may be glorified by means of it." (John 11:1-4)

Lord, Your death on the cross has brought us life. We thank You for our Easter life.

DAY OF EASTER 24

Prayer is a religious act, by which we reverence God and ask blessings from Him.
— *Treatise on Spiritual Life,* John Cardinal Bona (1609-1674)

Now Jesus loved Martha and her sister and Lazarus. So when he heard that he was ill, he stayed two days longer in the place where he was. Then after this he said to the disciples, "Let us go into Judea again." The disciples said to him, "Rabbi, the Jews were but now seeking to stone you, and are you going there again?" Jesus answered, "Are there any twelve hours in the day? If any one walks in the day, he does not stumble, because he sees the light of this world. But if any one walks in the night, he stumbles, because the light is not in him." (John 11:5-10)

Light of the World, be the light for all our paths.

DAY OF EASTER 25

Prayer is nothing else but the manifestation of the will or mind of God.
— *Holy Discoveries,* John Saltmarsh (c. 1610-1647)

Then he said to them, "Our friend Lazarus has fallen asleep, but I go to awake him out of sleep." The disciples said to him, "Lord, if he has fallen asleep, he will recover." Now Jesus had spoken of his death, but they thought that he meant taking rest in sleep. Then Jesus told them plainly, "Lazarus is dead; and for your sake I am glad that I was not there, so that you may believe. But let us go to him." Thomas, called the Twin, said to his fellow disciples, "Let us also go, that we may die with him." (John 11:11-16)

You died for us, O Jesus; help us die to self for You a little each day.

DAY OF EASTER 26

Prayer is the state of our humble presence before God.
— *Writings,* Marquis Gaston de Renty (1611-1649)

Now when Jesus came, he found that Lazarus had already been in the tomb four days. Bethany was near Jerusalem, about two miles off, and many of the Jews had come to Martha and Mary to console them concerning their brother. When Martha heard that Jesus was coming, she went and met him, while Mary sat in the house. Martha said to Jesus, "Lord, if you had been here, my brother would not have died. And even now I know that whatever you ask from God, God will give you." Jesus said to her, "Your brother will rise again." Martha said to him, "I know that he will rise again in the resurrection at the last day." (John 11:17-24)

In this Easter season, Lord, show us Your life-giving power.

DAY OF EASTER 27

Prayer is thinking of the presence of God; habitually to be delighted with His divine company, speaking humbly and conversing with Him lovingly at all times, at every minute, without rule or regulation, above all, in the time of

temptations, sorrows, dryness, aversion, even in unfaithfulness and sin.
— *Practice of the Presence of God,* Brother Lawrence (1611-1691)

Jesus said to her, "I am the resurrection and the life; he who believes in me, though he die, yet shall live, and whoever lives and believes in me shall never die. Do you believe this?" She said to him, "Yes, Lord; I believe that you are the Christ, the Son of God, he who is coming into the world." (John 11:25-27)

Christ our Savior, You bring us new life and joy this Easter. May You be praised.

DAY OF EASTER 28

Prayer is an ascent of the mind to God. All the forms of such ascent, adoration, confession, thanksgiving as well as petition, seeking for particular gifts, may be included under the general term of prayer. Prayer is in general the communion of the human soul with God.
— *Sermons,* Jeremy Taylor (1613-1667)

When she had said this, she went and called her sister Mary, saying quietly, "The Teacher is here and is calling for you." And when she heard it, she rose quickly and went to him. Now Jesus had not yet come to the village, but was still in the place where Martha had met him. When the Jews who were with her in the house, consoling her, saw Mary rise quickly and go out, they followed her, supposing that she was going to the tomb to weep there. Then Mary, when she came where Jesus was and saw him, fell at his feet, saying to him, "Lord, if you had been here, my brother would not have died." When Jesus saw her weeping, and the Jews who came with her also weeping, he was deeply moved in spirit and troubled; and he said, "Where have you laid him?" They said to him, "Lord, come and see." Jesus wept. So the Jews said, "See how he loved him!" (John 11:28-36)

Teach us Your way to inner peace, Lord.

DAY OF EASTER 29

By prayer, I do not mean any bodily exercise of the outward person; but the going forth of the Spirit of life towards the Fountain of life, for fulness and contentment. . . . Prayer is the breath of life, an effect of God's spiritual breathing, which no person can do properly without the Spirit's breathing

upon him. Therefore the Spirit is to be waited upon, for His breathings and holy fire, that the offering of prayer may be living, and pleasing to the living God.
— *Spiritual Journal,* Isaac Penington (1616-1679)

Martha, the sister of the dead man, said to Jesus, "Lord, by this time there will be an odor, for he has been dead four days." Jesus said to her, "Did I not tell you that if you would believe you would see the glory of God?" So they took away the stone. And Jesus lifted up his eyes and said, "Father, I thank thee that thou hast heard me. I knew that thou hearest me always, but I have said this on account of the people standing by, that they may believe that thou didst send me." When he had said this, he cried with a loud voice, "Lazarus, come out." The dead man came out, his hands and feet bound with bandages, and his face wrapped with a cloth. Jesus said to them, "Unbind him, and let him go." (John 11:39-44)

Lord, call us out of ourselves so that we may find You.

DAY OF EASTER 30

Why has God established prayer?
1. To communicate to His creatures the dignity of causality.
2. To teach us from whom our virtue comes.
3. To make us deserve other virtues by toiling.
But to keep His own preeminence, He grants the gift of prayer to whom He pleases.
— *Pensées,* Blaise Paschal (1623-1662)

"Let not your hearts be troubled; believe in God, believe also in me. In my Father's house are many rooms; if it were not so, would I have told you that I go to prepare a place for you? And when I go and prepare a place for you, I will come again and will take you to myself, that where I am you may be also. And you know the way where I am going." Thomas said to him, "Lord, we do not know where you are going; how can we know the way?" Jesus said to him, "I am the way, and the truth, and the life; no one comes to the Father, but by me. If you had known me, you would have known my Father also; henceforth you know him and have seen him." (John 14:1-7)

Help us, Lord, to follow the way You alone can show.

DAY OF EASTER 31

Prayer raises a person to an incomparable honor by making it converse with God; this causes the person to be venerable even to the angels.
— *Reign of God Through Mental Prayer,* Henri-Marie Boudon
(1624-1702)

Philip said to him, "Lord, show us the Father, and we shall be satisfied." Jesus said to him, "Have I been with you so long, and yet you do not know me, Philip? He who has seen me has seen the Father; how can you say, 'Show us the Father'? Do you not believe that I am in the Father and the Father in me? The words that I say to you I do not speak on my own authority; but the Father who dwells in me does his works. Believe me that I am in the Father and the Father in me; or else believe me for the sake of the works themselves." (John 14:8-11)

Lord, help me to pray to You in full confidence.

DAY OF EASTER 32

Prayer is to be understood as a discourse of our soul with God, the Author and Fountain of all good, to request of Him those things which we feel we want, and for which we aspire.
— *Discourse Concerning Prayer,* Symon Patrick (1626-1707)

"Truly, truly, I say to you, he who believes in me will also do the works that I do; and greater works than these will he do, because I go to the Father. Whatever you ask in my name, I will do it, that the Father may be glorified in the Son; if you ask anything in my name, I will do it." (John 14:12-14)

May we take You at Your word, Lord, and beg You to hear us?

DAY OF EASTER 33

True prayer, and that which is best, consists in whatever unites us to God, whatever enables us to delight in Him, to appreciate Him, to rejoice in His Glory, and to love Him as our very own.
— *Sermons,* Jacques Bénigne Bossuet (1627-1704)

"If you love me, you will keep my commandments. And I will pray the Father, and he will give you another Counselor, to be with you for ever, even the Spirit of truth, whom the world cannot receive, because it neither sees him nor knows him; you know him, for he dwells with you, and will be in you." (John 14:15-17)

Spirit of all Truth, be our only Guide this day.

DAY OF EASTER 34

Prayer is mother to the presence of God, in that it places the thought of God in the soul, leaves an ongoing memory of Him, and helps the person to nurture the divine presence until it becomes second nature.
— *True Perfection,* John Francis of Rheims (d. 1690)

"I will not leave you desolate; I will come to you. Yet a little while, and the world will see me no more, but you will see me; because I live, you will live also. In that day you will know that I am in my Father, and you in me, and I in you. He who has my commandments and keeps them, he it is who loves me; and he who loves me will be loved by my Father, and I will love him and manifest myself to him." Judas (not Iscariot) said to him, "Lord, how is it that you will manifest yourself to us, and not to the world?" Jesus answered him, "If a man loves me, he will keep my word, and my Father will love him, and we will come to him and make our home with him. He who does not love me does not keep my words; and the word which you hear is not mine but the Father's who sent me." (John 14:18-24)

Speak to me Your word, O Lord, so that I may walk in Your presence.

DAY OF EASTER 35

Prayer is a sincere, sound, loving pouring out of the heart or soul to God, through Christ, in the strength and assistance of the Holy Spirit, for such things as God has promised, or according to His Word, for the good of the church, with faith-filled obedience to the will of God.
— *Prayer,* John Bunyan (1629-1688)

"These things I have spoken to you, while I am still with you. But the Counselor, the Holy Spirit, whom the Father will send in my name, he will teach you all things, and bring to your remembrance all that I have said to you. Peace I leave with you; my peace I give to you; not as the world gives do I give to you. Let not your hearts be troubled, neither let them be afraid. You heard me say to you, 'I go away, and I will come to you.' If you loved me, you would have rejoiced, because I go to the Father; for the Father is greater than I. And now I have told you before it takes place, so that when it does take place, you may believe. I will no longer talk much with you, for the ruler of this world is coming. He has no power over me; but I do as the Father has commanded me, so that the world may know that I love the Father." (John 14:25-31)

Guide us, O gentle Spirit, in the way of inner peace.

DAY OF EASTER 36

Prayer is that blessed envoy between heaven and earth, keeping in touch with both worlds, and by a happy exchange and relationship carrying up the necessities of a person, and bringing down the goodness of God.
— *Sermon on Prayer,* Robert South (1634-1716)

"I am the true vine, and my Father is the vinedresser. Every branch of mine that bears no fruit, he takes away, and every branch that does bear fruit he prunes, that it may bear more fruit. You are already made clean by the word which I have spoken to you. Abide in me, and I in you. As the branch cannot bear fruit by itself, unless it abides in the vine, neither can you, unless you abide in me. I am the vine, you are the branches. He who abides in me, and I in him, he it is that bears much fruit, for apart from me you can do nothing. If a man does not abide in me, he is cast forth as a branch and withers; and the branches are gathered, thrown into the fire and burned." (John 15:1-6)

Cleanse us with Your saving word, O God, so that we may abide in You.

DAY OF EASTER 37

All prayer is to be given in a humble cry whenever you plead for something from the Father. The Greek word is *aitein,* that is, a prayer as a poor person prays. Praying is not speaking certain words alone but must include a desire for those things for which we pray; they must first be in our heart before we bring the word of them to our mouth, just as a poor person is truly sincere in his keen desire to receive what he needs.
— *Sermons,* Philip Jakob Spener (1635-1705)

"If you abide in me, and my words abide in you, ask whatever you will, and it shall be done for you. By this my Father is glorified, that you bear much fruit, and so prove to be my disciples. As the Father has loved me, so have I loved you; abide in my love. If you keep my commandments, you will abide in my love, just as I have kept my Father's commandments and abide in his love. These things I have spoken to you, that my joy may be in you, and that your joy may be full." (John 15:7-11)

You give peace and joy, Lord, to all who believe in You. May we lead others to Your joy.

DAY OF EASTER 38

As to the subject of your prayer, do not be afraid to maintain yourself in God's presence. Even if you do not do anything else, you would be making good use of your time. . . . Do not be troubled about speaking a lot to God. He does not have a need for your words or your thoughts, provided your heart belongs to Him.
— *Spiritual Letters,* Bl. Claude La Colombière (1641-1682)

"This is my commandment, that you love one another as I have loved you. Greater love has no man than this, that a man lay down his life for his friends. You are my friends if you do what I command you. No longer do I call you servants, for the servant does not know what his master is doing; but I have called you friends, for all that I have heard from my Father I have made known to you. You did not choose me, but I chose you and appointed you that you should go and bear fruit and that your fruit should abide; so that whatever you ask the Father in my name, he may give it to you. This I command you, to love one another." (John 15:12-17)

May I know the deep joy, Lord, that comes from doing Your will.

DAY OF EASTER 39

Prayer, the soul's sincere desire, spoken or unspoken, is the discourse of personal spirit to personal spirit.
— *Christographia,* E. B. Taylor (1642-1729)

"If the world hates you, know that it has hated me before it hated you. If you were of the world, the world would love its own; but because you are not of the world, but I chose you out of the world, therefore the world hates you. Remember the word that I said to you, 'A servant is not greater than his master.' If they persecuted me, they will persecute you; if they kept my word, they will keep yours also." (John 15:18-20)

O Jesus, help me today to be Your disciple in spirit and truth.

DAY OF EASTER 40

Prayer is the appeal of the heart to God, and the internal exercise of love. . . We should live by prayer just as we should also live by love.
— *A Method of Prayer,* Madame Guyon (1648-1717)

"I did not say these things to you from the beginning, because I was with you. But now I am going to him who sent me; yet none of you asks me, 'Where are you going?' But because I have said these things to you, sorrow has filled your hearts. Nevertheless I tell you the truth: it is to your advantage that I go away, for if I do not go away, the Counselor will not come to you; but if I go, I will send him to you. And when he comes, he will convince the world concerning sin and righteousness and judgment: concerning sin, because they do not believe in me; concerning righteousness, because I go to the Father, and you will see me no more; concerning judgment, because the ruler of this world is judged." (John 16:4-11)

Counselor Spirit, help me to follow Your daily guidance in my life.

DAY OF EASTER 41

Prayer is turning the mind and thoughts toward God. To pray means to stand before God with the mind, mentally to gaze unswervingly at Him, and to converse with Him in reverent fear and hope.
— *Spiritual Writings,* St. Dimitri of Rostov (1651-1709)

"I have yet many things to say to you, but you cannot bear them now. When the Spirit of truth comes, he will guide you into all the truth; for he will not speak on his own authority, but whatever he hears he will speak, and he will declare to you the things that are to come. He will glorify me, for he will take what is mine and declare it to you. All that the Father has is mine; therefore I said that he will take what is mine and declare it to you." (John 16:12-15)

Make Your call clear to me today, O God. Help me to do Your will.

DAY OF EASTER 42

To pray . . . is to desire; but it is to desire what God would have us desire. He who desires not from the bottom of his heart, offers a deceitful prayer.
— *Spiritual Letters,* Fénelon (1651-1715)

"A little while, and you will see me no more; again a little while, and you will see me." Some of his disciples said to one another, "What is this that he says to us, 'A little while, and you will not see me, and again a little while, and you will see me'; and, 'because I go to the Father'? They said, "What does he mean by 'a little while'? We do not know what he means." Jesus knew that they wanted to ask him; so he said to them, "Is this what you are asking yourselves, what I meant by saying, 'A little while, and you will not see me, and again a little while, and you will see me'? Truly, truly, I say to you, you will weep and lament, but the world will rejoice; you will be sorrowful, but your sorrow will turn into joy." (John 16:16-20)

Lord, help me to see You always in others.

DAY OF EASTER 43

Prayer is both the root and the salt of all divine action. Prayer may not be foreign to anything one does, and in prayer comes all union with the dear God. You must know that there is no better way to get a taste of eternal life than for one to humble oneself before God and truly pray, to remain constant in prayer and to walk constantly with the good God.
— *Sunday and Feast Day Sermons,* August H. Francke (1663-1727)

"So you have sorrow now, but I will see you again and your hearts will rejoice, and no one will take your joy from you. In that day you will ask nothing of me. Truly, truly, I say to you, if you ask anything of the Father, he will give it to you in my name. Hitherto you have asked nothing in my name; ask, and you will receive, that your joy may be full." (John 16:22-24)

May our personal sorrows lead us, O God, to receive Your gift of joy.

DAY OF EASTER 44

Prayer consists in the complete tending of the heart to the Supreme Good, which is God.
— *A Method of Prayer,* Johannes Kelpius (1673-1708)

"I have said this to you in figures; the hour is coming when I shall no longer speak to you in figures but tell you plainly of the Father. In that day you will ask in my name; and I do not say to you that I shall pray the Father for you; for the Father himself loves you, because you have loved me and have believed that I came from the Father. I came from the Father and have come into the world; again, I am leaving the world and going to the Father." (John 16:25-28)

By the outpouring of Your Easter gifts, O Lord, increase the family of Your believers.

DAY OF EASTER 45

The gift of prayer may be thus described: it is an ability to accommodate our thoughts to all the various parts and purposes of this service, and a readiness to express these thoughts before God in the best manner for the benefit of our own souls and the souls of others that join us.
— *A Guide to Prayer,* Isaac Watts (1674-1748)

His disciples said, "Ah, now you are speaking plainly, not in any figure! Now we know that you know all things, and need none to question you; by this we believe that you came from God." Jesus answered them, "Do you now believe? The hour is coming, indeed it has come, when you will be scattered, every man to his home, and will leave me alone; yet I am not alone, for the Father is with me. I have said this to you, that in me you may have peace. In the world you have tribulation; but be of good cheer, I have overcome the world." (John 16:29-33)

May Your Easter victory, O Jesus, be our daily peace.

DAY OF EASTER 46

All our life is nothing but prayer and thanksgiving, that is to say, we should plead with God every day in our prayers for His blessing, help, consolation, and grace, and when these are given, we should give thanks to Him with all our hearts. Therefore, O believer, when you awake in the morning from your sleep, let it be your first concern to raise your eyes to heaven.
— *Daily Handbook,* Johann F. Starck (1680-1756)

When Jesus had spoken these words, he lifted up his eyes to heaven and said, "Father, the hour has come: glorify thy Son that the Son may glorify thee, since thou hast given him power over all flesh, to give eternal life to all whom thou hast given him. And this is eternal life, that they know thee the only true God, and Jesus Christ whom thou hast sent. I glorified thee on earth, having accomplished the work which thou gavest me to do; and now, Father, glorify thou me in thy own presence with the glory which I had with thee before the world was made." (John 17:1-5)

Lord, may I know You as my one true God. Help me to recognize and reject all idols in my life.

DAY OF EASTER 47

The Spirit of Prayer is a reaching of the person out of this present life. It is an attending with all its desire after the life of God.
— *Serious Call to A Devout and Holy Life,* William Law (1686-1761)

"I have manifested thy name to the men whom thou gavest me out of the world; thine they were and thou gavest them to me, and they have kept thy word. Now they know that everything that thou hast given me is from thee; for I have given them the words which thou gavest me, and they have received them and know in truth that I came from thee; and they have believed that thou didst send me." (John 17:6-8)

With all Your disciples, Lord, may I know the central place of Your word in my life.

DAY OF EASTER 48

To pray is to listen to God in silence after we have spoken to Him; for He speaks in His turn during prayer, which is merely a dialogue, a conversation with God.
— *Spiritual Letters,* John Peter de Caussade (d. 1751)

"I am praying for them; I am not praying for the world but for those whom thou hast given me, for they are thine; all mine are thine, and thine are mine, and I am glorified in them. And now I am no more in the world, but they are in the world, and I am coming to thee. Holy Father, keep them in thy name, which thou hast given me, that they may be one, even as we are one. While I was with them, I kept them in thy name, which thou has given me; I have guarded them, and none of them is lost but the son of perdition, that the scripture might be fulfilled. But now I am coming to thee; and these things I speak in the world, that they may have my joy fulfilled in themselves.'' (John 17:9-13)

You are three persons in one, O God. Make us also one in You.

DAY OF EASTER 49

Prayer is a familiar talk and an intimate union with God. . . . We ought to pray in order to be perfectly united to God; and that which unites us to God is not so much our good thoughts as the good desires of our will.
— *The Great Means of Salvation,* St. Alphonsus Liguori (1696-1787)

"I have given them thy word; and the world has hated them because they are not of the world, even as I am not of the world. I do not pray that thou shouldst take them out of the world, but that thou shouldst keep them from the evil one. They are not of the world, even as I am not of the world. Sanctify them in the truth; thy word is truth. As thou didst send me into the world, so I have sent them into the world. And for their sake I consecrate myself, that they also may be consecrated in truth." (John 17:14-19)

Lord, our life and our world lack unity. Make us one in the unity of Your peace.

DAY OF EASTER 50

You do well to practice prayer in your own manner. Remain constant without ceasing and you cannot fail; God will make His own good word true for you. Pray and it will be given to you. No art is more simple and easier in the whole world than to pray poorly; that is no art. If we think that we cannot pray, it is a sign that we have not yet properly understood what it is to pray. Prayer means to turn to the ever-present God and to permit oneself to be seen by Him.
— *Spiritual Letters,* Gerhard Tersteegen (1697-1769)

"I do not pray for these only, but also for those who believe in me through their word, that they may all be one; even as thou, Father, art in me, and I in thee, that they also may be in us, so that the world may believe that thou hast sent me. The glory which thou hast given me I have given to them, that they may be one even as we are one, I in them and thou in me, that they may become perfectly one, so that the world may know that thou hast sent me and hast loved them even as thou hast loved me." (John 17:20-23)

In our love for You, O Jesus, help us to bring Your peace to others.

PENTECOST

Pentecost is the season of the Holy Spirit and the birth of the Church. The feast of Pentecost is the season which continually rejoices in the sending of the Holy Spirit by the Risen Lord. It is only through the risen and exalted humanity of the Easter Christ that the Spirit of Pentecost is sent. It is the Risen Lord who bestows the Spirit. Easter, Ascension and Pentecost are therefore only facets of the one great mystery of Christ the Lord among us.

While the Church at Pentecost time rejoices with her Risen Lord, two challenges are especially visible in the liturgical readings. Our Mother is concerned about our Christian living and our Christian mission. Both should be our joyful response to the God who saved us in Christ. Now, more than ever, we are called to live as children of God, grateful recipients of His life, forgiveness, peace and joy.

During Pentecost the Church invites us to pray over the *Acts of the Apostles* so that we may all be "filled with the Holy Spirit." (Acts 2:4)

The Octave of Pentecost was once observed as a separate season, but now the day after Pentecost resumes the season of the year. It could benefit us, however, to continue our meditation on the action of the Spirit with Peter and the disciples.

DAY OF PENTECOST

Whether we think of or speak to God, whether we act or suffer for Him, all is prayer, when we have no other purpose than His love, and the desire of pleasing Him. All that a Christian does, even in eating and sleeping, is prayer, when it is done in simplicity, according to the order of God, without either adding to or diminishing from it by his own choice.
— *Plain Account of Christian Perfection,* John Wesley (1703-1791)

When the day of Pentecost had come, they were all together in one place. And suddenly a sound came from heaven like the rush of a mighty wind, and it filled all the house where they were sitting. And there apeared to them tongues as of fire, distributing and resting on each one of them. And they were all filled with the Holy Spirit and began to speak in other tongues, as the Spirit gave them utterance. (Acts 2:1-4)

Send forth Your Spirit, Lord, so that your Church may experience a new Pentecost.

DAY AFTER PENTECOST 1

Prayer can be said by the mind without words. . . . The outward voice and word must agree with the interior intention because the word is nothing more than the revelation of the interior state. God sees through our heart. He looks at our heart and not at our words. Therefore words without the desire of the heart are useless.
— *Spiritual Doctrine,* St. Tikhon of Zadonsk (1724-1783)

Now there were dwelling in Jerusalem Jews, devout men from every nation under heaven. And at this sound the multitude came together, and they were bewildered, because each one heard them speaking in his own language. And they were amazed and wondered, saying, "Are not all these who are speaking Galileans? And how is it that we hear, each of us in his own native language?" (Acts 2:5-8)

May we also know Your mighty deeds in our lives so that we may truly be Your people.

DAY AFTER PENTECOST 2

Prayer is a religious act; but when it comes to praying, we easily forget that it is a supernatural act, which is therefore beyond our power, and which we cannot properly perform without the inspiration and help of grace.
— *How to Pray,* Jean Grou (1731-1803)

Peter, standing with the eleven, lifted up his voice and addressed them, "Men of Judea and all who dwell in Jerusalem, let this be known to you, and give ear to my words. For these men are not drunk, as you suppose, since it is only the third hour of the day; but this is what was spoken by the prophet Joel: 'And in the last days it shall be, God declares, that I will pour out my Spirit upon all flesh, and your sons and your daughters shall prophesy, and your young men shall see visions, and your old men shall dream dreams; yea, and on my menservants and my maidservants in those days I will pour out my Spirit; and they shall prophesy. And I will show wonders in the heaven above and signs on the earth beneath, blood, and fire, and vapor of smoke; the sun shall be turned into darkness and the moon into blood, before the day of the Lord comes, the great and manifest day. And it shall be that whoever calls on the name of the Lord shall be saved.' " (Acts 2:14-21)

Help us all to hear Your saving word today.

DAY AFTER PENTECOST 3

Prayer is a speaking to and a conversation of our soul with God concerning the matter of our salvation and perfection.
— *Institutes of Mystical Theology,* Dominikus Schramm (1722-1797)

"Men of Israel, hear these words: Jesus of Nazareth, a man attested to you by God with mighty works and wonders and signs which God did through him in your midst, as you yourselves know — that Jesus, delivered up according to the definite plan and foreknowledge of God, you crucified and killed by the hands of lawless men. But God raised him up, having loosed the pangs of death, because it was not possible for him to be held by it." (Acts 2:22-24)

Water flowed from Your side, O Jesus, at Your death on the cross. Now may the new fountain of the Spirit flow into our lives.

DAY AFTER PENTECOST 4

Prayer is not only the practice of the presence of God, it is the realization of His presence in our midst.
— *Sermons and Lectures,* Joseph Fort Newton (1725-1807)

"Brethren, I may say to you confidently of the patriarch David that he both died and was buried, and his tomb is with us to this day. Being therefore a prophet, and knowing that God had sworn with an oath to him that he would set one of his descendants upon his throne, he foresaw and spoke of the resurrection of the Christ, that he was not abandoned to Hades, nor did his flesh see corruption. This Jesus God raised up, and of that we all are witnesses. Being therefore exalted at the right hand of God, and having received from the Father the promise of the Holy Spirit, he has poured out this which you see and hear." (Acts 2:29-33)

Lord, may Your Spirit continue to work in the hearts of all who believe.

DAY AFTER PENTECOST 5

Prayer is the appeal of need to Him who alone can relieve it, the cry of sinfulness to Him who alone can pardon it.
— *Reflections on Prayer,* Hannah More (1745-1833)

Now when they heard this they were cut to the heart, and said to Peter and the rest of the apostles, "Brethren, what shall we do?" And Peter said to them, "Repent, and be baptized every one of you in the name of Jesus Christ for the forgiveness of your sins; and you shall receive the gift of the Holy Spirit. For the promise is to you and to your children and to all that are far off, every one whom the Lord our God calls to him." And he testified with many other words and exhorted them, saying, "Save yourselves from this crooked generation." So those who receive his word were baptized, and there were added that day about three thousand souls. And they devoted themselves to the apostles' teaching and fellowship, to the breaking of bread and the prayers. (Acts 2:37-42)

May the Good News of Pentecost change our lives.

DAY AFTER PENTECOST 6

Through prayer we are honored by dialogue with our all-good and life-giving God and Savior. But we must pray only until the moment when God the Holy Spirit covers us with His heavenly grace. When He honors us with a visit we must cease to pray. There is no reason to utter a prayer then.
— *Conversations,* St. Seraphim of Sarov (1759-1833)

And fear came upon every soul; and many wonders and signs were done through the apostles. And all who believed were together and had all things in common; and they sold their possessions and goods and distributed them to all, as any had need. And day by day, attending the temple together and breaking bread in their homes, they partook of food with glad and generous hearts, praising God and having favor with all the people. And the Lord added to their number day by day those who were being saved. (Acts 2:43-47)

Lord, you desire the whole world to be filled with Your Spirit. Help us all build a world of justice and peace.

ORDINARY TIME

At the end of the celebration of Easter and Pentecost we sense a certain shift in the fulness of joy that is expressed in the Liturgy of this great season. The Sundays and the time from now to the next Advent seem less colorful, even though several feasts brighten this period.

This impression fails to grasp the meaning of Sunday and the historical development of the Church Year. In fact, the cycle of Sundays was the first to be developed. In the earliest centuries the Church Year was a series of equal Sundays, among which were two exceptions: Easter and Pentecost. Little by little the other celebrations of the temporal cycle came about. They grew into Advent, Christmas, Epiphany, Lent, Eastertide. At present the old cycle of Sundays appears only between Epiphany and Lent and between Pentecost and the beginning of Advent. This original plan for the Sundays is still very rich in inspiration for Christian formation. It is the time for developing Christians in ongoing spiritual growth through the liturgical message and the Sacraments.

The presence of the Lord among us is no longer in exactly the same way as when He lived on earth. When He manifested himself after His Resurrection, He showed himself as the Lord. Nearly all the appearances of Christ end with a sacramental rite or a priestly mission. The disciples at Emmaus recognized the Lord in the breaking of the bread. The power to forgive sins was given at the appearance on the day of His Resurrection. St. Peter's pastoral role was bestowed at the Lake of Tiberias.

The Lord's presence now in our midst is continued in the Church through the sacraments and in the Scriptures. He intends that we should assemble on Sunday so that He can be among us through the proclamation of His word: through the breaking of the bread in which we can recognize Him; through the forgiveness of sins, His victory over death; through His minister, who continues in His role as the Christ who continues to save His people.

In our efforts to grow in a prayerful spirit, let us take our invitation from the Church herself. She gives us this invitation in the special readings chosen for the Holy Eucharist in this season. As the season unfolds its richness to us in the word of God, we can grow in depth as a prayerful person with Christ in the Church.

DAY OF ORDINARY TIME 1

To be a spiritual person and to pray are really one and the same thing. . . .

There is no genuine prayer, but the prayer we offer when we have the living thought of God attending, purifying and sanctifying all our other thoughts, feelings and intentions.
— *Selected Sermons,* Friedrich Schleiermacher (1768-1834)

Seeing the crowds, he went up on the mountain, and when he sat down his disciples came to him. And he opened his mouth and taught them, saying: "Blessed are the poor in spirit, for theirs is the kingdom of heaven. Blessed are those who mourn, for they shall be comforted. Blessed are the meek, for they shall inherit the earth. Blessed are those who hunger and thirst for righteousness, for they shall be satisfied. Blessed are the merciful, for they shall obtain mercy." (Matt. 5: 1-7)

Lord, teach me how to make Your mission my own in life.

DAY OF ORDINARY TIME 2

Prayer is the sincere desire of a person which is spoken or unspoken.
— *What Is Prayer?* James Montgomery (1771-1854)

"Blessed are the pure in heart, for they shall see God. Blessed are the peacemakers, for they shall be called sons of God. Blessed are those who are persecuted for righteousness' sake, for theirs is the kingdom of heaven. Blessed are you when men revile you and persecute you and utter all kinds of evil against you falsely on my account. Rejoice and be glad, for your reward is great in heaven, for so men persecuted the prophets who were before you." (Matt. 5:8-12)

May Your word, O Jesus, make a difference in my life today.

DAY OF ORDINARY TIME 5

Pray, pray incessantly, pray with fervor and with confidence. Be sincere in your wish to know the truth and firm in your resolution to follow it. . . . Without prayer I should be of little service.
— *Letters,* St. Elizabeth Ann Seton (1774-1821)

"If you are offering your gift at the altar, and there remember that your brother has something against you, leave your gift there before the altar and go; first be reconciled to your brother, and then come and offer your gift. Make friends quickly with your accuser, while you are going with him to court, lest your accuser hand you over to the judge, and the judge to the guard, and you be put in prison; truly, I say to you, you will never get out till you have paid the last penny." (Matt. 5:23-26)

Today, Lord, may I be truly reconciled with family and all my friends.

DAY OF ORDINARY TIME 6

Prayer is a person living in the presence of God.
— *Sermons,* Dr. Lyman Beecher (1775-1863)

"You have heard that it was said, 'An eye for an eye and a tooth for a tooth.' But I say to you, Do not resist one who is evil. But if any one strikes you on the right cheek, turn to him the other also; and if any one would sue you and take your coat, let him have your cloak as well; and if any one forces you to go one mile, go with him two miles. Give to him who begs from you, and do not refuse him who would borrow from you." (Matt. 5:38-42)

O gentle Jesus, help me to imitate Your modesty and humility in my life.

DAY OF ORDINARY TIME 7

The precious gift of prayer is the source of all the others, the continual cry of the soul to the divine Master. . . . There are no true Christians in the world, and no true religious, without the habit of prayer.
— *Spiritual Letters,* St. Madeleine Sophie Barat (1779-1865)

"You have heard that it was said, 'You shall love your neighbor and hate your enemy.' But I say to you, love your enemies and pray for those who persecute you, so that you may be sons of your Father who is in heaven; for he makes his sun rise on the evil and on the good, and sends rain on the just and on the unjust. For if you love those who love you, what reward have you? Do not even the tax collectors do the same? And if you salute only your brethren, what more are you doing than others? Do not even the Gentiles do the same? You, therefore, must be perfect, as your heavenly Father is perfect." (Matt. 5:43-48)

O God, may I truly call You Father as I strive to love all others as sister and brother.

DAY OF ORDINARY TIME 8

Prayer is the continual cry of the person to the Divine Master. In prayer be content to stay before God in a tranquil submission to all that He wills to work in you. If, however, you see that dryness and boredom are taking from you all sense of God's presence, then say a few Psalms or other passages of Holy Scripture, without pronouncing the words, just to turn aside laziness and draw yourself back.
— *Spiritual Letters,* St. Madeleine Sophie Barat (1779-1865)

"Beware of practicing your piety before men in order to be seen by them; for then you will have no reward from your Father who is in heaven. Thus, when you give alms, sound no trumpet before you, as the hypocrites do in the synagogues and in the streets, that they may be praised by men. Truly, I say to you, they have received their reward. But when you give alms, do not let your left hand know what your right hand is doing, so that your alms may be in secret; and your Father who sees in secret will reward you." (Matt. 6:1-4)

Free me of all hypocrisy, O God, so that I may come into Your presence with a clean heart.

DAY OF ORDINARY TIME 9

Prayer is an elevation, a tending of our mind and of our heart to God, to make known to Him our wants and to ask for His help. We do not see the good God, my children, but He sees us, He hears us, He desires that we should raise towards Him what is most beautiful in us, our mind and our heart.
— *Sermons,* St. John-Baptist Vianney (1786-1859)

"And when you pray, you must not be like the hypocrites; for they love to stand and pray in the synagogues and at the street corners, that they may be seen by men. Truly, I say to you, they have received their reward. But when you pray, go into your room and shut the door and pray to your Father who is in secret; and your Father who sees in secret will reward you. And in praying do not heap up empty phrases as the Gentiles do; for they think that they will be heard for their many words. Do not be like them, for your Father knows what you need before you ask him." (Matt. 6:5-8)

Teach me, O Lord, to understand that prayer is much more than words.

DAY OF ORDINARY TIME 10

He who gives up regularity in prayer has lost a principal means of reminding himself that spiritual life is obedience to a Lawgiver, not a mere feeling or a taste. Hence it is that so many persons fall away into a mere luxurious self-indulgent devotion, which they take for religion; they reject everything which implies self-denial, and regular prayer especially.
— *Sermons,* John Cardinal Newman (1801-1890)

"Pray then like this: Our Father who art in heaven, Hallowed be thy name. Thy kingdom come, Thy will be done, On earth as it is in heaven. Give us this day our daily bread; And forgive us our debts, As we also have forgiven our debtors; And lead us not into temptation, But deliver us from evil. For if you forgive men their trespasses, your heavenly Father also will forgive you; but if you do not forgive men their trespasses, neither will your Father forgive your trespasses." (Matt. 6:9-15)

Jesus, teach me to pray Your prayer as You want me to pray.

DAY OF ORDINARY TIME 11

Prayer is, if it may be said with reverence, conversing with God. We con verse with companions, and we use familiar language for that, because they are our companions. We converse with God, and then we use the lowliest, most reverent, calmest, concisest language we can, because He is God. Prayer, then, is divine discourse, differing from human as God differs from a person.
— *Sermons,* John Cardinal Newman (1801-1890)

"Do not lay up for yourselves treasures on earth, where moth and rust consume and where thieves break in and steal, but lay up for yourselves treasure in heaven, where neither moth nor rust consumes and where thieves do not break in and steal. For where your treasure is, there will your heart be also." (Matt. 6:19-21)

Help me to clarify my real personal values, Lord. May they be based on Gospel values.

DAY OF ORDINARY TIME 12

Prayer is the Regent of the world. Covered with humble apparel, the head

bent, the hand outstretched, she protects the universe by her beseeching power. . . . It is prayer which re-establishes our discourse with God, which recalls to us His action, which really storms Him without violating His liberty, and which is therefore the mother of faith.
— *Conferences,* Père Lacordaire (1802-1861)

"The eye is the lamp of the body. So, if your eye is sound, your whole body will be full of light; but if your eye is not sound, your whole body will be full of darkness. If then the light in you is darkness, how great is the darkness!" (Matt. 6:22-23)

Spirit of Truth, fill us with Your gifts of wisdom and prudence so that we may have an inner light.

DAY OF ORDINARY TIME 13

Prayer is an exercise of union with God. Its ultimate purpose is to strengthen our union with Him and make it permeate our days. Hence, its genuine fruits are union with God outside the time of mental prayer and a genuine effort to remove from us every hindrance to that union.
— *Spiritual Letters,* Ven. Francis Libermann (1803-1852)

"No one can serve two masters; for either he will hate the one and love the other, or he will be devoted to the one and despise the other. You cannot serve God and mammon." (Matt. 6:24)

O God, be my only master. May I serve You this day by striving to do Your will as I know it.

DAY OF ORDINARY TIME 14

Prayer is the lifting of our minds and hearts of God in order that we may render Him His due, make known our needs and implore His help.
— Early American Catechism (19th century)

"Therefore I tell you, do not be anxious about your life, what you shall eat or what you shall drink, nor about your body, what you shall put on. Is not life more than food, and the body more than clothing? Look at the birds of the air: they neither sow nor reap nor gather into barns, and yet your heavenly Father feeds them. Are you not of more value than they?" (Matt. 6:25-26)

Heavenly Father, give me what I need this day. May I be truly grateful for all Your gifts.

DAY OF ORDINARY TIME 15

Prayer is the contemplation of the facts of life from the highest point of view. It is the soliloquy of a beholding and jubilant soul. It is the spirit of God pronouncing his works good.
— *Essays,* Ralph Waldo Emerson (1803-1882)

"Judge not, that you be not judged. For with the judgment you pronounce you will be judged, and the measure you give will be the measure you get. Why do you see the speck that is in your brother's eye, but do not notice the log that is in your own eye? Or how can you say to your brother, 'Let me take the speck out of your eye,' when there is the log in your own eye? You hypocrite, first take the log out of your own eye, and then you will see clearly to take the speck out of your brother's eye." (Matt. 7:1-5)

Help me to care for others with Your gentleness and understanding, O Lord.

DAY OF ORDINARY TIME 16

Prayer is not an affair of words, but an action of the internal spirit. Words are but an imperfect instrument for the manifestation of the deeper movements of the soul.
— *Groundwork of the Christian Virtues,* William Ullathorne (1806-1889)

"Ask, and it will be given you; seek, and you will find; knock, and it will be opened to you. For every one who asks receives, and he who seeks finds, and to him who knocks it will be opened. Or what man of you, if his son asks him for bread, will give him a stone? Or if he asks for a fish, will give him a serpent? If you then, who are evil, know how to give good gifts to your children, how much more will your Father who is in heaven give good things to those who ask him! So whatever you wish that men would do to you, do so to them; for this is the law and the prophets." (Matt. 7:7-12)

Loving Father, help me pray with confidence for all good gifts.

DAY OF ORDINARY TIME 17

The soul of prayer is attention. As a body without a soul is dead, so is prayer without attention. Prayer said without attention is empty speech. He who prays in this way calls on God in vain.
— *On the Prayer of Jesus,* Ignatius Brianchaninov (1807-1867)

"Beware of false prophets, who come to you in sheep's clothing but inwardly are ravenous wolves. You will know them by their fruits. Are grapes gathered from thorns, or figs from thistles? So, every sound tree bears good fruit, but the bad tree bears evil fruit. A sound tree cannot bear evil fruit, nor can a bad tree bear good fruit. Every tree that does not bear good fruit is cut down and thrown into the fire. Thus you will know them by their fruits." (Matt. 7:15-20)

Purge me, O Lord, of all that keeps me at a distance from You.

DAY OF ORDINARY TIME 18

Prayer is not a matter of overcoming the reluctance of God; it is our benefiting from His great willingness.
— *Prayer,* Richard Chenevix Trench (1807-1886)

"Not every one who says to me, 'Lord, Lord,' shall enter the kingdom of heaven, but he who does the will of my Father who is in heaven. On that day many will say to me, 'Lord, Lord, did we not prophesy in your name, and cast out demons in your name, and do many mighty works in your name?' And then will I declare to them, "I never knew you; depart from me, you evildoer.' " (Matt. 7:21-23)

Change my life in such a way, Lord, that I may truly be Your disciple.

DAY OF ORDINARY TIME 19

Prayer is essentially turning to God with the conviction of need, and in full reliance that this need can be supplied.
— *The Christian Doctrine of Prayer,* James F. Clarke (1810-1888)

"Every one then who hears these words of mine and does them will be like a wise man who built his house upon the rock; and the rain fell, and the floods came, and the winds blew and beat upon that house, but it did not fall, because it had been founded on the rock. And every one who hears these words of mine and does not do them will be like a foolish man who built his house upon the sand; and the rain fell, and the floods came, and the winds blew and beat against that house, and it fell; and great was the fall of it." (Matt. 7:24-27)

Make me strong in doing Your will, O God, so nothing can separate me from You.

DAY OF ORDINARY TIME 20

True prayer is a struggle with God, in which a person triumphs through the triumph of God.
— *Journal,* Soren Kierkegaard (1813-1855)

When he came down from the mountain, great crowds followed him; and behold, a leper came to him and knelt before him, saying, "Lord, if you will, you can make me clean." And he stretched out his hand and touched him saying, "I will; be clean." And immediately his leprosy was cleansed. And Jesus said to him, "See that you say nothing to any one; but go, show yourself to the priest, and offer the gift that Moses commanded for a proof to the people." (Matt. 8:1-4)

Heal me inwardly, Lord, so that I may be clean in Your sight.

DAY OF ORDINARY TIME 21

The right relation in prayer is not when God hears what is prayed for, but when the person praying continues to pray until he is the one who hears, who hears what God wants. The important person, therefore, uses many words and therefore makes demands in his prayer. The true person of prayer listens to God only.
— *Edifying Discourses,* Soren Kierkegaard (1813-1855)

Now when Jesus saw great crowds around him, he gave orders to go over to the other side. And a scribe came up and said to him, "Teacher, I will follow you wherever you go." And Jesus said to him, "Foxes have holes, and birds of the air have nests; but the Son of man has nowhere to lay his head." Another of the disciples said to him, "Lord, let me first go and bury my father." But Jesus said to him, "Follow me, and leave the dead to bury their own dead." (Matt. 8: 18-22)

Shepherd of my life, teach me to follow You wherever You lead me.

DAY OF ORDINARY TIME 22

Christianity would teach us that prayer, blessed as it is in itself, reaches toward something more blessed, and is not in itself the height of blessedness.
— *Edifying Discourses,* Soren Kierkegaard (1813-1855)

And when he got into the boat, his disciples followed him. And behold, there arose a great storm on the sea, so that the boat was being swamped by the waves; but he was asleep. And they went and woke him, saying, "Save [us], Lord; we are perishing." And he said to them, "Why are you afraid, O men of little faith?" Then he rose and rebuked the winds and the sea; and there was a great calm. And the men marveled, saying, "What sort of man is this, that even winds and sea obey him?" (Matt. 8:23-27)

Save us, O God, for we will surely perish on our own.

DAY OF ORDINARY TIME 23

The whole function [of prayer] is expressed in a word; it is simply this — the child at his father's knee, his words stumbling over each other from very earnestness, and his wistful face pleading better than his hardly intelligible prayer.
— *The Spirit of Prayer,* Frederick W. Faber (1814-1863)

They brought to him a paralytic, lying on his bed; and when Jesus saw their faith he said to the paralytic, "Take heart, my son; your sins are forgiven" And behold, some of the scribes said to themselves, "This man is blaspheming." But Jesus, knowing their thoughts, said, "Why do you think evil in your hearts? For which is easier, to say, 'Your sins are forgiven,' or to say, "Rise and walk'? But that you may know that the Son of man has authority on earth to forgive sins" — he then said to the paralytic — "Rise, take up your bed and go home." And he rose and went home. When the crowds saw it, they were afraid, and they glorified God, who had given such authority to men. (Matt. 9:2-8)

O Good Lord, rescue us from our own sinfulness.

DAY OF ORDINARY TIME 24

To pray always is always to feel the sweet urgency of prayer, and to hunger after it. . . . In consequence of this attraction we acquire habits of prayer by having set times for it, whether mental or vocal. To pray always is, furthermore, to renew frequently our acts of pure intention for the glory of God, and thus to animate with the life of prayer our actions, conversations, studies, and sufferings.
— *The Spirit of Prayer,* Frederick William Faber (1814-1863)

As Jesus passed on from there, he saw a man called Matthew sitting at the tax office; and he said to him, "Follow me." And he rose and followed him. And as he sat at table in the house, behold, many tax collectors and sinners came and sat down with Jesus and his disciples. And when the Pharisees saw this, they said to his disciples, "Why does your teacher eat with tax collectors and sinners?" But when he heard it, he said, "Those who are well have no need of a physician, but those who are sick. Go and learn what this means, 'I desire mercy, and not sacrifice.' For I came not to call the righteous, but sinners." (Matt. 9:9-13)

Teach us, Lord, Your real message. Let us learn to love as You do.

DAY OF ORDINARY TIME 24

Prayer is the elevation of the mind and heart to God in praise and thanksgiving to Him and in entreaty for the blessings that we need, both spiritual and material. The essence of prayer is the spiritual elevation of the heart toward God.
— *Spiritual Doctrine,* Theophan the Recluse (1815-1894)

Then the disciples of John came to him, saying, "Why do we and the Pharisees fast, but your disciples do not fast?" And Jesus said to them, "Can the wedding guests mourn as long as the bridegroom is with them? The days will come, when the bridegroom is taken away from them, and then they will fast. And no one puts a piece of unshrunk cloth on an old garment, for the patch tears away from the garment, and a worse tear is made. Neither is new wine put into old wineskins; if it is, the skins burst, and the wine is spilled, and the skins are destroyed; but new wine is put into fresh wineskins, and so both are preserved." (Matt. 9:14-17)

Jesus, invigorate us with the wine of Your good news.

DAY OF ORDINARY TIME 25

External prayer, whether at home or in church, is only the verbal expression and manner of prayer. The essence of the heart of prayer is within the mind and heart of a person.
— *Spiritual Doctrine,* Theophan the Recluse (1815-1894)

And as Jesus passed on from there, two blind men followed him, crying aloud, "Have mercy on us, Son of David." When he entered the house, the blind men came to him; and Jesus said to them, "Do you believe that I am able to do this?" They said to him, "Yes, Lord." Then he touched their eyes, saying, "According to your faith be it done to you." And their eyes were opened. And Jesus sternly charged them, "See that no one knows it." But they went away and spread his fame through all that district. (Matt. 9:27-31)

Son of David, do have mercy on us and restore us to new life.

DAY OF ORDINARY TIME 27

Regarding prayer not so much as consisting of particular acts of devotion, but as the spirit of life, it seems to be the spirit of harmony with the will of God. It is the aspiration after all good, the wish, stronger than any earthly passion or desire, to live in His service only.
— *Sermons on Faith and Doctrine,* Benjamin Jowett (1817-1893)

And Jesus went about all the cities and villages, teaching in their synagogues and preaching the gospel of the kingdom, and healing every disease and every infirmity. When he saw the crowds, he had compassion for them, because they were harassed and helpless, like sheep without a shepherd. Then he said to his disciples, "The harvest is plentiful, but the laborers are few; pray therefore the Lord of the harvest to send out laborers into his harvest." (Matt. 9:35-38)

Good Shepherd, may Your call to follow You be heard by many young women and men today.

DAY OF ORDINARY TIME 28

The very act of prayer justifies God, honors God, and gives glory to God; for it confesses that God is what He is, a good God.
— *Westminster Sermons,* Charles Kingsley (1819-1875)

"Preach as you go, saying, The kingdom of heaven is at hand. Heal the sick, raise the dead, cleanse lepers, cast out demons. You received without paying, give without pay. Take no gold, nor silver nor copper in your belts, no bag for your journey, nor two tunics, nor sandals, nor a staff; for the laborer deserves his food. And whatever town or village you enter, find out who is worthy in it, and stay with him until you depart. As you enter the house, salute it. And if the house is worthy, let your peace come upon it; but if it is not worthy, let your peace return to you." (Matt. 10:7-13)

Lord, help us live Your Gospel in such a way that we may enlighten others.

DAY OF ORDINARY TIME 29

Prayer is an act of friendship, it is converse; an act of trust, of hope, of love.
— *The Still Hour,* Dr. Austin Phelps (1820-1890)

"A disciple is not above his teacher, nor a servant above his master; it is enough for the disciple to be like his teacher, and the servant like his master. If they have called the master of the house Beelzebul, how much more will they malign those of his household." (Matt. 10:24-25)

Our Teacher and our Guide, do not lose patience with us. We do want to model our lives after You.

DAY OF ORDINARY TIME 30

Prayer is a spiritual ointment, a treasured remedy which restores us to peace and courage. It reminds us of pardon and duty.
— *Personal Journal,* Henri-Frederic Amiel (1821-1881)

"Do not fear those who kill the body but cannot kill the soul; rather fear him who can destroy both soul and body in hell. Are not two sparrows sold for a penny? And not one of them will fall to the ground without your Father's will. But even the hairs of your head are all numbered. Fear not, therefore; you are of more value than many sparrows. So every one who acknowledges me before men, I also will acknowledge before my Father who is in heaven; but whoever denies me before men, I also will deny before my Father who is in heaven." (Matt. 10:28-33)

Loving Father, take away my fear. Replace it with confidence in You.

DAY OF ORDINARY TIME 31

Prayer is an act of humility and patience and the means of establishing a person in these virtues.
— *Justification and Reconciliation,* Albrecht Ritschl (1822-1889)

"Do not think that I have come to bring peace on earth; I have not come to bring peace, but a sword. For I have come to set a man against his father, and a daughter against her mother, and a daughter-in-law against her mother-in-law; and a man's foes will be those of his own household. He who loves father or mother more than me is not worthy of me; and he who loves son or daughter more than me is not worthy of me; and he who does not take his cross and follow me is not worthy of me. He who finds his life will lose it, and he who loses his life for my sake will find it." (Matt. 10:34-39)

Help me to get it straight, Lord. You must be first in my life in everything.

DAY OF ORDINARY TIME 32

Prayer is the great energy of love and this prayer is the voice of the Holy Ghost. We cannot intercede for one another simply in the strength of our old nature. We need the power of the Holy Ghost. It is the Holy Ghost who must enable us to sympathize, to feel so truly the needs of others as to pray for them properly.
— *The Way of Holiness,* Richard Meux Benson (1824-1915)

"He who receives you receives me, and he who receives me receives him who sent me. He who receives a prophet because he is a prophet shall receive a prophet's reward, and he who receives a righteous man because he is a righteous man shall receive a righteous man's reward. And whoever gives to one of these little ones even a cup of cold water because he is a disciple, truly, I say to you, he shall not lose his reward." (Matt. 10:40-42)

Help me, Lord, to pay loving attention to all the little people in my world today.

DAY OF ORDINARY TIME 33

Prayer is the ethical and religious act in which the union of the believing person and Christian with his God finds its strongest and best expression, and by

which this union is most profoundly realized and accomplished.
— *The Theology of Luther,* Julius Koestlin (1826-1902)

When John heard in prison about the deeds of the Christ, he sent word by his disciples and said to him, "Are you he who is to come, or shall we look for another?" And Jesus answered them, "Go and tell John what you hear and see: the blind receive their sight and the lame walk, lepers are cleansed and the deaf hear, and the dead are raised up, and the poor have good news preached to them. And blessed is he who takes no offense at me." (Matt. 11:2-6)

Jesus, help me to hear Your word clearly today so I may be made whole.

DAY OF ORDINARY TIME 34

Strictly speaking there is really only one legitimate object in prayer, and that is the desire for communion with God.
— *With Christ in the School of Prayer,* Andrew Murray (1828-1917)

As they went away, Jesus began to speak to the crowds concerning John: "What did you go out into the wilderness to behold? A reed shaken by the wind? Why then did you go out? To see a man clothed in soft raiment? Behold, those who wear soft raiment are in kings' houses. Why then did you go out? To see a prophet? Yes, I tell you, and more than a prophet. This is he of whom it is written, 'Behold, I send my messenger before thy face, who shall prepare thy way before thee.' " (Matt. 11:7-10)

Thank You, Lord, for the gift of faith and wisdom.

DAY OF ORDINARY TIME 35

Prayer is not monologue, but dialogue; God's voice in response to mine is its most essential part. Listening to God's voice is the secret of the assurance that He will listen to mine.
— *With Christ in the School of Prayer,* Andrew Murray (1828-1917)

"But to what shall I compare this generation? It is like children sitting in the market places and calling to their playmates, 'We piped to you, and you did not dance; we wailed, and you did not mourn.' For John came neither eating nor drinking, and they say, 'He has a demon'; the Son of man came eating and drinking, and they say, 'Behold, a glutton and a drunkard, a friend of tax collectors and sinners!' Yet wisdom is justified by her deeds." (Matt. 11:16-19)

Give me a good sense of humor, Lord, so that in all humility I may enjoy Your gift of wisdom.

DAY OF ORDINARY TIME 36

Prayer is the attending of the person toward its end. . . . Prayer is a focusing of the faculties of the person to the things concerning his end, under the form of a conversation with God . . . nothing other than an inner act of the person occupied with itself and with God.
— *Spiritual Works,* Pére Achille Desurmont (1828-1898)

At that time Jesus declared, "I thank thee, Father, Lord of heaven and earth, that thou hast hidden these things from the wise and understanding and revealed them to babes; yea, Father, for such was thy gracious will. All things have been delivered to me by my Father; and no one knows the Son except the Father, and no one knows the Father except the Son and any one to whom the Son chooses to reveal him." (Matt. 11:25-27)

Thank You, Lord, for calling me to faith in You. May I always give You praise and glory.

DAY OF ORDINARY TIME 37

Prayer is the lifting up of the mind and heart to God, the contemplation of God, the bold conversation of the creature with the Creator.
— *My Life in Christ,* John Sergieff of Cronstadt (1829-1908)

"Come to me, all who labor and are heavy laden, and I will give you rest. Take my yoke upon you, and learn from me; for I am gentle and lowly in heart, and you will find rest for your souls. For my yoke is easy, and my burden is light." (Matt. 11:28-30)

When I am tired and weary of life, Lord, let me find deep peace in You.

DAY OF ORDINARY TIME 38

All of the many phases of true prayer are included in the one idea of communing with God.
— *Prayer: Its Nature and Scope,* H. Clay Trumbull (1830-1903)

While he was still speaking to the people, behold, his mother and his brothers stood outside, asking to speak to him. But he replied to the man who told him, "Who is my mother, and who are my brothers?" And stretching out his hand toward his disciples, he said, "Here are my mother and my brothers! For whoever does the will of my Father in heaven is my brother, and sister, and mother." (Matt. 12:46-50)

Doing the will of God was everything for You, Jesus. May I learn to live my life this way too.

DAY OF ORDINARY TIME 39

To pray is simply to converse with God, to have a conversation with Him with adoration, praise, gratitude, petition and compunction.
— *Three Fundamental Principles of the Spiritual Life,* Moritz
      Meschler, S.J. (1830-1910)

He told them many things in parables, saying: "A sower went out to sow. And as he sowed, some seeds fell along the path, and the birds came and devoured them. Other seeds fell on rocky ground, where they had not much soil, and immediately they sprang up, since they had no depth of soil, but when the sun rose they were scorched; and since they had no root they withered away. Other seeds fell upon thorns, and the thorns grew up and choked them. Other seeds fell on good soil and brought forth grain, some a hundredfold, some sixty, some thirty. He who has ears, let him hear." (Matt. 13:3-9)

O Jesus, open my heart to receive the seed of Your love. May I be rich in Your goodness.

DAY OF ORDINARY TIME 40

Prayer is the whole spiritual action of the soul, turned toward God as its true and adequate object.
— *Sermons,* Canon F. W. Farrar (1831-1903)

Another parable he put before them saying, "The kingdom of heaven is like a grain of mustard seed which a man took and sowed in his field; it is the smallest of all seeds, but when it has grown it is the greatest of shrubs and becomes a tree, so that the birds of the air come and make nests in its branches." (Matt. 13:31-32)

O God, with You, little can be great. Help me to open to be Your Spirit present within all who believe.

DAY OF ORDINARY TIME 41

Prayer is the meeting of a human supplicant alone with God for supplication and communion at the mercy seat.
— *Lessons in the School of Prayer,* Dr. A. T. Pierson (1831-1896)

He told them another parable. "The kingdom of heaven is like leaven which a woman took and hid in three measures of flour, till it was all leavened." All this Jesus said to the crowds in parables; indeed he said nothing to them without a parable. This was to fulfill what was spoken by the prophet; "I will open my mouth in parables, I will utter what has been hidden since the foundation of the world." (Matt. 13:33-35)

Spirit of Life, open my mind so that I may hear the word of God.

DAY OF ORDINARY TIME 42

Pray simply. Do not expect to find in your heart any remarkable gift of prayer. Consider yourself unworthy of it. Then you will find peace. Use the empty cold dryness of your prayer as food for your humility. . . . This humble prayer, unlike the sweet one you delight in, will be acceptable to God.
— *Letters of Direction,* Macarius of Optino (1834-1860)

"The kingdom of heaven is like treasure hidden in a field, which a man found and covered up; then in his joy he goes and sells all that he has and buys that field. Again, the kingdom of heaven is like a merchant in search of fine pearls, who, on finding one pearl of great value, went and sold all that he had and bought it." (Matt. 13:44-46)

Thank You, Lord, for the treasure that is ours. May we prize faith in You above everything.

DAY OF ORDINARY TIME 43

Prayer, in its simplest definition, is merely a wish turned God-ward.
— *Letters,* Phillips Brooks (1835-1893)

"Again, the kingdom of heaven is like a net which was thrown into the sea and gathered fish of every kind; when it was full, men drew it ashore and sat down and sorted the good into vessels but threw away the bad. So it will be at the close of the age. The angels will come out and separate the evil from the righteous, and throw them into the furnace of fire; there men will weep and gnash their teeth." (Matt. 13:47-50)

Spirit of Truth, give me Your gift of discernment. Teach me to do what leads to You.

DAY OF ORDINARY TIME 44

Prayer is the creator as well as the channel of devotion.
— *The Essentials of Prayer,* E. M. Bounds (1835-1913)

When they had crossed over, they came to land at Gennesaret. And when the men of that place recognized him, they sent round to all that region and brought to him all that were sick, and besought him that they might only touch the fringe of his garment; and as many as touched it were made well. (Matt. 14:34-36)

Daily we are privileged to touch You, Lord, in Your word and in other people. May this privilege lead us all to You.

DAY OF ORDINARY TIME 45

To pray for everything simply means to have companionship with the Father in everything.
— *Value and Confidence in Prayer of Petition,* Martin Kohler (1835-1917)

And Jesus went on from there and passed along the Sea of Galilee. And he went up on the mountain, and sat down there. And great crowds came to him, bringing with them the lame, the maimed, the blind, the dumb, and many others, and they put them at his feet, and he healed them, so that the throng wondered, when they saw the dumb speaking, the maimed whole, the lame walking, and the blind seeing; and they glorified the God of Israel. (Matt. 15:29-31)

Save us, O Christ, because You truly are the Son of God.

DAY OF ORDINARY TIME 46

To pray is to draw near to Him, who searches the heart, to have an audience with God. . . . Prayer is the nearest approach to God, and the highest enjoyment of Him that we are capable of in this life.
— *The Throne of Grace,* Mosheim Rhodes (1837-1924)

And the Pharisees and Sadducees came, and to test him they asked him to show them a sign from heaven. He answered them, "When it is evening, you say, 'It will be fair weather; for the sky is red.' And in the morning, 'It will be stormy today, for the sky is red and threatening.' You know how to interpret the appearance of the sky, but you cannot interpret the signs of the times. An evil and adulterous generation seeks for a sign, but no sign shall be given to it except the sign of Jonah." So he left them and departed. (Matt. 16:1-4)

Strengthen my faith in You, O Christ, so that I may be able to understand the signs You give me.

DAY OF ORDINARY TIME 47

Prayer is conversation with God, familial conversation, and interior dialogue.
— *On the Philosophy of Religion,* Auguste Sabatier (1839-1901)

From that time Jesus began to show his disciples that he must go to Jerusalem and suffer many things from the elders and chief priests and scribes, and be killed and on the third day be raised. And Peter took him and began to rebuke him, saying, "God forbid, Lord! This shall never happen to you." But he turned and said to Peter, 'Get behind me, Satan! You are a hindrance to me; for you are not on the side of God, but of men." (Matt. 16:21-23)

Lord, teach me Your Father's way of judging so that my perspective on life may be like Yours.

DAY OF ORDINARY TIME 48

Prayer is religion in action, which means prayer is genuine religion. It is prayer that distinguishes the religious phenomenon from such similar or related phenomena as purely moral or aesthetic feeling. . . . Prayer is conversation with God, intimate familiarity, and inner dialogue with Him.
— *On the Philosophy of Religion,* Auguste Sabatier (1839-1901)

Then Jesus told his disciples, "If any man would come after me, let him deny himself and take up his cross and follow me. For whoever would save his life will lose it, and whoever loses his life for my sake will find it. For what will it profit a man, if he gains the whole world and forfeits his life? Or what shall a man give in return for his life? For the Son of man is to come with his angels in the glory of his Father, and then he will pay every man for what he has done." (Matt. 16:24-27)

Only if I carry my cross after You, Jesus, can I hope to enjoy Your glory. Help me.

DAY OF ORDINARY TIME 49

Prayer is the spiritual manifestation of desire.
— *The Book of the Spiritual Life,* Lady Emilia Dilke (1840-1904)

After six days Jesus took with him Peter and James and John his brother, and led them up a high mountain apart. And he was transfigured before them, and his face shone like the sun, and his garments became white as light. And behold, there appeared to them Moses and Elijah, talking with him. And Peter said to Jesus, "Lord, it is well that we are here; if you wish, I will make three booths here, one for you and one for Moses and one for Elijah." (Matt. 17:1-4)

Light before all light, send us Your Spirit of Truth so that we may see as You want us to see.

DAY OF ORDINARY TIME 50

Prayer is every kind of inward communion or conversation with the power recognized as divine. . . . Prayer is conversation with an ideal companion.
— *Psychology: Briefer Course,* William James (1842-1910)

He was still speaking, when lo, a bright cloud overshadowed them, and a voice from the cloud said, "This is my beloved Son, with whom I am well pleased; listen to him." When the disciples heard this, they fell on their faces, and were filled with awe. But Jesus came and touched them, saying, "Rise, and have no fear." And when they lifted up their eyes, they saw no one but Jesus only. (Matt. 17:5-8)

May I lift up my eyes always only to see You, O Jesus. You alone can show me Your way.

DAY OF ORDINARY TIME 51

Individual prayer is every communication of the person with God, all the elevation of the heart toward Him, that is free, personal, and not limited to any determined liturgical form.
— *Spiritual Life and Prayer,* Madame Cécile J. Bruyère (1845-1909)

Jesus commanded them, "Tell no one the vision, until the Son of man is raised from the dead." And the disciples asked him, "Then why do the scribes say that first Elijah must come?" He replied, "Elijah does come, and he is to restore all things; but I tell you that Elijah has already come, and they did not know him, but did to him whatever they pleased. So also the Son of man will suffer at their hands." (Matt. 17:9-12)

Teach us the plain truth, Lord. You alone know the secret wisdom which leads to salvation.

DAY OF ORDINARY TIME 52

Prayer is conversation with God, as free as that of children with their father, in which we speak with Him of what pertains to His glory, His generosity and the needs of our soul.
— *The Practice of Mental Prayer,* René de Maumigny, S.J. (d. 1917)

When they came to the crowd, a man came up to him and kneeling before him said, "Lord, have mercy on my son, for he is an epileptic and he suffers terribly; for often he falls into the fire, and often into the water. And I brought him to your disciples, and they could not heal him." And Jesus answered, "O faithless and perverse generation, how long am I to be with you? How long am I to bear with you? Bring him here to me." And Jesus rebuked him, and the demon came out of him, and the boy was cured instantly. (Matt. 17:14-18)

Lord, I do want to believe in You, but help me in my unbelief.

DAY OF ORDINARY TIME 53

Prayer is the communication of human need before God, the communication of satisfied need in the prayer of thanksgiving, and of need still felt in the prayer of petition.
— *The Community of the Christian With God,* Wilhelm Herrmann (1846-1922)

Then the disciples came to Jesus privately and said, "Why could we not cast it out?" He said to them, "Because of your little faith. For truly, I say to you, if you have faith as a grain of mustard seed, you will say to this mountain, 'Move from here to there,' and it will move; and nothing will be impossible to you." (Matt. 17:19-21)

O God, You and I are a majority. Nothing can defeat Your will and purpose. Make it mine too.

DAY OF ORDINARY TIME 54

This religious desire and effort of the soul to relate itself and all its interests to God and His will is prayer in the deepest sense. This is essential prayer. Uttered or unexpressed, it is equally prayer. It is the soul's desire after God going forth in manifestation.
— *The Essence of Religion,* Borden Parker Bowne (1847-1910)

When they came to Capernaum, the collectors of the half-shekel tax went up to Peter and said, "Does not your teacher pay the tax?" He said, "Yes." And when he came home, Jesus spoke to him first, saying, "What do you think, Simon? From whom do kings of the earth take toll or tribute? From their sons or from others?" And when he said, "From others," Jesus said to him, "Then the sons are free. However, not to give offense to them, go to the sea and cast a hook, and take the first fish that comes up, and when you open its mouth you will find a shekel; take that and give it to them for me and for yourself." (Matt. 17:24-27)

Teach me, good Jesus, to live as Your disciple and not as a stranger to You.

DAY OF ORDINARY TIME 55

Prayer is an art, this great and creative prayer, this intimate conversation with God.
— *The Soul of Prayer,* P. T. Forsyth (1848-1921)

At that time the disciples came to Jesus, saying "Who is the greatest in the kingdom of heaven?" And calling to him a child, he put him in the midst of them, and said, "Truly, I say to you, unless you turn and become like children, you will never enter the kingdom of heaven. Whoever humbles himself like this child, he is the greatest in the kingdom of heaven. Whoever receives one such child in my name receives me; but whoever causes one of these little ones who believe in me to sin, it would be better for him to have a great millstone fastened round his neck and to be drowned in the depth of the sea." (Matt. 18:1-6)

May my tendency to pride never defeat my good intentions. Teach me how to be humble.

DAY OF ORDINARY TIME 56

Prayer is a gift and sacrifice we make; sacrament is a gift and sacrifice that God makes. . . . in prayer we go to God; in sacrament He comes to us.
— *The Soul of Prayer,* P. T. Forsyth (1848-1921)

"Woe to the world for temptations to sin! For it is necessary that temptations come, and woe to the man by whom the temptation comes! And if your hand or your foot causes you to sin, cut it off and throw it away; it is better for you to enter life maimed or lame than with two hands or two feet to be thrown into the eternal fire. And if your eye causes you to sin, pluck it out and throw it away; it is better for you to enter life with one eye than with two eyes to be thrown into the hell of fire." (Matt. 18:7-9)

Let me learn to deny myself in little ways so that I will not disappoint You in big things, O God.

DAY OF ORDINARY TIME 57

If you cannot come to God with the occasions of your private life and affairs, then there is some unreality in the relation between you and Him.
— *The Soul of Prayer,* P. T. Forsyth (1848-1921)

"What do you think? If a man has a hundred sheep, and one of them has gone astray, does he not leave the ninety-nine on the mountains and go in search of the one that went astray? And if he finds it, truly, I say to you, he rejoices over it more than over the ninety-nine that never went astray. So it is not the will of my Father who is in heaven that one of these little ones should perish." (Matt. 18:12-14)

Help me, Lord, to truly rejoice with those who are pardoned. May I know the inner joy of being forgiven by You.

DAY OF ORDINARY TIME 58

Prayer is not only an intellectual act, but a colloquy with our living God. Two persons are necessarily engaged in it. . . . Being a conversation with God, prayer demands more listening to God rather than in speaking to Him.
— *Conferences,* Cardinal Mercier (1851-1926)

"If your brother sins against you, go and tell him his fault, between you and him alone. If he listens to you, you have gained your brother. But if he does not listen, take one or two others along with you, that every word may be confirmed by the evidence of two or three witnesses. If he refuses to listen to them, tell it to the church; and if he refuses to listen even to the church, let him be to you as a Gentile and a tax collector." (Matt. 18:15-17)

May the assembly of the faithful, Lord, practice Your compassion toward all in need.

DAY OF ORDINARY TIME 59

Prayer, understood properly, prepares the person for action, sustains us on life's road when tired and lonely, and arms us for battle when the enemy comes after us.
— *Conferences,* Desiré Joseph Mercier (1851-1926)

"Truly, I say to you, whatever you bind on earth shall be bound in heaven, and whatever you loose on earth shall be loosed in heaven. Again I say to you, if two of you agree on earth about anything they ask, it will be done for them by my Father in heaven. For where two or three are gathered in my name, there am I in the midst of them." Then Peter came up and said to him, "Lord, how often shall my brother sin against me, and I forgive him?

As many as seven times?" Jesus said to him, "I do not say to you seven times, but seventy times seven." (Matt. 18:18-22)

Make each of us, Lord, an instrument of Your peace and reconciliation today.

DAY OF ORDINARY TIME 60

Prayer winds in and out through our many actions, moral and all others, which forever are proceeding in our field of life. Prayer gathers them together in bundles and bears them into the storehouse of the Divine Reaper.
— *Conferences,* Desiré Joseph Mercier (1851-1926)

Children were brought to him that he might lay his hands on them and pray. The disciples rebuked the people; but Jesus said, "Let the children come to me, and do not hinder them; for to such belongs the kingdom of heaven." And he laid his hands on them and went away. (Matt. 19:13-15)

Touch me, gentle Jesus, as I need to be touched by You. Bless me and heal me.

DAY OF ORDINARY TIME 61

Prayer may be understood widely, so as to include every form of address from man to God, whatever its character. . . . In the larger sense of the word, as the spiritual language of the soul, prayer is conversation with God, often seeking no end beyond the pleasure of such conversation.
— *Doctrine of Christian Prayer,* James Hastings (1852-1922)

Jesus said to his disciples, "Truly, I say to you, it will be hard for a rich man to enter the kingdom of heaven. Again I tell you, it is easier for a camel to go through the eye of a needle than for a rich man to enter the kingdom of God." When the disciples heard this they were greatly astonished, saying, "Who then can be saved?" But Jesus looked at them and said to them, "With men this is impossible, but with God all things are possible." (Matt. 19:23-26)

Teach me to believe that all things are possible with You, God, and give me peace.

DAY OF ORDINARY TIME 62

Prayer is nothing at all except as on the one side there is a human "I," on the other a divine "Thou," and living fellowship between the two. Prayer is thus the psychological act by which the soul seeks and finds contact, conscious contact, or communion, with God. In the first instance it is not asking for anything, it is not petition; all it seeks is God himself.
— *Doctrine of Christian Prayer,* James Hastings (1852-1922)

Peter said in reply, "Lo, we have left everything and followed you. What then shall we have?" Jesus said to them, "Truly, I say to you, in the new world, when the Son of man shall sit on his glorious throne, you who have followed me will also sit on twelve thrones, judging the twelve tribes of Israel. And every one who has left houses or brothers or sisters or father or mother or children or lands, for my name's sake, will receive a hundredfold, and inherit eternal life." (Matt. 19:27-28)

Teach us, Lord, to turn loose all things which stand in our way. Draw us to You in love.

DAY OF ORDINARY TIME 63

The most fundamental need, duty, honor and happiness of man is not petition nor even contrition, nor again even thanksgiving; these are three kinds of prayer which indeed must never disappear out of our spiritual lives; but adoration.
— *The Life of Prayer,* Baron Friedrich von Hügel (1852-1925)

And as Jesus was going up to Jerusalem, he took the twelve disciples aside, and on the way he said to them, "Behold, we are going up to Jerusalem; and the Son of man will be delivered to the chief priests and scribes, and they will condemn him to death, and deliver him to the Gentiles to be mocked and scourged and crucified, and he will be raised on the third day." (Matt. 20:17-19)

To follow You closely, O Jesus, means to accept the cross. Help us overcome our fear of it.

DAY OF ORDINARY TIME 64

There is no doubt that the prayer of quiet, that certain formless recollection

and loving feeding upon the sense and presence of God . . . is a most legitimate prayer.
— *The Life of Prayer,* Baron Friedrich von Hügel (1852-1925)

Jesus called them to them and said, "You know that the rulers of the Gentiles lord it over them, and their great men exercise authority over them. It shall not be so among you; but whoever would be great among you must be your servant, and whoever would be first among you must be your slave; even as the Son of man came not to be served but to serve, and to give his life as a ransom for many." (Matt. 20:25-28)

Lord, You call us Your friends and Your disciples. Help us to know also that we are the servants of Your people.

DAY OF ORDINARY TIME 65

To pray means to relax one's heart, to say good-bye to concerns, to breathe out misery and trouble, to breathe in the pure mountain air and the power of another world.
— *More Joy,* Paul Wilhelm von Keppler (1852-1926)

And as they went out of Jericho, a great crowd followed him. And behold, two blind men sitting by the roadside, when they heard that Jesus was passing by, cried out, "Have mercy on us, Son of David!" The crowd rebuked them, telling them to be silent; but they cried out the more, "Lord, have mercy on us, Son of David!" And Jesus stopped and called them, saying, "What do you want me to do for you?" They said to him, "Lord, let our eyes be opened." And Jesus in pity touched their eyes, and immediately they received their sight and followed him. (Matt. 20:29-34)

Jesus, help us to see the way so that we may follow You in faith.

DAY OF ORDINARY TIME 66

Prayer is a devout and humble elevation of the mind to God so that we may manifest to Him our love and our personal desires.
— *Christian Asceticism,* Francis X. Mutz (1854-1925)

The blind and the lame came to him in the temple, and he healed them. But when the chief priests and the scribes saw the wonderful things that he did, and the children crying out in the temple, "Hosanna to the Son of David!"

they were indignant; and they said to him, "Do you hear what these are saying?" And Jesus said to them, "Yes; have you never read, 'Out of the mouth of babes and sucklings thou hast brought perfect praise'?" And leaving them, he went out of the city to Bethany and lodged there. (Matt. 21:14-17)

Praise and glory be to You, O Christ, our Savior. Help our lives to reflect our belief.

DAY OF ORDINARY TIME 67

Prayer is the raising of our soul to God to offer Him our adoration and ask His blessing so that we may grow in holiness for His glory.
— *The Spiritual Life,* Adolphe Tanquerey, S.S. (1854-1932)

In the morning, as he was returning to the city, he was hungry. And seeing a fig tree by the wayside he went to it, and found nothing on it but leaves only. And he said to it, "May no fruit ever come from you again!" And the fig tree withered at once, When the disciples saw it they marveled, saying, "How did the fig tree wither at once?" And Jesus answered them, "Truly, I say to you, if you have faith and never doubt, you will not only do what has been done to the fig tree, but even if you say to this mountain, 'Be taken up and cast into the sea,' it will be done. And whatever you ask in prayer, you will receive, if you have faith." (Matt. 21:18-22)

Jesus, let me experience Your confidence and enthusiasm for life.

DAY OF ORDINARY TIME 68

I don't think there is any ground for fear as to prayer, that it may be simply daydreaming. You prepare your meditation, which preparation is the homage and service of your mind; in the morning you set a light to the offering prepared on your altar, and let it burn quietly. That is all good, and an excellent way of praying. When God wants anything else He will let you know.
— *Letters,* Janet Erskine Stuart (1857-1914)

"Teacher, we know that you are true, and teach the way of God truthfully, and care for no man; for you do not regard the position of men. Tell us, then, what you think. Is it lawful to pay taxes to Caesar, or not?" But Jesus, aware of their malice, said, "Why put me to the test, you hypocrites? Show me the money for the tax." And they brought him a coin. And Jesus said to them,

"Whose likeness and inscription is this?" They said, "Caesar's." Then he said to them, "Render therefore to Caesar the things that are Caesar's, and to God the things that are God's." (Matt. 22:16-21)

Your wisdom, O Lord, is beyond comparison. Share with us the gifts we need for salvation.

DAY OF ORDINARY TIME 69

Prayer is the raising of the soul to God, to adore Him, to thank Him, to beg pardon and to ask for His blessing.
— *The Ways of Mental Prayer,* Vitalis Lehodey (1857-1948)

One of them, a lawyer, asked him a question, to test him. "Teacher, which is the great commandment in the law?" And he said to him, "You shall love the Lord your God with all your heart, and with all your soul, and with all your mind. This is the great and first commandment. And a second is like it, You shall love your neighbor as yourself. On these two commandments depend all the law and the prophets." (Matt. 22:35-40)

Teacher, give me the wisdom and trust to make Your law of love the norm for all my behavior.

DAY OF ORDINARY TIME 70

Prayer is the attention of the person lovingly fixed on God. The more loving that attention is, the more genuine is the prayer.
— *Letters,* Charles de Foucauld (1858-1916)

While the Pharisees were gathered together, Jesus asked them a question, saying, "What do you think of the Christ? Whose son is he?" They said to him, "The son of David." He said to them, "How is it then that David, inspired by the Spirit, calls him Lord, saying, 'The Lord said to my Lord, Sit at my right hand, till I put thy enemies under thy feet'? If David thus calls him Lord, how is he his son?" And no one was able to answer him a word, nor from that day did any one dare to ask him any more questions. (Matt. 22:41-46)

Spirit of Truth, reveal to me who Jesus is so that I may follow Him more closely.

DAY OF ORDINARY TIME 71

Prayer in the widest sense of the word can be either silent contemplation or contemplation accompanied by words, words of adoration, or love, or self-giving, the giving to God of everything that is in a person. They can be words of thanksgiving for the goodness of God, or for blessings given to oneself or other created beings. They may be words of regret in sorrow for one's own sins or those of another; they may also express a petition.
— *Letters,* Charles de Foucauld (1858-1916)

Therefore, since we are justified by faith, we have peace with God through the Lord Jesus Christ. Through him we have obtained access to this grace in which we stand, and we rejoice in our hope of sharing the glory of God. More than that, we rejoice in our sufferings, knowing that suffering produces endurance, and endurance produces character, and character produces hope, and hope does not disappoint us, because God's love has been poured into our hearts through the Holy Spirit which has been given to us. (Rom. 5:1-5)

Holy Spirit of God, lead us into Your truth and fill us with enthusiasm for the Christian way.

DAY OF ORDINARY TIME 72

Prayer is any conversation between a person and God. Hence it is that state in which the person looks wordlessly on God, occupied completely with contemplating Him, telling Him with glances that he loves Him, while speaking no words, not even in one's thoughts.
— *Letters,* Charles de Foucauld (1858-1916)

While we were still weak, at the right time Christ died for the ungodly. Why, one will hardly die for a righteous man — though perhaps for a good man one will dare even to die. But God shows his love for us in that while we were yet sinners Christ died for us. Since, therefore, we are now justified by his blood, much more shall we be saved by him from the wrath of God. For if while we were enemies we were reconciled to God by the death of his Son, much more, now that we are reconciled, shall we be saved by his life. Not only so, but we also rejoice in God through our Lord Jesus Christ, through whom we have now received our reconciliation. (Rom. 5:6-11)

Lord Jesus Christ, help me to properly thank You for Your death for me.

DAY OF ORDINARY TIME 73

Prayer is like the expression of our inner life as children of God, like the result of our divine relationship with Christ, the spontaneous flowering of the gifts of the Holy Ghost. And that is why it is so essential and so fruitful.
— *Spiritual Letters,* Dom Columba Marmion (1858-1923)

As one man's trespass led to condemnation for all men, so one man's act of righteousness leads to acquittal and life for all men. For as by one man's disobedience many were made sinners, so by one man's obedience many will be made righteous. Law came in, to increase the trespass; but where sin increased, grace abounded all the more, so that, as sin reigned in death, grace also might reign through righteousness to eternal life through Jesus Christ our Lord. (Rom. 5:18-21)

Son of God, may Your example of obedience to Your Father challenge me to walk in righteousness.

DAY OF ORDINARY TIME 74

Method is one thing, prayer another. The method ought to vary according to the aptitude and needs of persons, while prayer (I am speaking of ordinary prayer) remains substantially always the same for every soul: a conversation in which the child of God pours out his soul before his Heavenly Father, and listens to Him in order to please Him.
— *Christ the Life of the Soul,* Dom Columba Marmion (1858-1923)

What shall we say then? Are we to continue in sin that grace may abound? By no means! How can we who died to sin still live in it? Do you not know that all of us who have been baptized into Christ Jesus were baptized into his death? We were buried therefore with him by baptism into death, so that as Christ was raised from the dead by the glory of the Father, we too might walk in newness of life. (Rom. 6:1-4)

By baptism we have died with You, O Christ. Help us to live each day in this awareness.

DAY OF ORDINARY TIME 75

Prayer is worship, addressed to the Father, in the name of Christ, and in the power of the Holy Spirit.
— *Effective Praying,* Henry W. Frost (1858-1927)

For if we have been united with him in a death like his, we shall certainly be united with him in a resurrection like his. We know that our old self was crucified with him so that the sinful body might be destroyed, and we might no longer be enslaved to sin. For he who has died is freed from sin. But if we have died with Christ, we believe that we shall also live with him. For we know that Christ being raised from the dead will never die again; death no longer has dominion over him. The death he died he died to sin, once for all, but the life he lives he lives to God. So you also must consider yourselves dead to sin and alive to God in Christ Jesus. (Rom. 6:5-11)

Help me die a little each day so that I may live out my calling.

DAY OF ORDINARY TIME 76

Prayer is going to God or elevation of mind and heart to Him. But our going to God depends on grace drawing. "Draw me, and we will run." Prayer is therefore God's work and ours.
— *Spiritual Writings,* Mother Mary St. Peter (1859-1942)

When you were slaves of sin, you were free in regard to righteousness. But then what return did you get from the things of which you are now ashamed? The end of those things is death. But now that you have been set free from sin and have become slaves of God, the return you get is sanctification and its end, eternal life. For the wages of sin is death, but the free gift of God is eternal life in Christ Jesus our Lord. (Rom. 6:20-23)

Lord, You are my only master. May I hear Your voice only, and respond to it in deed.

DAY OF ORDINARY TIME 77

Prayer is not necessarily petition, the asking for benefits. Any intercourse of a human soul with higher powers may rightly be termed prayer. For the monotheist prayer is intercourse with God.
— *The Nature of Belief,* Martin C. D'Arcy (1859-1940)

I know that nothing good dwells within me, that is, in my flesh. I can will what is right, but I cannot do it. For I do not do the good I want, but the evil I do not want is what I do. Now if I do what I do not want, it is no longer I that do it, but sin which dwells within me. (Rom. 7:18-20)

O God, save me from myself. Help me to overcome my lethargy and do Your will.

DAY OF ORDINARY TIME 78

To pray is to converse with God himself, honoring Him with the virtue of religion and entering into intimate and familiar union with Him by means of the three theological virtues which, since they cause us to share in the mutual knowledge and love of the three divine Persons, unite us with them in ever-increasing measures, and by means of the seven gifts of the Holy Spirit which place us under the loving guidance and influence of this divine Consoler.
— *Stages in Prayer,* Juan Arintero (1860-1928)

But you are not in the flesh, you are in the Spirit, if in fact the Spirit of God dwells in you. Any one who does not have the Spirit of Christ does not belong to him. But if Christ is in you, although your bodies are dead because of sin, your spirits are alive because of righteousness. If the Spirit of him who raised Jesus from the dead dwells in you, he who raised Christ Jesus from the dead will give life to your mortal bodies also through his Spirit who dwells in you. (Rom. 8:9-11)

Holy Spirit of God, lead me to those actions which flow from Your grace alone.

DAY OF ORDINARY TIME 79

The joy of communion and intercourse with God is the central feature of prayer.
— *Pathways to the Reality of God,* Rufus Jones (1863-1948)

I consider that the sufferings of this present time are not worth comparing with the glory that is to be revealed to us. For the creation waits with eager longing for the revealing of the sons of God; for the creation was subjected to futility, not of its own will but by the will of him who subjected it in hope; because the creation itself will be set free from its bondage to decay and obtain the glorious liberty of the children of God. We know that the whole creation has been groaning in travail together until now; and not only the creation, but we ourselves, who have the first fruits of the Spirit, groan inwardly as we wait for adoption as sons, the redemption of our bodies. For in this hope we were saved. Now hope that is seen is not hope. For who hopes for what he sees? But if we hope for what we do not see, we wait for it with patience. (Rom. 8:18-25)

Keep hope alive in me, Lord, so that I may always persevere.

DAY OF ORDINARY TIME 80

Prayer is an act of the virtue of religion whereby we acknowledge that God is the maker and mover of all things.
— *The Craft of Prayer,* Vincent McNabb, O.P. (1864-1943)

Likewise the Spirit helps us in our weakness; for we do not know how to pray as we ought, but the Spirit himself intercedes for us with sighs too deep for words. And he who searches the hearts of men knows what is the mind of the Spirit, because the Spirit intercedes for the saints according to the will of God. (Rom. 8:26-27)

Pray within me today, Holy Spirit, so that I may be able to present my true self to God in prayer.

DAY OF ORDINARY TIME 81

Prayer in its essence is an intelligent asking for what God has not yet given us. There are things a good God could not give us. There are things a wise God could not give us. These we should not ask for.
— *The Craft of Prayer,* Vincent McNabb, O.P. (1864-1943)

We know that in everything God works for good with those who love him, who are called according to his purpose. For those whom he foreknew he also predestined to be conformed to the image of his Son, in order that he might be the first-born among many brethren. And those whom he predestined he also called; and those whom he called he also justified; and those whom he justified he also glorified. (Rom. 8:28-30)

Let me clearly see Your purpose for me, O God, so that I may live each day for You.

DAY OF ORDINARY TIME 82

What is prayer? It is, when we comprehend it in its deepest and most partic-

ular meaning, a dialogue between our innermost self and Almighty God, a genuine and true experience. It is an uplifting of the human person to the highest reality, God condescending and bending toward the individual human person.
— *Instruction on Prayer,* Wilhelm Bousset (1865-1920)

Who shall separate us from the love of Christ? Shall tribulation, or distress, or persecution, or famine, or nakedeness, or peril, or sword? As it is written, "For thy sake we are being killed all the day long; we are regarded as sheep to be slaughtered." No, in all these things we are more than conquerors through him who loved us. For I am sure that neither death, nor life, nor angels, nor principalities, nor things present, nor things to come, nor powers, nor height, nor depth, nor anything else in all creation, will be able to separate us from the love of God in Christ Jesus our Lord. (Rom. 8:35-39)

Keep me in Your love always, O Lord Jesus Christ.

DAY OF ORDINARY TIME 83

Why is poetry incapable of apprehending God as prayer apprehends Him? Because not only contemplation, but the humblest prayer worthy of the name is a supernatural gift of God.
— *Prayer and Poetry,* Henri Brémond (1865-1933)

The word is near you, on your lips and in your heart (that is, the word of faith which we preach); because, if you confess with your lips that Jesus is Lord and believe in your heart that God raised him from the dead, you will be saved. For man believes with his heart and so is justified, and he confesses with his lips and so is saved. The scripture says, "No one who believes in him will be put to shame." For there is no distinction between Jew and Greek; the same Lord is Lord of all and bestows his riches upon all who call upon him. For, "every one who calls upon the name of the Lord will be saved." (Rom. 10:8-13)

May my daily life reflect, O Jesus, what I believe in my heart.

DAY OF ORDINARY TIME 84

Prayer, in the sense of union with God, is the most crucifying thing there is. One must do it for God's sake, but one will not get any satisfaction out of it,

in the sense of feeling "I am good at prayer."
— *Spiritual Letters,* John Chapman (1865-1933)

O the depth of the riches and wisdom and knowledge of God! How unsearchable are his judgments and how inscrutable his ways! "For who has known the mind of the Lord, or who has been his counselor?" "Or who has given a gift to him that he might be repaid?" For from him and through him and to him are all things. To him be glory for ever. Amen. (Rom. 11:33-36)

Guide of my life, give me Your counsel always. May my whole life be to Your glory.

DAY OF ORDINARY TIME 85

Prayer is conversation, habitual and loving discourse with God, with the Master of our inner life. . . . It is docility to God.
— *Spiritual Writings,* Léonce de Grandmaison (1868-1927)

I appeal to you therefore, brethren, by the mercies of God, to present your bodies as a living sacrifice, holy and acceptable to God, which is your spiritual worship. Do not be conformed to this world but be transformed by the renewal of your mind, that you may prove what is the will of God, what is good and acceptable and perfect. (Rom. 12:1-2)

Spirit of Truth, renew the resolve of my heart so that I may live a life worthy of You.

DAY OF ORDINARY TIME 86

Praying is identifying oneself with the divine will by the deliberate renunciation of one's own will, not by killing one's desire but by freely giving in to a stronger will.
— *Lord, Teach Us to Pray,* Paul Claudel (1868-1955)

For as in one body we have many members, and all the members do not have the same function, so we, though many, are one body in Christ, and individually members one of another. Having gifts that differ according to the grace given to us, let us use them: if prophecy, in proportion to our faith; if service, in our serving; he who teaches, in his teaching; he who exhorts, in his exhortation; he who contributes, in liberality; he who gives aid, with zeal; he who does acts of mercy, with cheerfulness. (Rom. 12:4-8)

Lord, each of us is unique. Each has gifts from You. May we all praise You in our diversity.

DAY OF ORDINARY TIME 87

To pray is to be present to oneself, to give oneself over, to lay oneself open, to make oneself look to God in all sincerity and peace and simplicity and humility and purity.
— *Lord, Teach Us to Pray,* Paul Claudel (1868-1955)

Let love be genuine; hate what is evil, hold fast to what is good; love one another with brotherly affection; outdo one another in showing honor. Never flag in zeal, be aglow with the Spirit, serve the Lord. Rejoice in your hope, be patient in tribulation, be constant in prayer. Contribute to the needs of the saints, practice hospitality. (Rom. 12:9-13)

May the light of Your Spirit burn brightly in our hearts, O God, so that all will be led to You.

DAY OF ORDINARY TIME 88

For me prayer is a lifting up of the heart, a look toward heaven, a cry of gratitude and love shouted out both when in sorrow and in joy; in a word, something beautiful and supernatural, which causes my soul to expand and unites it to God.
— *Autobiography,* St. Thérèse of Lisieux (1873-1897)

Bless those who persecute you; bless and do not curse them. Rejoice with those who rejoice, weep with those who weep. Live in harmony with one another; do not be haughty, but associate with the lowly; never be conceited. Repay no one evil for evil, but take thought for what is noble in the sight of all. If possible, so far as it depends upon you, live peaceably with all. (Rom. 12:14-18)

May Your peace rule the lives of all Your people. You alone bring true peace to us, Lord.

DAY OF ORDINARY TIME 89

When I pray, I simply say what I want to God, and He always understands

126

me. For me, prayer is an outburst of my heart, a simple glance raised to heaven, a cry of gratitude and love in the midst of troubles as well as in the midst of joy. In short, prayer is a noble and supernatural reality which enlarges the person and unites him with God.
— *Autobiography,* St. Thérèse of Lisieux (1873-1897)

Owe no one anything, except to love one another; for he who loves his neighbor has fulfilled the law. The commandments, "You shall not commit adultery, You shall not kill, You shall not steal, You shall not covet," and any other commandment, are summed up in this sentence, "You shall love your neighbor as yourself." Love does no wrong to a neighbor; therefore love is the fulfilling of the law. (Rom. 13:8-10)

O Jesus, may I know the love You call us to show to all our sisters and brothers.

DAY OF ORDINARY TIME 90

Worship, or prayer, is the special sphere of the will in religion. It is an act of approach to God; and while this act involves a lifting of thought to God, it is more than an act of thought — it intends to institute some communication or transaction with God wherein will answers will.
— *The Meaning of God in Human Experience,* W. E. Hocking
      (1873-1966)

Besides this you know what hour it is, how it is full time now for you to wake from sleep. For salvation is nearer to us now than when we first believed; the night is far gone, the day is at hand. Let us then cast off the works of darkness and put on the armor of light; let us conduct ourselves becomingly as in the day, not in reveling and drunkenness, not in debauchery and licentiousness, not in quarreling and jealousy. But put on the Lord Jesus Christ, and make no provision for the flesh, to gratify its desires. (Rom. 13:11-14)

You call us each day to the light of a new day, O God. May we not disappoint You by wandering in darkness.

DAY OF ORDINARY TIME 91

Prayer seems to be essentially a tending of the spirit toward the immaterial foundation of the world. In general, it consists in a complaint, a cry of anguish, a demand for help. Sometimes it becomes a peaceful contemplation

of the immanent and transcendent principle of all reality. One can define it equally as an uplifting of the person to God.
— *Prayer,* Dr. Alexis Carrel (1873-1944)

None of us lives to himself, and none of us dies to himself. If we live, we live to the Lord, and if we die, we die to the Lord; so then, whether we live or whether we die, we are the Lord's. For to this end Christ died and lived again, that he might be Lord both of the dead and of the living. (Rom. 14:7-9)

Help me to choose life, O Jesus, the life You came to give to all.

DAY OF ORDINARY TIME 92

Prayer should be understood, not as a mere rote recitation of a formula, but as a spiritual lifting up, an absorption of consciousness in the contemplation of a principle both innate to and transcending of our natural universe. . . . It is a world unknown to philosophers and scientists, and closed to them. But the simple seem to feel God as simply as the heat of the sun or the warmth of a friend.
— *Prayer,* Dr. Alexis Carrel (1873-1944)

We who are strong ought to bear with the failings of the weak, and not to please ourselves; let each of us please his neighbor for his good, to edify him. For Christ did not please himself; but, as it is written, "The reproaches of those who reproached thee fell on me." For whatever was written in former days was written for our instruction, that by steadfastness and by the encouragement of the scriptures we might have hope. May the God of steadfastness and encouragement grant you to live in such harmony with one another, in accord with Christ Jesus, that together you may with one voice glorify the God and Father of our Lord Jesus Christ. (Rom. 15:1-6)

May the wisdom of Your good news touch many hearts today, O Jesus.

DAY OF ORDINARY TIME 93

Prayer is the endeavor of a person to reach out to God, to converse with an invisible being, maker of all things, supreme wisdom, truth, beauty and strength, father and redeemer of every human person.
— *Prayer,* Dr. Alexis Carrel (1873-1944)

Now to him who is able to strengthen you according to my gospel and the preaching of Jesus Christ, according to the revelation of the mystery which was kept secret for long ages but is now disclosed and through the prophetic writings is made known to all nations, according to the command of the eternal God, to bring about the obedience of faith — to the only wise God be glory for evermore through Jesus Christ! Amen. (Rom. 16:25-27)

All praise, honor and glory be to You, Lord Jesus Christ.

DAY OF ORDINARY TIME 94

Prayer always remains a true mutual expression, a real communication, even sometimes a real combat between a person and Almighty God.
— *The Problem of Prayer,* Fernand Menagoz (b. 1873)

Has not God made foolish the wisdom of the world? For since, in the wisdom of God, the world did not know God through wisdom, it pleased God through the folly of what we preach to save those who believe. For Jews demand signs and Greeks seek wisdom, but we preach Christ crucified, a stumbling block to Jews and folly to Gentiles, but to those who are called, both Jews and Greeks, Christ the power of God and the wisdom of God. For the foolishness of God is wiser than men, and the weakness of God is stronger than men. (1 Cor. 1:20-25)

Give us the only sign we need or can trust, O God, which is Your holy word.

DAY OF ORDINARY TIME 95

Whenever the insistence is on the point that God answers prayer, we are off the track. The meaning of prayer is that we get hold of God, not of the answer.
— *Knocking at God's Door,* Oswald Chambers (1874-1917)

Consider your call, brethren; not many of you were wise according to worldly standards, not many were powerful, not many were of noble birth; but God chose what is foolish in the world to shame the wise, God chose what is weak in the world to shame the strong, God chose what is low and despised in the world, even things that are not, to bring to nothing things that are, so that no human being might boast in the presence of God. He is the source of your life in Christ Jesus, whom God made our wisdom, our righteousness and sanctification and redemption; therefore, as it is written, "Let him who boasts, boast of the Lord." (I Cor. 1:26-31)

We are truly wise, O God, because You called us and gave us the wisdom of Your Spirit.

DAY OF ORDINARY TIME 96

Prayer is nothing other than the adhesion of our will to God's. Whatever be the form of the prayer, the substance of it is always the submission of the will of a person to the Will of God.
— *World Intangible,* Robert H. J. Steuart (1874-1948)

When I came to you, brethren, I did not come proclaiming to you the testimony of God in lofty words or wisdom. For I decided to know nothing among you except Jesus Christ and him crucified. And I was with you in weakness and in much fear and trembling; and my speech and my message were not in plausible words of wisdom, but in demonstration of the Spirit and of power, that your faith might not rest in the wisdom of men but in the power of God. (I Cor. 2:1-5)

All my trust is in Your Spirit, O God. May He always guide me in my thoughts and speech.

DAY OF ORDINARY TIME 97

Any act, which in its first intention means that we deliberately place our wills in line with God's, that we wish thereby to bring about adhesion of them to His, is prayer, real prayer in its most fundamental significance, for it contains that essence of true prayer which must underlie all its forms.
— *Diversity in Holiness,* Robert H. J. Steuart (1874-1948)

Among the mature we do impart wisdom, although it is not a wisdom of this age or of the rulers of this age, who are doomed to pass away. But we impart a secret and hidden wisdom of God, which God decreed before the ages for our glorification. None of the rulers of this age understood this; for if they had, they would not have cruficied the Lord of glory. But, as it is written, "What no eye has seen, nor ear heard, nor the heart of man conceived, what God has prepared for those who love him," God has revealed to us through the Spirit. For the Spirit searches everything, even the depths of God. (1 Cor. 2:6-10)

Spirit of Wisdom, may we always treasure the power of this gift You share with us.

DAY OF ORDINARY TIME 98

Prayer is evoked by the need to feel oneself not entirely dependent upon the necessity which reigns in the world and upon the power of fate which belongs to this world. Prayer is conversation with the Existent One who is exalted above the world cycle, above the falsity and wrongness in which the world is submerged.
— *The Realm of the Spirit,* Nicholas Berdyaev (1874-1948)

What person knows a man's thoughts except the spirit of the man which is in him? So also no one comprehends the thoughts of God except the Spirit of God. Now we have received not the spirit of the world, but the Spirit which is from God, that we might understand the gifts bestowed on us by God. And we impart this in words not taught by human wisdom but taught by the Spirit, interpreting spiritual truths to those who possess the Spirit. The unspiritual man does not receive the gifts of the Spirit of God, for they are folly to him, and he is not able to understand them because they are spiritually discerned. The spiritual man judges all things, but is himself to be judged by no one. "For who has known the mind of the Lord so as to instruct him?" But we have the mind of Christ. (1 Cor. 2:11-16)

Lord, we praise You for all Your gifts to us.

DAY OF ORDINARY TIME 99

The essence of prayer is conversation, communion. Aware of God, looking at Him with the eyes of my soul, I reach toward Him — to converse with Him, to give Him what I have, to identify my will with His. Communion of spirit with spirit, of man with God, this is prayer.
— *A Primer of Prayer,* Joseph McSorley (1874-1963)

According to the grace of God given to me, like a skilled master builder I laid a foundation, and another man is building upon it. Let each man take care how he builds upon it. For no other foundation can any one lay than that which is laid, which is Jesus Christ. Now if any one builds on the foundation with gold, silver, precious stones, wood, hay, straw — each man's work will become manifest; for the Day will disclose it, because it will be revealed with fire, and the fire will test what sort of work each one has done. If the work which any man has built on the foundation survives, he will receive a reward. If any man's work is burned up, he will suffer loss, though he himself will be saved, but only as through fire. (1 Cor. 3:10-15)

Spirit of Light, give us the gift of discernment. May we know Your truth.

DAY OF ORDINARY TIME 100

Prayer is a divine action in the human person. . . . Through prayer, God comes into a person, giving that person His powers and forming it in accord with His will; this is the final and genuine meaning of prayer.
— *Twelve Addresses on the Christian Religion,* Karl Girgensohn
    (1875-1925)

Do you not know that you are God's temple and that God's Spirit dwells in you? If any one destroys God's temple, God will destroy him. For God's temple is holy, and that temple you are. Let no one deceive himself. If any one among you thinks that he is wise in this age, let him become a fool that he may become wise. For the wisdom of this world is folly with God. For it is written, "He catches the wise in their craftiness," and again, "The Lord knows that the thoughts of the wise are futile." So let no one boast of men. For all things are yours, whether Paul or Apollos or Cephas or the world or life or death or the present or the future, all are yours; and you are Christ's; and Christ is God's. (1 Cor. 3:16-23)

Thank you, Lord, for allowing Your Holy Spirit to dwell in my heart.

DAY OF ORDINARY TIME 101

In a most general sense, prayer is the conversation of our little human souls with God. Therefore it includes all the work done by God himself through, in, and with the souls which are self-given to Him in prayer. . . . Prayer is a purely spiritual activity; and its real doer is God himself, the one inciter and mover of our souls.
— *Concerning the Inner Life,* Evelyn Underhill (1875-1941)

This is how one should regard us, as servants of Christ and stewards of the mysteries of God. Moreover it is required of stewards that they be found trustworthy. But with me it is a very small thing that I should be judged by you or by any human court. I do not even judge myself. I am not aware of anything against myself, but I am not thereby acquitted. It is the Lord who judges me. Therefore do not pronounce judgment before the time, before the Lord comes, who will bring to light the things now hidden in darkness and will disclose the purposes of the heart. Then every man will receive his commendation from God. (1 Cor. 4:1-5)

O Lord and Master, teach me true obedience. May Your will be my command.

DAY OF ORDINARY TIME 102

True Christian prayer is usually in the plural. . . . It is true that in the secret of our rooms many of us use the first person singular in our petitions; perhaps we do it unknowingly, but let us be under no illusion, our prayer when very secret and most personal is still a groaning of the Spirit who asks for the saints according to God's plan. We pray with others because they also, perhaps at the very same moment, ask of God the things we seek in prayer.
— *The Soul and the Spiritual Life,* Dom Anscar Vonier (1875-1938)

I think that God has exhibited us apostles as last of all, like men sentenced to death; because we have become a spectacle to the world, to angels and to men. We are fools for Christ's sake, but you are wise in Christ. We are weak, but you are strong. You are held in honor, but we in disrepute. To the present hour we hunger and thirst, we are ill-clad and buffeted and homeless, and we labor, working with our hands. When reviled, we bless; when persecuted, we endure; when slandered, we try to conciliate; we have become, and are now, as the refuse of the world, the offscouring of all things. (1 Cor. 4:9-13)

To be a fool before the world for love of You, O Christ, is the highest honor.

DAY OF ORDINARY TIME 103

Prayer in its essence is communion with God. The simplest analogy, that of loving, trustful intercourse between friend and friend, is also the most profound.
— *Creative Prayer,* Emily Herman (1876-1923)

I do not write this to make you ashamed, but to admonish you as my beloved children. For though you have countless guides in Christ, you do not have many fathers. For I became your father in Christ Jesus through the gospel. I urge you, then, be imitators of me. (1 Cor. 4:14-16)

Holy Spirit of Wisdom, be our only guide. Teach us the right path. Help us to discern the best way to love.

DAY OF ORDINARY TIME 104

The secret of prayer is to give over to God the gift of oneself by an act of

love; it is to freely give soul and body to the Divine Will and to all It wills.
— *The Gift of Oneself,* Joseph Schryvers (1876-1945)

Your boasting is not good. Do you not know that a little leavens the whole lump? Cleanse out the old leaven that you may be a new lump, as you really are unleavened. For Christ, our paschal lamb, has been sacrificed. Let us, therefore, celebrate the festival, not with the old leaven, the leaven of malice and evil, but with the unleavened bread of sincerity and truth. (1 Cor. 5:6-8)

Purge from us, O Lord, all that is not of You. Let us eat Your bread of sincerity.

DAY OF ORDINARY TIME 105

Prayer is the attempt to establish contact between man and the Divine Person whose message or meaning all phenomena express. It is simply communication between man and God, or rather, we should say between God and man, for God begins it, and man's prayers to God are always a response to God's prayer to man.
— *Intelligent Prayer,* Lewis Machlachlan (d. 1951)

Though I am free from all men, I have made myself a slave of all, that I might win the more. To the Jews I became as a Jew, in order to win Jews; to those under the law I became as one under the law — though not being myself under the law — that I might win those under the law. To those outside the law I became as one outside the law — not being without law toward God but under the law of Christ — that I might win those outside the law. To the weak I became weak, that I might win the weak. I have become all things to all men, that I might by all means save some. I do it all for the sake of the gospel, that I may share in its blessings. (1 Cor. 9:19-23)

May the challenge of Your holy gospel, O Christ, always rule my life.

DAY OF ORDINARY TIME 106

Prayer is not asking God for anything, but it is really a sort of exercise in communion and submission. . . . Prayer is communion with God.
— *The Reality of the Religious Life,* Henry Bett (b. 1876)

Do you not know that in a race all the runners compete, but only one receives the prize? So run that you may obtain it. Every athlete exercises self-control

134

in all things. They do it to receive a perishable wreath, but we an imperishable. Well, I do not run aimlessly, I do not box as one beating the air; but I pommel my body and subdue it, lest after preaching to others I myself should be disqualified. (1 Cor. 9:24-27)

O Lord, You call me to a daily self-discipline so that I may always be ready to win the race for You.

DAY OF ORDINARY TIME 107

When we pray it is not a matter of convincing God, of inclining Him, of changing His providential attitude. It is simply a matter of raising our will to the level of His will so as to will with Him what He has willed to give us.
— *Christian Perfection and Contemplation,* Reginald Garrigou-
    Lagrange (1877-1964)

We must not put the Lord to the test, as some of them did and were destroyed by serpents; nor grumble, as some of them did and were destroyed by the Destroyer. Now these things happened to them as a warning, but they were written down for our instruction, upon whom the end of the ages has come. Therefore let any one who thinks that he stands take heed lest he fall. No temptation has overtaken you that is not common to man. God is faithful, and he will not let you be tempted beyond your strength, but with the temptation will also provide the way of escape, that you may be able to endure it. (1 Cor. 10:9-13)

Lead us not into temptation, O Lord, but deliver us from every evil.

DAY OF ORDINARY TIME 108

It may seem to us that the will of God changes when our prayer is heard and granted; but it is our will alone that rises up to God. We begin to will in time what God has willed for us from all eternity.
— *Christian Perfection and Contemplation,* Reginald Garrigou-
    Lagrange (1877-1964)

So, whether you eat or drink, or whatever you do, do all to the glory of God. Give no offense to Jews or to Greeks or to the church of God, just as I try to please all men in everything I do, not seeking my own advantage, but that of many, that they may be saved. Be imitators of me, as I am of Christ. (1 Cor. 10:31-33, 11:1)

To imitate You, O Christ, by walking in Your footsteps is my daily desire. Help me to know Your will for me today.

DAY OF ORDINARY TIME 109

Prayer is necessary to obtain the help of God, as seed is necessary for the crops. Even though the best seed may be used, if there is lacking favorable growing conditions, the seed produces nothing, and thousands of seeds are lost; true, humble confident prayer, by which we ask for ourselves what is necessary for salvation, is never lost. It is heard in this manner, in so far as it obtains for us the grace to go on.
— *Christian Perfection and Contemplation,* Reginald Garrigou-
     Lagrange (1877-1964)

For I received from the Lord what I also delivered to you, that the Lord Jesus on the night when he was betrayed took bread, and when he had given thanks, he broke it, and said, "This is my body which is for you, Do this in re-membrance of me." In the same way also the cup, after supper, saying, "This cup is the new covenant in my blood. Do this, as often as you drink it, in remembrance of me." For as often as you eat this bread and drink the cup, you proclaim the Lord's death until he comes. Whoever, therefore, eats the bread or drinks the cup of the Lord in an unworthy manner will be guilty of profaning the body and blood of the Lord. Let a man examine himself, and so eat of the bread and drink of the cup. For any one who eats and drinks without discerning the body eats and drinks judgment upon himself. (1 Cor. 11:23-29)

O Lord, I am not worthy.

DAY OF ORDINARY TIME 110

Prayer is the chief agency and activity whereby men align themselves with God's purpose. Prayer does not consist in battering the walls of heaven for personal benefits or the success of our plans. Rather it is the committing of ourselves for the carrying out of His purposes.
— *The Catechism Today,* G. Ashton Oldham (b. 1877)

There are varieties of gifts, but the same Spirit; and there are varieties of service, but the same Lord; and there are varieties of working, but it is the same God who inspires them all in every one. To each is given the manifesta-tion of the Spirit for the common good. To one is given through the Spirit the utterance of wisdom, and to another the utterance of knowledge according to the same Spirit, to another gifts of healing by the one Spirit, to another the working of miracles, to another prophecy, to another the ability to distinguish between spirits, to another various kinds of tongues, to another the interpretation of tongues. All these are inspired by one and the same Spirit, who apportions to each one individually as he wills. (1 Cor. 12:4-11)

May You be glorified, O God, in all Your gifts.

DAY OF ORDINARY TIME 111

Prayer is the soul getting in contact with the God in whom it believes. . . . True prayer is deliberately putting ourselves at God's disposal.
— *The Meaning of Prayer,* Harry Emerson Fosdick (1878-1969)

Now you are the body of Christ and individually members of it. And God has appointed in the church first apostles, second prophets, third teachers, then workers of miracles, then healers, helpers, administrators, speakers in various kinds of tongues. Are all apostles? Are all prophets? Are all teachers? Do all work miracles? Do all possess gifts of healing? Do all speak with tongues? Do all interpret? But earnestly desire the higher gifts. (1 Cor. 12:27-31)

Each of us, Lord, has a special gift from You. Help us to use that gift for Your glory and the good of others.

DAY OF ORDINARY TIME 112

To pray is to let Jesus come into our hearts. . . . To most of us prayer is burdensome because we have not learned that prayer consists in telling Jesus what we or others lack.
— *The Christian Life,* Ole Hallesby (1879-1961)

If I speak in the tongues of men and of angels, but have not love, I am a noisy gong or a clanging cymbal. And if I have prophetic powers, and understand all mysteries and all knowledge, and if I have all faith, so as to remove mountains, but have not love, I am nothing. If I give away all I have, and if I deliver my body to be burned, but have not love, I gain nothing. Love is patient and kind; love is not jealous or boastful; it is not arrogant or rude. Love does not insist on its own way; it is not irritable or resentful; it does not rejoice at wrong, but rejoices in the right. Love bears all things, believes all things, hopes all things, endures all things. (1 Cor. 13:1-7)

Teach me to love, O loving Christ, and I will have the greatest gift of all.

DAY OF ORDINARY TIME 113

Prayer is essentially a seeing, a tasting, that is to say, a kind of intuition relating to certain superior qualities in things. It cannot, therefore, be attained directly by any process of reasoning, nor by any human endeavor. It is a gift, like life itself.
— *The Divine Milieu,* Pierre Teilhard de Chardin (1881-1955)

Love never ends; as for prophecies, they will pass away; as for tongues, they will cease; as for knowledge, it will pass away. For our knowledge is imperfect and our prophecy is imperfect; but when the perfect comes, the imperfect will pass away. When I was a child, I spoke like a child; when I became a man, I gave up childish ways. For now we see in a mirror dimly, but then face to face. Now I know in part; then I shall understand fully, even as I have been fully understood. So faith, hope, love abide, these three; but the greatest of these is love. (1 Cor. 13:8-13)

Lord, never allow me to forget the innocence and enthusiasm of my youth.

DAY OF ORDINARY TIME 114

By prayer we understand nothing else but that supreme prayer which is made in the secret recesses of the heart, in so far as it tends to contemplation and union with God. . . . Finally, the life of prayer, alone, by supernaturally renewing our will power, enables us to change the truth into human acts.
— *Prayer and Intelligence,* Jacques Maritain (1882-1973)

Make love your aim, and earnestly desire the spiritual gifts, especially that you may prophesy. For one who speaks in a tongue speaks not to men but to God; for no one understands him, but he utters mysteries in the Spirit. On the other hand, he who prophesies speaks to men for their upbuilding and encouragement and consolation. He who speaks in a tongue edifies himself, but he who prophesies edifies the church. Now I want you all to speak in tongues, but even more to prophesy. He who prophesies is greater than he who speaks in tongues, unless some one interprets, so that the church may be edified. (1 Cor. 14:1-5)

Holy Spirit of God, share with me whatever gift You please. But do fill me with Your love.

DAY OF ORDINARY TIME 115

There is no prayer, no contemplation, unless Christ is in the soul, and unless there is an imitation of Christ, a participation in His states and in His life, and in His prayer. Saint Paul calls this a tracing of His image, which must be present in the depths of our persons.
— *Notes on the Lord's Prayer,* Raïssa Maritain (1883-1960)

Therefore, he who speaks in a tongue should pray for the power to interpret. For if I pray in a tongue, my spirit prays but my mind is unfruitful. What am I to do? I will pray with the spirit and I will pray with the mind also; I will sing with the spirit and I will sing with the mind also. Otherwise, if you bless with the spirit, how can any one in the position of an outsider say the "Amen" to your thanksgiving when he does not know what you are saying? For you may give thanks well enough, but the other man is not edified. (1 Cor. 14:13-17)

Teach me Your way of prayer, Spirit of God, so that You will always be glorified by me.

DAY OF ORDINARY TIME 116

Prayer is the Holy of Holies where God is present in our midst, not as an object of study, but as a real presence.
— *Spiritual Letters,* Albert Peyriguère (1883-1960)

Blessed be the God and Father of our Lord Jesus Christ, the Father of mercies and God of all comfort, who comforts us in all our affliction, so that we may be able to comfort those who are in any affliction, with the comfort with which we ourselves are comforted by God. For as we share abundantly in Christ's sufferings, so through Christ we share abundantly in comfort too. If we are afflicted, it is for your comfort and salvation; and if we are comforted, it is for your comfort, which you experience when you patiently endure the same sufferings that we suffer. Our hope for you is unshaken; for we know that as you share in our sufferings, you will also share in our comfort. (2 Cor. 1:3-7)

O Good Shepherd, lead us to quiet pastures and let us know Your comforting Spirit.

DAY OF ORDINARY TIME 117

Prayer may be simply defined as the appeal of the soul to God.
— *The Practice of Prayer,* Albert D. Belden (1883-   )

Are we beginning to commend ourselves again? Or do we need, as some do, letters of recommendation to you, or from you? You yourselves are our letter of recommendation, written on your hearts, to be known and read by all men; and you show that you are a letter from Christ delivered by us, written not with ink but with the Spirit of the living God, not on tablets of stone but on tablets of human hearts. Such is the confidence that we have through Christ toward God. Not that we are competent of ourselves to claim anything as coming from us; our competence is from God, who has qualified us to be ministers of a new covenant, not in a written code but in the Spirit; for the written code kills, but the Spirit gives life. (2 Cor. 3:1-7)

If You approve of us, O Lord, we need nothing else in life.

DAY OF ORDINARY TIME 118

Prayer at its highest is a two-way conversation — and for me that most important part is listening to God's replies.
— *Practicing His Presence,* Frank C. Laubach (1884-1964)

But we have this treasure in earthen vessels, to show that the transcendent power belongs to God and not to us. We are afflicted in every way, but not crushed; perplexed, but not driven to despair; persecuted, but not forsaken; struck down, but not destroyed; always carrying in the body the death of Jesus, so that the life of Jesus may also be manifested in our bodies. For while we live we are always being given up to death for Jesus' sake, so that the life of Jesus may be manifested in our mortal flesh. So death is at work in us, but life in you. (2 Cor. 4:7-12)

Let me die a little more to self today, O Jesus, so that I may truly carry my cross with You.

DAY OF ORDINARY TIME 119

Prayer is man's effort to establish contact with God.
— *An Autobiography of Prayer,* Albert Edward Day (1884-1960)

Since we have the same spirit of faith as he had who wrote, "I believed, and so I spoke," we too believe, and so we speak, knowing that he who raised the Lord Jesus will raise us also with Jesus and bring us with you into his presence. For it is all for your sake, so that as grace extends to more and more people it may increase thanksgiving, to the glory of God. So we do not lose heart. Though our outer nature is wasting away, our inner nature is being renewed every day. (2 Cor. 4:13-16)

Do not allow us to lose heart, Lord, but fill us with the strength of the Holy Spirit.

DAY OF ORDINARY TIME 120

Prayer at its best is the deliberate establishment of those attitudes of personality through which the order of God can possess the world. . . . Prayer is worship plus petition.
— *The Issues of Life,* Henry N. Wiemann (1884-1975)

For we know that if the earthly tent we live in is destroyed, we have a building from God, a house not made with hands, eternal in the heavens. Here indeed we groan, and long to put on your heavenly dwelling, so that by putting it on we may not be found naked. For while we are still in this tent, we sigh with anxiety; not that we would be unclothed, but that we would be further clothed, so that what is mortal may be swallowed up by life. He who has prepared us for this very thing is God, who has given us the Spirit as a guarantee. (2 Cor. 5:1-5)

Do not permit us, O Lord, to be too concerned about bodily life that we forget the life we have with You.

DAY OF ORDINARY TIME 121

In private prayer a person faces God. God has created him and called him into a special relationship in grace with Him. It is by virtue of this relationship, in which God meets each one of us personally, that we come up to the dignity of being individuals at all, of being individual persons. This reality comes to fulfillment in personal prayer, which is a dialogue between a person and God.
— *Prayer in Practice,* Romano Guardini (1885-1968)

The love of Christ controls us, because we are convinced that one has died for all; therefore all have died. And he died for all, that those who live might live no longer for themselves but for him who for their sake died and was raised. From now on, therefore, we regard no one from a human point of view; even though we once regarded Christ from a human point of view, we regard him thus no longer. Therefore, if any one is in Christ, he is a new creation; the old has passed away, behold, the new has come. (2 Cor. 5:14-17)

May Your creative love, O Christ, make me into a new creation.

DAY OF ORDINARY TIME 122

Prayer itself is the unfolding of our mind before the most High and in His presence. It begins by a desire on the part of the soul to put itself in the presence of its Creator; in its development it tends to become an interchange of thought and affection between the soul and God.
— *Progress Through Mental Prayer,* Edward Leen (1885-1944)

We put no obstacle in any one's way, so that no fault may be found with our ministry, but as servants of God we commend ourselves in every way: through great endurance, in afflictions, hardships, calamities, beatings, imprisonments, tumults, labors, watching, hunger; by purity, knowledge, forbearance, kindness, the Holy Spirit, genuine love, truthful speech, and the power of God; with the weapons of righteousness for the right hand and for the left; in honor and dishonor, in ill repute and good repute. We are treated as impostors, and yet are true; as unknown, and yet well known; as dying, and behold we live; as punished, and yet not killed; as sorrowful, yet always rejoicing; as poor, yet making many rich; as having nothing, and yet possessing everything. (2 Cor. 6:3-10)

In You, O Lord God, we have all we need.

DAY OF ORDINARY TIME 123

Prayer is the spiritual longing of a finite being to return to its origin. . . . Praying means elevating oneself to the eternal, elevating the content of one's wishes and hopes into the Spiritual Presence; bringing one's own personal center before God, willing to accept the divine acceptance of prayer.
— *The Dynamics of Faith,* Paul Tillich (1886-1965)

The point is this: he who sows sparingly will also reap sparingly, and he who sows bountifully will also reap bountifully. Each one must do as he has made up his mind, not reluctantly or under compulsion, for God loves a cheerful giver. And God is able to provide you with every blessing in abundance, so that you may always have enough of everything and may provide in abundance for every good work. As it is written, "He scatters abroad, he gives to the poor; his righteousness endures for ever." (2 Cor. 9:6-9)

May the seed of Your word, O Christ, take root in my life. May all my actions proceed from faith.

DAY OF ORDINARY TIME 124

Prayer understood as a conversation between two beings . . . is blasphemous and ridiculous. If, however, it is understood as the elevation of the heart, namely, the center of the personality, to God, it is a revelatory event.
— *Systematic Theology,* Paul Tillich (1886-1965)

He who supplies seed to the sower and bread for food will supply and multiply your resources and increase the harvest of your righteousness. You will be enriched in every way for great generosity, which through us will produce thanksgiving to God; for the rendering of this service not only supplies the wants of the saints but also overflows in many thanksgivings to God. Under the test of this service, you will glorify God by your obedience in acknowledging the gospel of Christ, and by the generosity of your contribution for them and for all others; while they long for you and pray for you, because of the surpassing grace of God in you. Thanks be to God for his inexpressible gift! (2 Cor. 9:10-14)

Thanksgiving and praise to You, O God, for all Your gifts.

DAY OF ORDINARY TIME 125

It is God himself who prays through us, when we pray to Him. . . . We cannot bridge the gap between God and ourselves even through the most intensive and frequent prayers; the gap between God and ourselves can only be bridged by God.
— *The Dynamics of Faith,* Paul Tillich (1886-1965)

I wish you would bear with me in a little foolishness. Do bear with me! I feel a divine jealousy for you, for I betrothed you to Christ to present you as a pure bride to her one husband. But I am afraid that as the serpent deceived Eve by his cunning, your thoughts will be led astray from a sincere and pure devotion to Christ. For if some one comes and preaches another Jesus than the one we preached, or if you receive a different spirit from the one you received, or if you accept a different gospel from the one you accepted, you submit to it readily enough. (2 Cor. 11:1-4)

Keep me faithful and true to You, O Christ. You alone are my God.

DAY OF ORDINARY TIME 126

Prayer is but thinking toward God.
— *A Diary of Private Prayer,* John Baillie (1886-1960)

I must boast; there is nothing to be gained by it, but I will go on to visions and revelations of the Lord. I know a man in Christ who fourteen years ago was caught up to the third heaven — whether in the body or out of the body I do not know, God knows. And I know that this man was caught up into Paradise — whether in the body or out of the body I do not know, God knows — and he heard things that cannot be told, which man may not utter. On behalf of this man I will boast, but on my own behalf I will not boast, except of my weaknesses. (2 Cor. 12:1-5)

O God, in my weakness may I experience Your power in my life.

DAY OF ORDINARY TIME 127

Prayer means that we address ourselves to him who has already spoken to us in the Gospel and in the Law. . . . Prayer is neither an arbitrary act nor a step to be taken blindly. When we pray, we cannot venture according to whim in this or that direction, with just any sort of request. For God commands a person to follow Him and to take the place that He has assigned to him. It is a matter ruled by God, not by our own initiative.
— *Prayer According to the Catechism of the Reformation,* Karl Barth
    (1886-1968)

Though if I wish to boast, I shall not be a fool, for I shall be speaking the truth. But I refrain from it, so that no one may think more of me than he sees in me or hears from me. And to keep me from being too elated by the abundance of revelation, a thorn was given me in the flesh, a messenger of Satan, to harass me, to keep me from being too elated. Three times I besought the Lord about this, that it should leave me; but he said to me, "My grace is sufficient for you, for my power is made perfect in weakness." I will all the more gladly boast of my weaknesses, that the power of Christ may rest upon me. For the sake of Christ, then, I am content with weaknesses, insults, hardships, persecutions, and calamities; for when I am weak, then I am strong. (2 Cor. 12:6-10)

In You alone, O my God, I place my trust.

DAY OF ORDINARY TIME 128

Prayer begins with the intention in which a person desires and seeks to find new clarity about the fact that "God is the one who rules.". . . . Prayer is the ultimate example of God's grace for us. . . . In prayer God invites us to dwell with Him.
— *Prayer According to the Catechism of the Reformation,* Karl Barth (1886-1968)

Examine yourselves, to see whether you are holding to your faith. Test yourselves. Do you not realize that Jesus Christ is in you? — unless indeed you fail to meet the test! I hope you will find out that we have not failed. But we pray God that you may not do wrong — not that we may appear to have met the test, but that you may do what is right, though we may seem to have failed.
For we cannot do anything against the truth, but only for the truth. For we are glad when we are weak and you are strong. What we pray for is your improvement. (2 Cor. 13:5-9)

Spirit of Truth, enlighten my mind so that I may honestly examine my life before God.

DAY OF ORDINARY TIME 129

In prayer the soul comes to God, to find Him and be with Him.
— *The Elements of the Spiritual Life,* F. P. Harton (1889-   )

We have not ceased to pray for you, asking that you may be filled with the knowledge of his will in all spiritual wisdom and understanding, to lead a life worthy of the Lord, fully pleasing to him, bearing fruit in every good work and increasing in the knowledge of God. May you be strengthened with all power, according to his glorious might, for all endurance and patience with joy, giving thanks to the Father, who has qualified us to share in the inheritance of the saints in light. He has delivered us from the dominion of darkness and transferred us to the kingdom of his beloved Son, in whom we have redemption, the forgiveness of sins. (Col. 1:9-14)

Spirit of Light, give us Your light and fill us with spiritual wisdom and understanding.

DAY OF ORDINARY TIME 130

Prayer is not only the continuation of the creative process until the soul once again hands its separate power back to its Creator: prayer is the redemptive process also. However far the soul has wandered, the path of prayer is the way home.
— *A Preface to Prayer,* Gerald Heard (1889-1972)

He is the image of the invisible God, the first-born of all creation; for in him all things were created, in heaven and on earth, visible and invisible, whether thrones or dominions or principalities or authorities — all things were created through him and for him. He is before all things, and in him all things hold together. He is the head of the body, the church; he is the beginning, the first-born from the dead, that in everything he might be preeminent. For in him all the fulness of God was pleased to dwell, and through him to reconcile to himself all things, whether on earth or in heaven, making peace by the blood of his cross. (Col. 1:15-20)

O Christ, You are the beginning and end for all creation. May we praise and glorify You.

DAY OF ORDINARY TIME 131

Prayer is not asking for things — not even for the best things; it is going where they are. The word, with its inevitable sense and stain of supplication, is therefore best abandoned. It is meditation and contemplation; it is opening another aperture of the mind, using another focus, that is the real re-creative process.
— *A Preface to Prayer,* Gerald Heard (1889-1972)

As therefore you received Christ Jesus the Lord, so live in him, rooted and built up in him and established in the faith, just as you were taught, abounding in thanksgiving. . . . For in him the whole fulness of deity dwells bodily, and you have come to fulness of life in him, who is the head of all rule and authority. In him also you were circumcised with a circumcision made without hands, by putting off the body of flesh in the circumcision of Christ; and you were buried with him in baptism, in which you were also raised with him through faith in the working of God, who raised him from the dead. And you,

146

who were dead in trespasses and the uncircumcision of your flesh, God made alive together with him, having canceled the bond which stood against us with its legal demands; this he set aside, nailing it to the cross. (Col. 2:6-7, 9-14)

Cleanse from our hearts, O Christ, every trace of sin.

DAY OF ORDINARY TIME 132

Constant interior prayer is a constant desire of the human spirit for God. To succeed in this consoling practice we must pray more often to God to teach us to pray constantly. Pray more, and pray more fervently. It is prayer itself which will show you how it can be achieved unceasingly; but it will take a period of time.
— *The Way of a Pilgrim,* anon. (c. 1890)

Put to death therefore what is earthly in you: fornication, impurity, passion, evil desire, and covetousness, which is idolatry. On account of these the wrath of God is coming. In these you once walked, when you lived in them. But now put them all away: anger, wrath, malice, slander, and foul talk from your mouth. Do not lie to one another, seeing that you have put off the old nature with its practices and have put on the new nature, which is being renewed in knowledge after the image of its creator. Here there cannot be Greek and Jew, circumcised and uncircumcised, barbarian, Scythian, slave, free man, but Christ is all, and in all. (Col. 3:5-11)

Each of us is different and unique, Lord, but in You we will find our common bond.

DAY OF ORDINARY TIME 133

. . . truly to pray means to direct the thought and the memory, constantly to the recollection of God, to walk in His divine Presence; to awaken oneself to His love by thinking about Him, and to join the Name of God with one's breathing and the rhythm of one's heart.
— *The Way of a Pilgrim,* anon. (c. 1890)

Put on then, as God's chosen ones, holy and beloved, compassion, kindness, lowliness, meekness, and patience, forbearing one another and, if one has a complaint against another, forgiving each other; as the Lord has forgiven you, so you also must forgive. And above all these put on love, which binds

147

everything together in perfect harmony. Let the peace of Christ rule in your hearts, to which indeed you were called in the one body. And be thankful. Let the word of Christ dwell in you richly, as you teach and admonish one another in all wisdom, and sing psalms and hymns and spiritual songs with thankfulness in your hearts to God. And whatever you do, in word or deed, do everything in the name of the Lord Jesus, giving thanks to God the Father through him. (Col. 3:12-17)

May our life today, O Christ, be one prayer of praise and glory to You.

DAY OF ORDINARY TIME 134

Prayer is the opening of the soul to God so He can speak to us.
— *Prayer and the Common Life,* Georgia Harkness (1891-1974)

It is my prayer that your love may abound more and more, with knowledge and all discernment, so that you may approve what is excellent, and may be pure and blameless for the day of Christ, filled with the fruits of righteousness which come through Jesus Christ, to the glory and praise of God. . . . It is my eager expectation and hope that I shall not be at all ashamed, but that with full courage now as always Christ will be honored in my body, whether by life or by death. For to me to live is Christ, and to die is gain. If it is to be life in the flesh, that means fruitful labor for me. Yet which I shall choose I cannot tell. I am hard pressed between the two. My desire is to depart and be with Christ, for that is far better. (Phil. 1:9-11, 20-23)

Let me hear Your voice today, O Lord, so that I may live this day for You.

DAY OF ORDINARY TIME 135

The Christian who prays, recollects himself, and discovers himself, gathers himself together, frees himself from all useless masters, from all secret controls, from all defeating desires which split him in pieces and prevent him from being his real self.
— *The Prayer of All Things,* Pierre Charles (1892-1954)

Have this mind among yourselves, which is yours in Christ Jesus, who, though he was in the form of God, did not count equality with God a thing to be grasped, but emptied himself, taking the form of a servant, being born in the likeness of men. And being found in human form he humbled himself and became obedient unto death, even death on a cross. Therefore God has highly exalted him and bestowed on him the name which is above every name, that at the name of Jesus every knee should bow, in heaven and on earth and under the earth, and every tongue confess that Jesus Christ is Lord, to the glory of God the Father. (Phil. 2:5-11)

Teach me Your loving and gentle ways, O Jesus.

DAY OF ORDINARY TIME 136

Prayer is a living relation of a person with God, a direct and living relationship, a haven, a mutual dialogue, a conversation, a spiritual interchange, an association, a fellowship, a communion, a discourse, a union, an intimacy of one person with another.
— *Prayer,* Friedrich Heiler (1892-   )

Do all things without grumbling or questioning, that you may be blameless and innocent, children of God without blemish in the midst of a crooked and perverse generation, among whom you shine as lights in the world, holding fast the word of life, so that in the day of Christ I may be proud that I did not run in vain or labor in vain. Even if I am to be poured as a libation upon the sacrificial offering of your faith, I am glad and rejoice with you all. Likewise you also should be glad and rejoice with me. (Phil. 2:14-18)

As a trusting child, O Lord, help me to turn my life over to You.

DAY OF ORDINARY TIME 137

Prayer is an ongoing communion of the religious person with God, seen as personal and present in experience, a communion which mirrors the kinds of relationships of ordinary human persons. This is prayer in its basic reality.
— *Prayer,* Friedrich Heiler (1892-   )

I count everything as loss because of the surpassing worth of knowing Christ Jesus my Lord. For his sake I have suffered the loss of all things, and count them as refuse, in order that I may gain Christ and be found in him, not having a righteousness of my own, based on law, but that which is through faith in Christ, the righteousness from God that depends on faith; that I may know him and the power of his resurrection, and may share his sufferings, becoming like him in his death, that if possible I may attain the resurrection from the dead. (Phil. 3:8-11)

Lord, I fear the cross in my life. By Your Spirit help me to overcome my fear.

DAY OF ORDINARY TIME 138

Prayer is not the searching for a God who is reluctant to be known. The very desire to pray is God himself in us drawing us to approach Him.
— *In Defense of Prayer,* E. J. Bicknell (1893-   )

Not that I have already obtained this or am already perfect; but I press on to make it my own, because Christ Jesus has made me his own. Brethren, I do not consider that I have made it my own; but one thing I do, forgetting what lies behind and straining forward to what lies ahead, I press on toward the goal for the prize of the upward call of God in Christ Jesus. Let those of us who are mature be thus minded; and if in anything you are otherwise minded, God will reveal that also to you. Only let us hold true to what we have attained. (Phil. 3:12-16)

Help me, O Jesus, to keep my eyes firmly fixed on You.

DAY OF ORDINARY TIME 139

Prayer is a movement of mind and soul into the Source of all being, that which we call God.
— *Prayer and Meditation,* F. C. Happold (1893-   )

Join in imitating me, and mark those who so live as you have an example in us. For many, of whom I have often told you and now tell you even with tears, live as enemies of the cross of Christ. Their end is destruction, their god is the belly, and they glory in their shame, with minds set on earthly things. But our commonwealth is in heaven, and from it we await a Savior, the Lord Jesus Christ, who will change our lowly body to be like his glorious body, by the power which enables him even to subject all things to himself. (Phil. 3:17-21)

May Your Holy Spirit, O Lord, create a new spirit in me, an obedient spirit intent on doing Your will.

DAY OF ORDINARY TIME 140

Without desire lifted up to God, there can be and there is no real prayer to God.
— *The Expositor,* James Morrison (1893-   )

Rejoice in the Lord always; again I will say, Rejoice. Let all men know your forbearance. The Lord is at hand. Have no anxiety about anything, but in everything by prayer and supplication with thanksgiving let your requests be made known to God. And the peace of God, which passes all understanding, will keep your hearts and your minds in Christ Jesus. (Phil. 4:4-7)

Preserve my heart and mind, O God, so that I may always rejoice in Christ Jesus.

DAY OF ORDINARY TIME 141

The essence of prayer is best described by means of verbs, thanking, calling, complaining, lamenting, rejoicing, approaching, pouring out one's heart, adoring, weeping, praising. . . .
— *The Roads of Prayer,* Kornelis H. Miskotte (1894-1972)

Blessed be the God and Father of our Lord Jesus Christ, who has blessed us in Christ with every spiritual blessing in the heavenly places, even as he chose us in him before the foundation of the world, that we should be holy and blameless before him. He destined us in love to be his sons through Jesus Christ, according to the purpose of his will, to the praise of his glorious grace which he freely bestowed on us in the Beloved. In him we have redemption through his blood, the forgiveness of our trespasses, according to the riches of his grace which he lavished upon us. For he has made known to us in all wisdom and insight the mystery of his will, according to his purpose which he set forth in Christ as a plan for the fullness of time, to unite all things in him, things in heaven and things on earth. (Eph. 1:3-10)

Lord, help me pray, "Amen, Alleluia."

DAY OF ORDINARY TIME 142

To pray means to refuse to compromise. It is an act of freedom with respect to what is, what is given in the midst of necessities and compulsions. Prayer

embraces the drama of our becoming persons in God's sight.
— *The Roads of Prayer,* Kornelis H. Miskotte (1894-1972)

I have heard of your faith in the Lord Jesus and your love toward all the
saints, I do not cease to give thanks for you, remembering you in my
prayers, that the God of our Lord Jesus Christ, the Father of glory, may give
you a spirit of wisdom and of revelation in the knowledge of him, having the
eyes of your hearts enlightened, that you may know what is the hope to which
he has called you, what are the riches of his glorious inheritance in the
saints, and what is the immeasurable greatness of his power in us who believe, according to the working of his great might which he accomplished in
Christ when he raised him from the dead and made him sit at his right hand
in the heavenly places. (Eph. 1:15-20)

Increase my faith, O God.

DAY OF ORDINARY TIME 143

Prayer is infinite creation, the supreme art. Over and over again we experience an eager upsurge toward God, followed only by a falling away from His
light. . . . Prayer cannot fail to revive in us the divine breath which God
breathed into Adam's nostrils and by virtue of which Adam became a living
soul.
— *Spiritual Writings,* Archimandrite Sophroney (1896-   )

God, who is rich in mercy, out of the great love with which he loved us, even
when we were dead through our trespasses, made us alive together with
Christ (by grace you have been saved), and raised us up with him, and made
us sit with him in the heavenly places of Christ Jesus, that in the coming
ages he might show the immeasurable riches of his grace in kindness toward
us in Christ Jesus. For by grace you have been saved through faith; and this
is not your own doing, it is the gift of God — not because of works, lest any
man should boast. For we are his workmanship, created in Christ Jesus for
good works, which God prepared beforehand, that we should walk in them.
(Eph. 2:4-10)

O God, may You be praised and glorified in all Your good gifts.

DAY OF ORDINARY TIME 144

Prayer is the process of becoming at home with God. . . . Prayer is the God-

ward reach of a person's soul. It exists on many levels and has many degrees of intensity and power. Prayer is communion with God, contact with God, the feeling of the presence of God, our intimate oneness with God.
— *Making Prayer Real,* Lynn James Radcliffe (1896-   )

Remember that you were at that time separated from Christ, alienated from the commonwealth of Israel, and strangers to the covenants of promise, having no hope and without God in the world. But now in Christ Jesus you who once were far off have been brought near in the blood of Christ. For he is our peace, who has made us both one, and has broken down the dividing wall of hostility, by abolishing in his flesh the law of commandments and ordinances, that he might create in himself one new man in place of the two, so making peace, and might reconcile us both to God in one body through the cross, thereby bringing the hostility to an end. (Eph. 2:12-16)

May You be my peace, O Lord.

DAY OF ORDINARY TIME 145

Prayer is not only the act of conscious self-identification with a desire; it is the offering of the desire to a Divine Being who is recognized as personal and as able to respond.
— *Prayer and Experience,* S. H. Mellone (1896-   )

To me, though I am the very least of all the saints, this grace was given, to preach to the Gentiles the unsearchable riches of Christ, and to make all men see what is the plan of the mystery hidden for ages in God who created all things; that through the church the manifold wisdom of God might now be made known to the principalities and powers in the heavenly places. This was according to the eternal purpose which he has realized in Christ Jesus our Lord, in whom we have boldness and confidence of access through our faith in him. (Eph. 3:8-12)

Fill me, O Lord, with a deep reverence for the mystery You are in my life.

DAY OF ORDINARY TIME 146

To pray means communion with God in wonder, intimacy, love. It means a long journey full of events, strains, discoveries, pain, and deep peace.
— *Christian Prayer,* Franz M. Moschner (1896-   )

I bow my knees before the Father, from whom every family in heaven and on earth is named, that according to the riches of his glory he may grant you to be strengthened with might through his Spirit in the inner man, and that Christ may dwell in your hearts through faith; that you, being rooted and grounded in love, may have power to comprehend with all the saints what is the breadth and length and height and depth, and to know the love of Christ which surpasses knowledge, that you may be filled with all the fulness of God. (Eph. 3:14-19)

My Lord and my God, I adore You.

DAY OF ORDINARY TIME 147

Prayer is a conversation with God. We speak to Him and He speaks to us. But this conversation is not like a casual conversation between friends. We do not speak to God simply in order to exchange views with Him, but rather to grow in the knowledge of His viewpoint and to make it our own.
— *The Mass and the Life of Prayer,* Anthony Thorold (1896-   )

I therefore, a prisoner for the Lord, beg you to lead a life worthy of the calling to which you have been called, with all lowliness and meekness, with patience, forbearing one another in love, eager to maintain the unity of the Spirit in the bond of peace. There is one body and one Spirit, just as you were called to the one hope that belongs to your call, one Lord, one faith, one baptism, one God and Father of us all, who is above all through all and in all. (Eph. 4:1-6)

Help me, Lord God, to hear Your call more clearly.

DAY OF ORDINARY TIME 148

Prayer is the unveiling of ourselves before God. . . . We must lay before Him what is in us, not what ought to be in us.
— *Letters to Malcolm,* C. S. Lewis (1898-1963)

His gifts were that some should be apostles, some prophets, some evangelists, some pastors and teachers, to equip the saints for the work of ministry, for building up the body of Christ, until we all attain to the unity of the faith and of the knowledge of the Son of God, to mature manhood, to the measure of the stature of the fulness of Christ; so that we may no longer be children, tossed to and fro and carried about with every wind of doctrine, by the cunning of men, by their craftiness in deceitful wiles. Rather, speaking the truth in love, we are to grow up in every way into him who is the head, into Christ, from whom the whole body, joined and knit together by every joint with which it is supplied, when each part is working properly, makes bodily growth and upbuilds itself in love. (Eph. 4:11-16)

Help me, Lord, to use my gifts.

DAY OF ORDINARY TIME 149

Prayer in the sense of petition, asking for things, is a small part of it; confession and penitence are its threshold, adoration its sanctuary, the presence and vision and enjoyment of God its bread and wine. In it God shows himself to us. That He answers prayer is a corollary — not necessarily the most important one — from that revelation. What He does is learned from what He is.
— *The World's Last Night*, C. S. Lewis (1898-1963)

Let no evil talk come out of your mouths, but only such as is good for edifying, as fits the occasion, that it may impart grace to those who hear. And do not grieve the Holy Spirit of God, in whom you are sealed for the day of redemption. Let all bitterness and wrath of anger and clamor and slander be put away from you, with all malice, and be kind to one another, tender-hearted, forgiving one another, as God in Christ forgave you. Therefore be imitators of God, as beloved childen. And walk in love, as Christ loved us and gave himself up for us, a fragrant offering and sacrifice to God. (Eph. 4:29-32; 5:1-2)

Show me Your ways, O Christ.

DAY OF ORDINARY TIME 150

Now the moment of prayer is for me — or involves for me as its condition — the awareness, the reawakened awareness, that this "real world" and "real self" are very far from being rock-bottom realities. . . . And in prayer this real I struggles to speak, for once, from his real being, and to address, for once, not the other actors, but — what shall I call Him? The Author, for He invented us all? The Producer, for He controls all? Or the Audience, for He watches, and will judge, the performance?
— *Letters to Malcolm*, C. S. Lewis (1898-1963)

Once you were darkness, but now you are light in the Lord; walk as children of light (for the fruit of light is found in all that is good and right and true), and try to learn what is pleasing to the Lord. Take no part in the unfruitful works of darkness, but instead expose them. For it is a shame even to speak of the things that they do in secret; but when anything is exposed by the light it becomes visible, for anything that becomes visible is light. Therefore it is said, "Awake, O sleeper, and arise from the dead, and Christ shall give you light." (Eph. 5:8-14)

Spirit of Light, shine brightly in my heart today.

DAY OF ORDINARY TIME 151

Prayer is the meeting of the human personality with the divine, in a great silence where all else is hushed, for God is speaking.
— *A Map of Life,* Frank Sheed (1897-1981)

Look carefully then how you walk, not as unwise men but as wise, making the most of the time, because the days are evil. Therefore do not be foolish, but understand what the will of the Lord is. And do not get drunk with wine, for that is debauchery; but be filled with the Spirit, addressing one another in psalms and hymns and spiritual songs, singing and making melody to the Lord with all your heart, always and for everything giving thanks in the name of our Lord Jesus Christ to God the Father. (Eph. 5:15-20)

May Your Holy Spirit teach me how to walk in Your ways, O God.

DAY OF ORDINARY TIME 152

Prayer is not a vain attempt to change God's will; it is a filial desire to learn God's will and to share it.
— *Prayer,* George A. Buttrick (1899-1979)

Stand therefore, having girded your loins with truth, and having put on the breastplate of righteousness, and having shod your feet with the equipment of the gospel of peace; above all taking the shield of faith, with which you can quench all the flaming darts of the evil one. And take the helmet of salvation, and the sword of the Spirit, which is the word of God. Pray at all times in the Spirit, with all prayer and supplication. To that end keep alert with all perseverance, making supplication for all the saints, and also for me, that utterance may be given me in opening my mouth boldly to proclaim the mystery of the gospel, for which I am an ambassador in chains; that I may declare it boldly, as I ought to speak. (Eph. 6:14-20)

May the word of Your good news always illumine my life.

DAY OF ORDINARY TIME 153

Prayer is listening as well as speaking, receiving as well as asking; and its deepest mood is friendship held in reverence.
— *Prayer,* George A. Buttrick (1899-1979)

I would have you know, brethren, that the gospel which was preached by me is not man's gospel. For I did not receive it from man, nor was I taught it, but it came through a revelation of Jesus Christ. For you have heard of my former life in Judaism, how I persecuted the church of God violently and tried to destroy it; and I advanced in Judaism beyond many of my own age among my people, so extremely zealous was I for the traditions of my fathers. (Gal. 1:11-14)

Fill my heart, O God, with a burning zeal to know and do Your will.

DAY OF ORDINARY TIME 154

Prayer is more than a lighted candle; it is the contagion of health. It is the pulse of life.
— *Prayer,* George A. Buttrick (1899-1979)

If, in our endeavor to be justified in Christ, we ourselves were found to be sinners, is Christ then an agent of sin? Certainly not! But if I build up again those things which I tore down, then I prove myself a transgressor. For I through the law died to the law, that I might live to God. I have been crucified with Christ; it is no longer I who live, but Christ who lives in me; and the life I now live in the flesh I live by faith in the Son of God, who loved me and gave himself for me. I do not nullify the grace of God; for if justification were through the law, then Christ died to no purpose. (Gal. 2:17-21)

May Christ Jesus live in me always.

DAY OF ORDINARY TIME 155

Prayer grows out of an imperative urgency, sometimes pointed, sometimes diffused. . . . Prayer often yields a buoyancy and joyousness of spirit as the overtone of a relaxed confidence in God.
— *Deep Is the Hunger,* Howard Thurman (1899-1980)

Before faith came, we were confined under the law, kept under restraint until faith should be revealed. So that the law was our custodian until Christ came, that we might be justified by faith. But now that faith has come, we are no longer under a custodian; for in Christ Jesus you are all sons of God, through faith. For as many of you as were baptized into Christ have put on Christ. There is neither Jew nor Greek, there is neither slave nor free, there is neither male nor female; for you are all one in Christ Jesus. (Gal. 3:23-28)

May we all be one in You and in Your Church, O Christ.

DAY OF ORDINARY TIME 156

Prayer is an approach to the living God.
— *Mount of Olives,* James Hamilton (1900-1968)

For you were called to freedom, brethren; only do not use your freedom as an opportunity for the flesh, but through love be servants of one another. For the whole law is fulfilled in one word, "You shall love your neighbor as yourself." But if you bite and devour one another take heed that you are not consumed by one another. But I say, walk by the Spirit, and do not gratify the desires of the flesh. For the desires of the flesh are against the Spirit, and the desires of the Spirit are against the flesh; for these are opposed to each other, to prevent you from doing what you would. But if you are led by the Spirit you are not under the law. (Gal. 5:13-18)

Spirit of Love, may Your love rule my life daily.

DAY OF ORDINARY TIME 157

Prayer is first and foremost that which God does for us, and to us, and in us. . . . Praying, on our part, is our response to God's prevenience.
— *Teach Us to Pray,* Charles F. Whiston (1900-   )

The fruit of the Spirit is love, joy, peace, patience, kindness, goodness, faithfulness, gentleness, self-control; against such there is no law. And those who belong to Christ Jesus have crucified the flesh with its passions and desires. If we live by the Spirit, let us also walk by the Spirit. Let us have no self-conceit, no provoking of one another, no envy of one another. (Gal. 5:22-26)

Come, Holy Spirit, fill my heart with Your fruits.

DAY OF ORDINARY TIME 158

Prayer is the life of every Christian. Without prayer, without contact with God, this life dies. Prayer is a contact of love between God and a person.
— *Poustinia,* Catherine de Hueck Doherty (1900-   )

Brethren, if a man is overtaken in any trespass, you who are spiritual should restore him in a spirit of gentleness. Look to yourself, lest you too be tempted. Bear one another's burdens, and so fulfil the law of Christ. For if any one thinks he is something, when he is nothing, he deceives himself. But let each one test his own work, and then his reason to boast will be in himself alone and not in his neighbor. For each man will have to bear his own load. (Gal. 6:1-5)

O God, You alone are my only real strength.

DAY OF ORDINARY TIME 159

We must all lead one another to the top of the mountain to pray, because prayer is dynamic, and prayer is holy. It is a contact with God; it is a union with Him. As a person grows in union with God he comes to know that it is prayer which includes all righteousness, and from which stems all the goodness that God wants to give mankind. What is this prayer, what is this union with God, then? It is a man or a woman moved with his or her whole being to communicate with the loving God, to respond to God's great love.
— *The Gospel Without Compromise,* Catherine de Hueck Doherty
        (1900-   )

Let him who is taught the word share all good things with him who teaches. Do not be deceived; God is not mocked, for whatever a man sows, that he will also reap. For he who sows to his own flesh will from the flesh reap corruption; but he who sows to the Spirit will from the Spirit reap eternal life. And let us not grow weary in well-doing, for in due season we shall reap, if we do not lose heart. So then, as we have opportunity, let us do good to all men, and especially to those who are of the household of faith. (Gal. 6:6-10)

May the seed of Your word, O God, take root deep in my heart.

DAY OF ORDINARY TIME 160

To speak or to listen to Me [Jesus] are two different kinds of prayer. My Lord Jesus, which do You prefer? That which listens to Me.
— *Spiritual Diary,* Sr. Mary of the Holy Trinity (1901-1942)

We give thanks to God always for you all, constantly mentioning you in our prayers, remembering before our God and Father your work of faith and labor of love and steadfastness of hope in our Lord Jesus Christ. For we know, brethren beloved by God, that he has chosen you; for our gospel came to you not only in word, but also in power and in the Holy Spirit and with full conviction. You know what kind of men we proved to be among you for your sake. And you became imitators of us and of the Lord, for you received the word in much affliction, with joy inspired by the Holy Spirit. . . . (1 Thes. 1:2-6)

Lord, may we enjoy the gifts of Your Spirit so that we may imitate Your Son Jesus.

DAY OF ORDINARY TIME 161

Prayer, as the Catechism tells us, is "raising the heart and mind to God" — there need be no words, but only an inexpressible adherence to God, an attitude of mind and heart, a simple wordless desire to be one with Him. This makes it inevitable that one recognizes His will for one at the moment in every circumstance, and knows that every act, however trivial, done in this spirit, is done for His glory and is prayer.
— *Personal Letters,* Caryll Houselander (1901-1954)

May the Lord make you increase and abound in love to one another and to all men, as we do to you, so that he may establish your hearts unblamable in holiness before our God and Father, at the coming of the Lord Jesus with all his saints. Finally, brethren, we beseech and exhort you in the Lord Jesus, that as you learned from us how you ought to live and to please God, just as you are doing, you do so more and more. For you know what instructions we gave you through the Lord Jesus. (1 Thes. 3:12-13; 4:1-2)

Teach us to love others, O good Jesus, as You have loved us.

DAY OF ORDINARY TIME 162

To live the life of prayer means to emerge from my drowse, to awaken to the communing, guiding, healing, clarifying, transforming current of God's Holy Spirit in which I am immersed.
— *Dimensions of Prayer,* Douglas Steere (1901-   )

Rejoice always, pray constantly, give thanks in all circumstances; for this is the will of God in Christ Jesus for you. Do not quench the Spirit, do not despise prophesying, but test everything; hold fast what is good, abstain from every form of evil. May the God of peace himself sanctify you wholly; and may your spirit and soul and body be kept sound and blameless at the coming of our Lord Jesus Christ. He who calls you is faithful, and he will do it. (1 Thes. 15:16-24)

Holy Lord, may Your Spirit keep us faithful to You in every way.

DAY OF ORDINARY TIME 163

Prayer then is simply a form of waking up out of the dull sleep in which our life has been spent in half-intentions, half-resolutions, half-creations, half-loyalties, and a becoming actively aware of the real character of that which we are and of that which we are over against. . . . Prayer is an attempt to get ourselves into that active cooperation with God where we may discern what is authentic and be made ready to carry it out.
— *Dimensions of Prayer,* Douglas Steere (1901-   )

Everything created by God is good, and nothing is to be rejected if it is received with thanksgiving; for then it is consecrated by the word of God and prayer. If you put these instructions before the brethren, you will be a good minister of Christ Jesus, nourished on the words of the faith and of the good doctrine which you have followed. Have nothing to do with godless and silly myth. Train yourself in godliness; for while bodily training is of some value, godliness is of value in every way, as it holds promise for the present life and also for the life to come. The saying is sure and worthy of full acceptance. For to this end we toil and strive, because we have our hope set on the living God, who is the Savior of all men, especially of those who believe. (1 Tim. 4:4-10)

Spirit of God, deepen our faith.

DAY OF ORDINARY TIME 164

Prayer is the breath of the soul, as essential as breath to the body. . . . It is through prayer that we come to know God, not only to know about Him, but to know Him personally, in experience.
— *The Practice of Prayer,* George Appleton (1901-   )

As for you, man of God, shun all this; aim at righteousness, godliness, faith, love, steadfastness, gentleness. Fight the good fight of the faith; take hold of the eternal life to which you were called when you made the good confession in the presence of many witnesses. In the presence of God who gives life to all things, and of Christ Jesus who in his testimony before Pontius Pilate made the good confession, I charge you to keep the commandment unstained and free from reproach until the appearing of our Lord Jesus Christ. (1 Tim. 6:11-14)

Keep us faithful, O God, so that we may deserve to be Your friends.

DAY OF ORDINARY TIME 165

Prayer is communication between God and ourselves, in which God takes the initiative to bring us into communion with himself.
— *Spiritual Renewal Through Personal Groups,* John L. Casteel
       (1903-   )

We are bound to give thanks to God always for you, brethren beloved by the Lord, because God chose you from the beginning to be saved through sanctification by the Spirit and belief in the truth. To this he called you through our gospel, so that you may obtain the glory of our Lord Jesus Christ. So then, brethren, stand firm and hold to the traditions which you were taught by us, either by word of mouth or by letter. Now may our Lord Jesus Christ himself, and God our Father, who loved us and gave us eternal comfort and good hope through grace, comfort your hearts and establish them in every good work and word. (2 Thes. 2:13-17)

Gentle Jesus, be our source of consolation this day.

DAY OF ORDINARY TIME 166

Prayer is humanity's communion and meeting with God. It is the way in which a person crosses over from his bodily person with its trials, to the spir-

itual person, with its inner peace.
— *Way of the Ascetics,* Tito Colliander (1904-   )

The grace of God has appeared for the salvation of all men, training us to renounce irreligion and worldly passions, and to live sober, upright, and godly lives in this world, awaiting our blessed hope, the appearing of the glory of our great God and Savior Jesus Christ, who gave himself for us to redeem us from all iniquity and to purify for himself a people of his own who are zealous for good deeds. (Titus 2:11-14)

O God, we thank You for all Your graces and blessings.

DAY OF ORDINARY TIME 167

Prayer is a gift of God, and we shall never really pray, unless continually we ask God for His gift of prayer. . . . For me what is the greatest about prayer is that I belong to Jesus Christ. . . . To live as a child of God in Christ means to be with Him, to speak with Him, to speak with Him personally. It is always to be one of the family, always at home with everybody and at the same time always at home with God.
— *Joy of the Cross,* Madeleine Delbrel (1904-1964)

When the goodness and loving kindness of God our Savior appeared, he saved us, not because of deeds done by us in righteousness, but in virtue of his own mercy, by the washing of regeneration and renewal in the Holy Spirit, which he poured out upon us richly through Jesus Christ our Savior, so that we might be justified by his grace and become heirs in hope of eternal life. (Titus 3:4-7)

For our baptism, O Lord, we are grateful. Help us live accordingly.

DAY OF ORDINARY TIME 168

Prayer is an act of the virtue of religion; it is an act of an intellectually endowed person by which the person turns toward God by acknowledging and praising His limitless perfection explicitly or implicitly and by subjecting oneself to that perfection in faith, hope and charity. Prayer, then, is an act by which mankind as a whole actualizes itself and by which this thus actualized human person is subjected and, as it were, given over to God.
— *Theological Investigations,* Karl Rahner, S.J. (1904-1984)

Do not be ashamed then of testifying to our Lord, nor of me his prisoner, but share in suffering for the gospel in the power of God, who saved us and called us with a holy calling, not in virtue of our works but in virtue of his own purpose and the grace which he gave us in Christ Jesus ages ago, and now has manifested through the appearing of our Savior Christ Jesus, who abolished death and brought life and immortality to light through the gospel. For this gospel I was appointed a preacher and apostle and teacher, and therefore I suffer as I do. But I am not ashamed, for I know whom I have believed, and I am sure that he is able to guard until that Day what has been entrusted to me. (2 Tim. 1:8-12)

Help me, O God, to hear Your call to follow the Gospel today.

DAY OF ORDINARY TIME 169

Prayer is the opening of the heart to God.
— *On Prayer,* Karl Rahner, S.J. (1904-1984)

Remember Jesus Christ, risen from the dead, descended from David, as preached in my gospel, the gospel for which I am suffering and wearing fetters like a criminal. But the word of God is not fettered. Therefore I endure everything for the sake of the elect, that they also may obtain salvation in Christ Jesus with its eternal glory. The saying is sure: If we have died with him, we shall also live with him; if we endure, we shall also reign with him; if we deny him, he also will deny us; if we are faithless, he remains faithful — for he cannot deny himself. (2 Tim. 2:8-13)

Teach me to die to self, Lord, for I also want life with You.

DAY OF ORDINARY TIME 170

Prayer is something more than an external action done out of a sense of duty, an act in which we tell God different things He already knows, a kind of daily roll call in the presence of the Sovereign who awaits, morning and evening, the obedience of His subjects. . . . Prayer is communication in which the word of God takes the initiative and we are at first only listeners.
— *Prayer,* Hans Urs von Balthasar (1905-   )

Now you have observed my teaching, my conduct, my aim in life, my faith, my patience, my love, my steadfastness, my persecutions, my sufferings, what befell me at Antioch, at Iconium, and at Lystra, what persecutions I endured; yet from them all the Lord rescued me. Indeed all who desire to live a godly life in Christ Jesus will be persecuted, while evil men and imposters will go on from bad to worse, deceivers and deceived. But as for you, continue in what you have learned and have firmly believed, knowing from whom you learned it and how from childhood you have been acquainted with the sacred writings which are able to instruct you for salvation through faith in Christ Jesus. All scripture is inspired by God and profitable for teaching, for reproof, for correction, and for training in righteousness, that the man of God may be complete, equipped for every good work. (2 Tim. 3:10-17)

We thank You for Your word, Lord.

DAY OF ORDINARY TIME 171

The purpose of prayer is the contemplation of God and the consequent conversation with Him.
— *God's Encounter With Man,* Maurice Nedoncelle, S.J. (1905-   )

I charge you in the presence of God and of Christ Jesus who is to judge the living and the dead, and by his appearing and his kingdom: preach the word, be urgent in season and out of season, convince, rebuke, and exhort, be unfailing in patience and in teaching. For the time is coming when people will not endure sound teaching, but having itching ears they will accumulate for themselves teachers to suit their own likings, and will turn away from listening to the truth and wander into myths. As for you, always be steady, endure suffering, do the work of an evangelist, fulfill your ministry. I am already on the point of being sacrificed; the time of my departure has come. I have fought the good fight, I have finished the race, I have kept the faith. Henceforth there is laid up for me the crown of righteousness, which the Lord, the righteous judge, will award to me on that Day, and not only to me but also to all who have loved his appearing. (2 Tim. 4:1-8)

Keep me faithful to You always, O God.

DAY OF ORDINARY TIME 172

Prayer creates or discovers a shining vocation in created beings; it does not merely exalt the person who is praying, it also illuminates those for whom he is interceding. It drives anxiety from the soul; it is the sovereign remedy for selfishness; it renews the face of the earth.
— *God's Encounter With Man,* Maurice Nedoncelle, S.J. (1905-   )

In many and various ways God spoke of old to our fathers by the prophets; but in these last days he has spoken to us by a Son, whom he appointed the heir of all things, through whom also he created the world. He reflects the glory of God and bears the very stamp of his nature, upholding the universe by his word of power. When he had made purification for sins, he sat down at the right hand of the Majesty on high, having become as much superior to angels as the name he has obtained is more excellent than theirs. (Heb. 1:1-4)

You continue to speak to us each day, Lord. Help me to hear Your voice clearly today.

DAY OF ORDINARY TIME 173

God's great gift to us is our unlimited power of detachment. Prayer is undoubtedly an expression of our acceptance of this requirement and of his incentive, both from God.
— *God's Encounter With Man,* Maurice Nedoncelle, S.J. (1905-   )

Since therefore the children share in flesh and blood, he himself likewise partook of the same nature, that through death he might destroy him who has the power of death, that is, the devil, and deliver all those who through fear of death were subject to lifelong bondage. For surely it is not with angels that he is concerned but with the descendants of Abraham. Therefore he had to be made like his brethren in every respect, so that he might become a merciful and faithful high priest in the service of God, to make expiation for the sins of the people. For because he himself has suffered and been tempted, he is able to help those who are tempted. (Heb. 2:14-18)

Lord, You know what is in us. Help us do Your will today.

DAY OF ORDINARY TIME 174

True prayer does not depend either on the individual person or the whole fellowship of the faithful, but only on the knowledge that our heavenly Father knows our needs. This makes God the only object of our prayers, and frees us from a false trust in our own prayerful endeavors.
— *The Cost of Discipleship,* Dietrich Bonhoeffer (1906-1945)

Therefore, as the Holy Spirit says, "Today, when you hear his voice, do not harden your hearts as in the rebellion, on the day of testing in the wilderness,

166

where your fathers put me to the test and saw my works for forty years. Therefore I was provoked with that generation, and said, 'They always go astray in their hearts; they have not known my ways.' As I swore in my wrath, 'They shall never enter my rest.' " Take care, brethren, lest there be in any of you an evil, unbelieving heart, leading you to fall away from the living God. But exhort one another every day, as long as it is called "today," that none of you may be hardened by the deceitfulness of sin. For we share in Christ, if only we hold our first confidence firm to the end. . . . (Heb. 3:7-14)

Today, O God, is Your gift to us. Help us spend it with You.

DAY OF ORDINARY TIME 175

Behind all words and gestures, behind all thoughts and feelings, there is an inner center of prayer where we can meet one another in the presence of God.
— *The Golden String,* Bede Griffiths (1906-   )

Let us therefore strive to enter that rest, that no one fall by the same sort of disobedience. For the word of God is living and active, sharper than any two-edged sword, piercing to the division of soul and spirit, of joints and marrow, and discerning the thoughts and intentions of the heart. And before him no creature is hidden, but all are open and laid bare to the eyes of him with whom we have to do. (Heb. 4:11-13)

Spirit of God, teach us to know Your word and to do Your will.

DAY OF ORDINARY TIME 176

Prayer is an act by which a person opens himself to the total values for wholeness that exists in each situational moment of his life. It is an affirmation (reaffirmation) of a fundamental dedication to each moment's emergent highest value. Prayer is the act of loving God with as much of the all (of heart, soul, strength, mind) as can possibly be brought into consciousness.
— *Man the Choicemaker,* Elizabeth B. Howes (1907-   )

Every high priest chosen from among men is appointed to act on behalf of men in relation to God, to offer gifts and sacrifices for sins. He can deal gently with the ignorant and wayward, since he himself is beset with weakness. Because of this he is bound to offer sacrifice for his own sins as well as for those of the people. And one does not take the honor upon himself, but he is called by God, just as Aaron was. (Heb. 5:1-4)

Renew the grace of office in all Your priests, O Jesus. May they serve faithfully and generously.

DAY OF ORDINARY TIME 177

Unless we meet God in prayer we never meet Him, for prayer is meeting God. Unless we meet Him, He can never become real to us.
— *Making Religion Real,* Nels Ferre (1908-   )

Since then we have a great high priest who has passed through the heavens, Jesus, the Son of God, let us hold fast our confession. For we have not a high priest who is unable to sympathize with our weaknesses, but one who in every respect has been tempted as we are, yet without sin. Let us then with confidence draw near to the throne of grace, that we may receive mercy and find grace to help in time of need. (Heb. 4:14-16)

Without You, Lord, we are lost. With You we can do all things.

DAY OF ORDINARY TIME 178

True prayer, when it is that kind which asks, is for courage to endure, never for permission to survive.
— *Recipes for Happiness,* William Purcell (1909-   )

Christ did not exalt himself to be made a high priest, but was appointed by him who said to him, "Thou art my Son, today I have begotten thee"; as he says also in another place, "Thou art a priest for ever, after the order of Melchizedek." In the days of his flesh, Jesus offered up prayers and supplications, with loud cries and tears, to him who was able to save him from death, and he was heard for his godly fear. Although he was a Son, he learned obedience through what he suffered; and being made perfect he became the source of eternal salvation to all who obey him, being designated by God a high priest after the order of Melchizedek. (Heb. 5:5-10)

Intercede for us, O Jesus, with Your Father. Then we will surely be heard.

DAY OF ORDINARY TIME 179

Prayer is disciplined opening of the self to God. My social, verbal, officious, work-a-day self has something closed and set about it. It is a mass of pre-dispositions, preconceptions, inhibitions, settled beliefs and expectations. There is a convenient fixity about it. . . . But that fixity must never be suffered to become final. This would be death. Prayer is the persistent effort to guard against that death.
— *The Religious Way,* Gregory Vlastos (1909-   )

Men indeed swear by a greater than themselves, and in all their disputes an oath is final for confirmation. So when God desired to show more convincingly to the heirs of the promise the unchangeable character of his purpose, he interposed with an oath, so that through two unchangeable things, in which it is impossible that God should prove false, we who have fled for refuge might have strong encouragement to seize the hope set before us. We have this as a sure and steadfast anchor of the soul, a hope that enters into the inner shrine behind the curtain, where Jesus has gone as a forerunner on our behalf, having become a high priest for ever after the order of Melchizedek. (Heb. 6:16-20)

Be the anchor of my life, O Jesus, so I will not founder.

DAY OF ORDINARY TIME 180

Prayer consists in giving attention. It is the direction of all the attention of which the person is capable toward God. The quality of the attention greatly determines the quality of the prayer. Warmth of heart cannot be substituted for it.
— *Waiting on God,* Simone Weil (1909-1943)

The former priests were many in number, because they were prevented by death from continuing in office; but he holds his priesthood permanently, because he continues for ever. Consequently he is able for all time to save those who draw near to God through him, since he always lives to make intercession for them. For it was fitting that we should have such a high priest, holy, blameless, unstained, separated from sinners, exalted above the heavens. He has no need, like those high priests, to offer sacrifices daily, first for his own sins and then for those of the people; he did this once for all when he offered up himself. Indeed, the law appoints men in their weakness as high priests, but the word of the oath, which came later than the law, appoints a Son who has been made perfect for ever. (Heb. 7:23-28)

We thank You for Your Son, O God.

DAY OF ORDINARY TIME 181

Prayer results from the totality of our relationship with God. . . . What we
pray is what we are. . . . The depth of our faith is the depth of our prayer.
The vitality of our hope is the vitality of our prayer. The tenderness of our
love is the tenderness of our prayer.
— *Letters From the Desert,* Carlo Carretto (1910-   )

When Christ appeared as a high priest of the good things that have come,
then through the greater and more perfect tent (not made with hands, that
is, not of this creation) he entered once for all into the Holy Place, taking not
the blood of goats and calves but his own blood, thus securing an eternal redemption. For if the sprinkling of defiled persons with the ashes of a heifer
sanctifies for the purification of the flesh, how much more shall the blood of
Christ, who through the eternal Spirit offered himself without blemish to
God, purify your conscience from dead works to serve the living God. (Heb.
9:11-14)

We praise and glorify You, O God, for the purifying sacrifice of Your Son.

DAY OF ORDINARY TIME 182

In true prayer a person uses the energy of his mind to direct the movement
of his living toward the finest goals he can create.
— *Understanding Prayer,* Edgar N. Jackson (1910-   )

Christ has entered, not into a sanctuary made with hands, a copy of the true
one, but into heaven itself, now to appear in the presence of God on our
behalf. Nor was it to offer himself repeatedly, as the high priest enters the
Holy Place yearly with blood not his own; for then he would have had to suffer repeatedly since the foundation of the world. But as it is, he has appeared
once for all at the end of the age to put away sin by the sacrifice of himself.
And just as it is appointed for men to die once, and after that comes judgment, so Christ, having been offered once to bear the sins of many, will appear a second time, not to deal with sin but to save those who are eagerly
waiting for him. (Heb. 9:24-28)

Come, Lord Jesus, and take us with You, when You are ready.

DAY OF ORDINARY TIME 183

Prayer is really believing that we are living in the mystery of God, that we are engulfed in that mystery.
— *Prayer,* Henry Le Saux, O.S.B. (1910-   )

Since we have confidence to enter the sanctuary by the blood of Jesus, by the new and living way which he opened for us through the curtain, that is, through his flesh, and since we have a great priest over the house of God, let us draw near with a true heart in full assurance of faith, with our hearts sprinkled clean from an evil conscience and our bodies washed with pure water. Let us hold fast the confession of our hope without wavering, for he who promised is faithful; and let us consider how to stir up one another to love and good works, not neglecting to meet together, as is the habit of some, but encouraging one another, and all the more as you see the Day drawing near. (Heb. 10:19-25)

Dawn from on high, fill us with Your light and new life.

DAY OF ORDINARY TIME 184

Prayer is movement. This movement does not mean that prayer consists in doing things, in a kind of permanent activity in which the person concerned has constantly to be thinking of new acts to undertake, either spiritually or bodily. Prayer is movement in the sense that it is growth, in the sense that all life is movement. . . . The idea of spiritual growth then is at the root of prayer.
— *Life and Fire of Love,* Herbert M. Waddams (1911-   )

Recall the former days when, after you were enlightened, you endured a hard struggle with sufferings, sometimes being publicly exposed to abuse and affliction and sometimes being partners with those so treated. For you had compassion on the prisoners, and you joyfully accepted the plundering of your property, since you knew that you yourselves had a better possession and an abiding one. Therefore do not throw away your confidence, which has a great reward. For you have need of endurance, so that you may do the will of God and receive what is promised. (Heb. 10:32-36)

Endurance is Your gift to us, O Lord. Help us persevere in Your ways.

DAY OF ORDINARY TIME 185

Prayer in its simplest expression does not attempt to change God's will or to bring Him down to the level of human whims and fancies; prayer molds the human will upon the divine. A life of constant prayer is not simply a passive attitude of a soul looking toward God, but of frequent acts of petition the underlying theme of which is always "Thy will be done."
— *The Crown of Life,* Conrad Pepler (1912-   )

Faith is the assurance of things hoped for, the conviction of things not seen. For by it the men of old received divine approval. By faith we understand that the world was created by the word of God, so that what is seen was made out of things which do not appear. By faith Abel offered to God a more acceptable sacrifice than Cain, through which he received approval as righteous, God bearing witness by accepting his gifts; he died, but through his faith he is still speaking. . . . And without faith it is impossible to please him. For whoever would draw near to God must believe that he exists and that he rewards those who seek him. (Heb. 11:1-6)

Spirit of God, increase our faith. By it, help us draw near to our God.

DAY OF ORDINARY TIME 186

Prayer covers all our speaking to God.
— *Prayer: An Adventure in Living,* Abbot B. C. Butler (1912-   )

By faith Abraham obeyed when he was called to go out to a place which he was to receive as an inheritance; and he went out, not knowing where he was to go. By faith he sojourned in the land of promise, as in a foreign land, living in tents with Isaac and Jacob, heirs with him of the same promise. For he looked forward to the city which has foundations, whose builder and maker is God. By faith Sarah herself received power to conceive, even when she was past the age, since she considered him faithful who had promised. (Heb. 11:8-11)

On our pilgrimage of life, O God, help us place all our faith and hope in You alone.

DAY OF ORDINARY TIME 187

Prayer is a religious activity. Even petitionary prayer for temporal benefits

is, in essence, not an attempt to force God's hand, but an appeal to His good pleasure. It recognizes God as the source of all good, and as himself the supreme Good.
— *Prayer: An Adventure in Living,* Abbot B. C. Butler (1912-   )

These all died in faith, not having received what was promised, but having seen it and greeted it from afar, and having acknowledged that they were strangers and exiles on the earth. For people who speak thus make it clear that they are seeking a homeland. If they had been thinking of that land from which they had gone out, they would have had opportunity to return. But as it is, they desire a better country, that is, a heavenly one. Therefore God is not ashamed to be called their God, for he has prepared for them a city. (Heb. 11:13-16)

We long for You, O Lord. Help us on our daily journey to come home to You.

DAY OF ORDINARY TIME 188

Prayer is a difficult, often a lost and cloudy and a hidden road which we see backwards better than forwards. This sense of blindness, of not knowing, "Am I praying or not?"; this torture of not knowing what prayer is or is meant to be, is all part of the life, the confusing, crucified life of prayer.
— *Spiritual Letters,* Mother Maria Gysi (1912-   )

Since we are surrounded by so great a cloud of witnesses, let us also lay aside every weight, and sin which clings so closely, and let us run with perseverance the race that is set before us, looking to Jesus the pioneer and perfecter of our faith, who for the joy that was set before him endured the cross, despising the shame, and is seated at the right hand of the throne of God. Consider him who endured from sinners such hostility against himself, so that you may not grow weary or fainthearted. In your struggle against sin you have not yet resisted to the point of shedding your blood. (Heb. 12:1-4)

O God, You have given us a glorious throng of witnesses to the faith. Help us join that number.

DAY OF ORDINARY TIME 189

Prayer is the search for God, encounter with God, and going beyond this encounter in communion. Thus it is an activity, a state and also a situation; a

situation both with respect to God and to the created world.
— *Courage to Pray,* Anthony Bloom (1914-   )

For the moment all discipline seems painful rather than pleasant; later it yields the peaceful fruit of righteousness to those who have been trained by it. Therefore lift your drooping hands and strengthen your weak knees, and make straight paths for your feet, so that what is lame may not be put out of joint but rather be healed. Strive for peace with all men, and for the holiness without which no one will see the Lord. See to it that no one fail to obtain the grace of God; that no "root of bitterness" spring up and cause trouble, and by it the many become defiled; that no one be immoral or irreligious like Esau, who sold his birthright for a single meal. For you know that afterward, when he desired to inherit the blessing, he was rejected, for he found no chance to repent, though he sought it with tears. (Heb. 12:11-17)

Fill me, Lord, with a deep and honest sorrow for all my sins.

DAY OF ORDINARY TIME 190

A very important thing is that a meeting face to face with God is always a moment of judgment for us. We cannot meet God in prayer or in meditation or in contemplation and not be either saved or condemned.
— *Courage to Pray,* Anthony Bloom (1914-   )

Do not neglect to show hospitality to strangers, for thereby some have entertained angels unawares. Remember those who are in prison, as though in prison with them; and those who are ill-treated, since you also are in the body. Let marriage be held in honor among all, and let the marriage bed be undefiled; for God will judge the immoral and adulterous. Keep your life free from love of money, and be content with what you have; for he has said, "I will never fail you nor forsake you." Hence we can confidently say, "The Lord is my helper, I will not be afraid; what can man do to me?" (Heb. 13:2-6)

Purify our love, Lord. May our love for You and our love for family and friends be pleasing to You.

DAY OF ORDINARY TIME 191

Prayer is then not just a formula in words, or a series of desires springing up in the heart — it is the orientation of our whole body, mind and spirit to God

in silence, attention, and adoration. All good meditative prayer is a conversion of our entire self to God.
— *Thoughts in Solitude,* Thomas Merton (1915-1968)

Remember your leaders, those who spoke to you the word of God; consider the outcome of their life, and imitate their faith. Jesus Christ is the same yesterday and today and for ever. Do not be led away by diverse and strange teachings; for it is well that the heart be strengthened by grace, not by foods, which have not benefited their adherents. (Heb. 13:7-9)

May Your word always be food for our life, O God.

DAY OF ORDINARY TIME 192

Prayer and love are really learned in the hour when prayer becomes impossible and your heart turns to stone. If you have never had any distractions you don't know how to pray. For the secret of prayer is a hunger for God and for the vision of God, a hunger that lies far deeper than the level of language or affection. And a person whose memory and imagination are persecuting him with a crowd of useless or even evil thoughts and images may sometimes be forced to pray far better, in the depths of his murdered heart, than one whose mind is swimming with clear concepts and brilliant purposes and easy acts of love.
— *Thoughts in Solitude,* Thomas Merton (1915-1968)

May the God of peace who brought again from the dead our Lord Jesus, the great shepherd of the sheep, by the blood of the eternal covenant, equip you with everything good that you may do his will, working in you that which is pleasing in his sight, through Jesus Christ; to whom be glory for ever and ever. Amen. (Heb. 13:20-21)

Shepherd of our souls, lead us to Your peace today.

DAY OF ORDINARY TIME 193

We do not pray for the sake of praying, but for the sake of being heard. We do not pray in order to listen to ourselves praying but in order that God may hear us and answer us. Also, we do not pray in order to receive just any answer: it must be God's answer. . . . It is the will to pray that is the essence of prayer, and the desire to find God, to see Him and to love Him is the one thing that matters. If you have desired to know Him and love Him, you have

already done what was expected of you, and it is much better to desire God without being able to think clearly of Him, than to have marvelous thoughts about Him without desiring to enter into union with His will.
— *New Seeds of Contemplation,* Thomas Merton (1915-1968)

Count it all joy, my brethren, when you meet various trials, for you know that the testing of your faith produces steadfastness. And let steadfastness have its full effect, that you may be perfect and complete, lacking in nothing. If any of you lacks wisdom, let him ask God, who gives to all men generously and without reproaching, and it will be given him. But let him ask in faith, with no doubting, for he who doubts is like a wave of the sea that is driven and tossed by the wind. For that person must not suppose that a double-minded man, unstable in all his ways, will receive anything from the Lord. (James 1:2-8)

Spirit of Wisdom, take away all doubt from my heart.

DAY OF ORDINARY TIME 194

Prayer is freedom and affirmation growing out of nothingness into love. Prayer is the flowering of our inmost freedom, in response to the Word of God. Prayer is not only dialogue with God: it is the communion of our freedom with His ultimate freedom, His infinite spirit. It is the elevation of our limited freedom into the infinite freedom of the divine love. Prayer is the encounter of our freedom with the all-embracing charity which knows no limit and knows no obstacle. Prayer is an emergence into this area of infinite freedom. Prayer then is not an abject procedure although sometimes it may spring from our abjection.
— *Contemplation in a World of Action,* Thomas Merton (1915-1968)

Blessed is the man who endures trial, for when he has stood the test he will receive the crown of life which God has promised to those who love him. Let no one say when he is tempted, "I am tempted by God"; for God cannot be tempted with evil and he himself tempts no one; but each person is tempted when he is lured and enticed by his own desire. Then desire when it has conceived gives birth to sin; and sin when it is full-grown brings forth death. (James 1:12-15)

In daily trial, O God, help me place all my trust in You.

DAY OF ORDINARY TIME 195

Prayer is nothing other than a period especially set aside to bring into action our gift of faith, with the desire of reaching God through the hidden knowledge prayer gives us, and of loving Him more deeply, thinking of God with loving attention.
— *Letters to the Little Brothers,* René Voillaume (1915-   )

Be doers of the word, and not hearers only, deceiving yourselves. For if any one is a hearer of the word and not a doer, he is like a man who observes his natural face in a mirror; for he observes himself and goes away and at once forgets what he was like. But he who looks into the perfect law, the law of liberty, and perseveres, being no hearer that forgets but a doer that acts, he shall be blessed in his doing. If any one thinks he is religious, and does not bridle his tongue but deceives his heart, this man's religion is vain. Religion that is pure and undefiled before God and the Father is this: to visit orphans and widows in their affliction, and to keep oneself unstained from the world. (James 1:22-27)

You alone, Lord, can make me a true believer and a real doer. Help me today.

DAY OF ORDINARY TIME 196

Prayer is above all waiting. It is permitting the "Come, Lord" of the Apocalypse to surge up in oneself day after day. . . . Prayer is a step from doubt toward faith, a creative waiting to discern in every event the Creator at work now. It is hidden wonder and gratitude for the gift of life.
— *Living Today for God,* Roger Schutz (1915-   )

What does it profit, my brethren, if a man says he has faith but has not works? Can his faith save him? If a brother or sister is ill-clad and in lack of daily food, and one of you says to them, "Go in peace, be warmed and filled," without giving them the things needed for the body, what does it profit? So faith by itself, if it has no works, is dead. But some one will say, "You have faith and I have works." Show me your faith apart from your works, and I by my works will show you my faith. (James 2:14-18)

Increase my faith, Holy Spirit of God. Only then will my poor works be pleasing to You.

DAY OF ORDINARY TIME 197

Prayer seems to us to be the confrontation of two desires: man's desire and the desire of God, or rather the assumption of man's desire into that of God.
— *The Rediscovery of Prayer,* Bernard Bro (1915-   )

Let not many of you become teachers, my brethren, for you know that we who teach shall be judged with greater strictness. For we all make many mistakes, and if any one makes no mistakes in what he says he is a perfect man, able to bridle the whole body also. If we put bits into the mouths of horses that they may obey us, we guide their whole bodies. Look at the ships also; though they are so great and are driven by strong winds, they are guided by a very small rudder wherever the will of the pilot directs. So the tongue is a little member and boasts of great things. How great a forest is set ablaze by a small fire! (James 3:1-5)

Holy Guide for all people, gently guide me today.

DAY OF ORDINARY TIME 198

The practice of prayer and meditation is as complex and varied as human life itself. As we confront the reality of the Other, we bring every part of our being, our ideas and thoughts, our plans for the day, for the week, for our entire life to the Other. We disclose our fears, our hopes, our human love, our thirst for more than human love, our anger and vengeance, our depression, sorrow and lostness, the values that are important to us, our adoration and joy and thanksgiving.
— *The Other Side of Silence,* Morton Kelsey (1917-   )

The tongue is a fire. The tongue is an unrighteous world among our members, staining the whole body, setting on fire the cycle of nature, and set on fire by hell. For every kind of beast and bird, of reptile and sea creature, can be tamed and has been tamed by humankind, but no human being can tame the tongue — a restless evil, full of deadly poison. With it we bless the Lord and Father, and with it we curse men, who are made in the likeness of God. From the same mouth come blessing and cursing. My brethren, this ought not to be so. (James 3:6-10)

Our gift of speech is Your gift to us, O Lord. Help us use it in praise of You.

DAY OF ORDINARY TIME 199

The sum of the matter is that prayer is the directing of the will in praise toward God, and that this leads eventually to the soul's rest in God, which is the end of mankind.
— *Approach to Prayer,* Hubert van Zeller (1919-   )

Who is wise and understanding among you? By his good life let him show his works in the meekness of wisdom. But if you have bitter jealousy and selfish ambition in your hearts, do not boast and be false to the truth. This wisdom is not such as comes down from above, but is earthly, unspiritual, devilish. For where jealousy and selfish ambition exist, there will be disorder and every vile practice. But the wisdom from above is first pure, then peaceable, gentle, open to reason, full of mercy and good fruits, without uncertainty or insincerity. And the harvest of righteousness is sown in peace by those who make peace. (James 3:13-18)

Spirit of Wisdom, teach us Your truth so that we may walk in Your ways.

DAY OF ORDINARY TIME 200

Prayer is a fundamental style of thinking, passionate and compassionate, responsible and thankful, that is deeply rooted in our humanity.
— *Paths in Spirituality,* John MacQuarrie (1919-   )

God opposes the proud, but gives grace to the humble. Submit yourselves therefore to God. Resist the devil and he will flee from you. Draw near to God and he will draw near to you. Cleanse your hands, you sinners, and purify your hearts, you men of double mind. Be wretched and mourn and weep. Let your laughter be turned to mourning and your joy to dejection. Humble yourselves before the Lord and he will exalt you. (James 4:6-10)

Teach us to be humble and gentle of heart, O Jesus, so that we may become more like You.

DAY OF ORDINARY TIME 201

Prayer is the responsibility to meet others with all I have . . . to expect to meet God in the way, not to turn aside from the way. All else is exercise toward that or reflection in depth upon it.
— *Honest to God,* John A. T. Robinson (1919-   )

Come now, you who say, "Today or tomorrow we will go into such and such a town and spend a year there and trade and get gain"; whereas you do not know about tomorrow. What is your life? For you are a mist that appears for a little time and then vanishes. Instead you ought to say, "If the Lord wills, we shall live and we shall do this or that." As it is, you boast in your arrogance. All such boasting is evil. Whoever knows what is right to do and fails to do it, for him it is sin. (James 4:13-17)

Teach us to know Your will, O God, so that we may fulfill it and do right before You.

DAY OF ORDINARY TIME 202

Prayer is not a matter of pleasant contemplation. To pray — and by that I do not mean merely an isolated religious act, but, more comprehensively, every serious use of the name of God, every act of appealing to Him, of speaking of Him, of thinking about Him, since it is prayer that first makes plain what it means to say "God" — and to pray, then, is to submit oneself, so it seems, to a durability test.
— *On Prayer,* Gerhard Ebeling (1920-   )

Be patient, therefore, brethren, until the coming of the Lord. Behold, the farmer waits for the precious fruit of the earth, being patient over it until it receives the early and the late rain. You also be patient. Establish your hearts, for the coming of the Lord is at hand. Do not grumble, brethren, against one another, that you may not be judged; behold, the Judge is standing at the doors. As an example of suffering and patience, brethren, take the prophets who spoke in the name of the Lord. Behold, we call those happy who were steadfast. (James 5:7-11)

By Your life and death, Jesus, You taught us patience. Help me practice it today.

DAY OF ORDINARY TIME 203

Talking to God is not an impossible feat. People do so when they pray. . . . Prayer cannot be understood as praying to someone "out there" who is "there" in the way in which the planets are "there."
— *The Concept of Prayer,* D. Z. Phillips (1921-   )

Is any one among you suffering? Let him pray. Is any cheerful? Let him sing praise. Is any among you sick? Let him call for the elders of the church, and let them pray over him, anointing him with oil in the name of the Lord; and the prayer of faith will save the sick man, and the Lord will raise him up; and if he has committed sins, he will be forgiven. Therefore confess your sins to one another, and pray for one another, that you may be healed. The prayer of a righteous man has great power in its effects. (James 5:13-16)

You alone, O God, can heal Your people. May we all know health of body and spirit.

DAY OF ORDINARY TIME 204

God, who gave us minds for thinking and bodies for working, would defeat His own purpose if He permitted us to obtain through prayer what may come through work and intelligence. Prayer is a marvelous and necessary supplement of our feeble efforts, but it is a dangerous substitute. I am certain we need to pray for God's help and guidance in this integration struggle, but we are gravely misled if we think the struggle will be won only by prayer.
— *Strength to Love,* Martin Luther King (1929-1968)

Blessed be the God and Father of our Lord Jesus Christ! By his great mercy we have been born anew to a living hope through the resurrection of Jesus Christ from the dead, and to an inheritance which is imperishable, undefiled, and unfading, kept in heaven for you, who by God's power are guarded through faith for a salvation ready to be revealed in the last time. In this you rejoice, though now for a little while you may have to suffer various trials, so that the genuineness of your faith, more precious than gold which though perishable is tested by fire, may redound to praise and glory and honor at the revelation of Jesus Christ. (1 Peter 1:3-7)

In all trials, O God, be my deliverer.

DAY OF ORDINARY TIME 205

To pray is to intend to hear God and to respond to God. . . . Prayer is a consent that is grounded in the expectation that God speaks to us and we can hear Him.
— *History of Christian Spirituality,* Urban T. Homes (1930-1981)

Gird up your minds, be sober, set your hope fully upon the grace that is coming to you at the revelation of Jesus Christ. As obedient children, do not be conformed to the passions of your former ignorance, but as he who called you is holy, be holy yourselves in all your conduct; since it is written, "You shall be holy, for I am holy." And if you invoke as Father him who judges each one impartially according to his deeds, conduct yourselves with fear throughout the time of your exile. You know that you were ransomed from the futile ways inherited from your fathers, not with perishable things such as silver or gold, but with the precious blood of Christ, like that of a lamb without blemish or spot. (1 Peter 1:13-19)

You alone are holy, O Lord. Share Your life with us today.

DAY OF ORDINARY TIME 206

True prayer consists in getting out of God's way, and allowing the Eternal Good to flow into the life.
— *Hidden Power for Human Problems,* Frederick W. Bailes
    (Contemporary)

Put away all malice and all guile and insincerity and envy and all slander. Like newborn babes, long for the pure spiritual milk, that by it you may grow up to salvation; for you have tasted the kindness of the Lord. Come to him, to that living stone, rejected by men but in God's sight chosen and precious; and like living stones be yourselves built into a spiritual house, to be a holy priesthood, to offer spiritual sacrifices acceptable to God through Jesus Christ. (1 Peter 2:1-5)

As a child trusting its parents, help me, O Lord, to place all my trust in You.

DAY OF ORDINARY TIME 207

Prayer has to be actively carried on apart with God, an activity directed toward God, of the heart, mind, soul, and I think, of the body too.
— *The Wonder of Prayer,* Shelton H. Bishop (Contemporary)

You are a chosen race, a royal priesthood, a holy nation, God's own people, that you may declare the wonderful deeds of him who called you out of darkness into his marvelous light. Once you were no people but now you are God's people; once you had not received mercy but now you have received mercy. Beloved, I beseech you as aliens and exiles to abstain from the passions of the flesh that wage war against your soul. Maintain good conduct among the Gentiles, so that in case they speak against you as wrongdoers, they may see your good deeds and glorify God on the day of visitation. (1 Peter 2:9-12)

Claim us once more, O God, as Your people. In You alone is our salvation.

DAY OF ORDINARY TIME 208

Prayer is the outpouring of the soul before a living God, the crying to God "out of the depths."
— *The Struggle of Prayer,* Donald G. Bloesch (Contemporary)

What credit is it, if when you do wrong and are beaten for it you take it patiently? But if when you do right and suffer for it you take it patiently, you have God's approval. For to this you have been called, because Christ also suffered for you, leaving you an example, that you should follow in his steps. He committed no sin; no guile was found on his lips. When he was reviled, he did not revile in return; but when he suffered, he did not threaten; but he trusted to him who judges justly. He himself bore our sins in his body on the tree, that we might die to sin and live to righteousness. By his wounds you have been healed. For you were straying like sheep, but have now returned to the Shepherd and Guardian of your souls. (1 Peter 2:20-25)

Loving Shepherd, hold us all to Your heart this day.

DAY OF ORDINARY TIME 209

Christian prayer is an openness setting the Christian free to receive God. It is the basic quality of our Christian life. . . . Prayer is a believer's attempt to break out of his ordinary existence in order to become open to God. In his innermost self, he must be open to receive God.
— *Christian Prayer,* Ladislaus Boros (Contemporary)

In your hearts reverence Christ as Lord. Always be prepared to make a defense to any one who calls you to account for the hope that is in you, yet do it with gentleness and reverence; and keep your conscience clear, so that, when you are abused, those who revile your good behavior in Christ may be put to shame. For it is better to suffer for doing right, if that should be God's will, than for doing wrong. For Christ also died for sins once for all, the righteous for the unrighteous, that he might bring us to God, being put to death in the flesh but made alive in the spirit. (1 Peter 3:15-18)

Redeemer of all people, save us from our sins. Make us one with You.

DAY OF ORDINARY TIME 210

To pray is to risk encounter with God and to stand in truth before Him. . . . Prayer is not a hobby but a life, and to live is to change. . . . Prayer springs from God's life in us. The living God who gives that life himself undertakes the pruning needed for its increase; He prunes through the experience of prayer and the diminishments we suffer in our lives.
— *Prayer: Our Journey Home,* Sr. Maria Boulding (Contemporary)

The end of all things is at hand; therefore keep sane and sober for your prayers. Above all hold unfailing your love for one another, since love covers a multitude of sins. Practice hospitality ungrudgingly to one another. As each has received a gift, employ it for one another, as good stewards of God's varied grace: whoever speaks, as one who utters oracles of God; whoever renders service, as one who renders it by the strength which God supplies; in order that in everything God may be glorified through Jesus Christ. To him belong glory and dominion for ever and ever. Amen. (1 Peter 4:7-11)

Whatever You call us to do today, O Lord, help us do it for love of You.

DAY OF ORDINARY TIME 211

Prayer is a journey to meet the absolute mysteriousness of God, the mysteriousness of His love for us and His action in us. As long as thoughts and words help us to meet Him in a communion of love we should use them, but for very many people who pray regularly the point is soon reached when we sense that we can get closer to God without them.
— *Prayer: Our Journey Home,* Sr. Maria Boulding (Contemporary)

Rejoice in so far as you share Christ's sufferings, that you may also rejoice and be glad when his glory is revealed. If you are reproached for the name of Christ, you are blessed, because the spirit of glory and of God rests upon you. But let none of you suffer as a murderer, or a thief, or a wrongdoer, or a mischiefmaker; yet if one suffers as a Christian, let him not be ashamed, but under that name let him glorify God. For the time has come for judgment to begin with the household of God; and if it begins with us, what will be the end of those who do not obey the gospel of God? . . . Therefore let those who suffer according to God's will do right and entrust their souls to a faithful Creator. (1 Peter 4:13-19)

O Jesus, You suffered death on a cross for us. Help us carry our cross for You today.

DAY OF ORDINARY TIME 212

Listening to God is prayer, but most of our prayer is apt to be either asking God something or telling God something rather than listening; . . . or our words may be expressions of love, of confession, or of thanksgiving. If that is all, something is missing. Prayer should be, is, a two-way street. Prayer, to be complete, must be some sort of communication with, or being with, God and not just our words to Him.
— *Hidden in Plain Sight,* Avery Brooke (Contemporary)

Humble yourselves therefore under the mighty hand of God, that in due time he may exalt you. Cast all your anxieties on him, for he cares about you. Be sober, be watchful. Your adversary the devil prowls around like a roaring lion, seeking some one to devour. Resist him, firm in your faith, knowing that the same experience of suffering is required of your brotherhood throughout the world. And after you have suffered a little while, the God of all grace, who has called you to his eternal glory in Christ, will himself restore, establish, and strengthen you. To him be the dominion for ever and ever. Amen. (1 Peter 5:6-11)

Each day, Lord, You ask us all to be watchful. May Your Spirit guide us in this effort.

DAY OF ORDINARY TIME 213

I want to say a little about the importance of giving time to prayer. God can give himself at any time, be it during the time of prayer or during activity. But He is most likely to visit us in this special way during prayer because only then are we likely to let Him in and our deep self respond to His visit.
— *Guidelines for Mystical Prayer,* Ruth Burrows (Contemporary)

His divine power has granted to us all things that pertain to life and godliness, through the knowledge of him who called us to his own glory and excellence, by which he has granted to us his precious and very great promises, that through these you may escape from the corruption that is in the world because of passion, and become partakers of the divine nature. For this very reason make every effort to supplement your faith with virtue, and virtue with knowledge, and knowledge with self-control, and self-control with steadfastness, and steadfastness with godliness, and godliness with brotherly affection, and brotherly affection with love. (2 Peter 1:3-7)

Spirit of God, shower Your precious gifts on us all, so that we may live godly lives.

DAY OF ORDINARY TIME 214

Prayer is tending the presence of God. Prayer is tending toward the presence of God. Prayer is paying attention to the presence of God. Prayer is intending God's presence. Prayer is being tender with — being a tender of — God's presence. Prayer is living with the tension of God's presence. Prayer is living intensely with God's presence.
— *Prayer From Where You Are,* James Carroll (Contemporary)

If these things are yours and abound, they keep you from being ineffective or unfruitful in the knowledge of our Lord Jesus Christ. For whoever lacks these things is blind and shortsighted and has forgotten that he was cleansed from his old sins. Therefore, brethren, be the more zealous to confirm your call and election; for if you do this you will never fall; so there will be richly provided for you an entrance into the eternal kingdom of our Lord and Savior Jesus Christ. (2 Peter 1:8-11)

You call us to goodness and greatness, O God. Like Jesus, may we know Your will for us.

DAY OF ORDINARY TIME 215

Prayer is a thirsting for God, a seeking for God, a wanting to be with Him, a form of loving companionship, a form of personal presence — God present to me in love, I present to God in love. Prayer is a love. It is a love-dialogue during which I in a special way open myself to God's word, to His speaking to me, and during which I respond with a word of my own. This word of mine is basically a yes, a yes to what God wants of me, a yes which is meant to include all the other words I may authentically utter in prayer.
— *Response in Christ,* Edward Carter, S.J. (Contemporary)

When he received honor and glory from God the Father and the voice was borne to him by the Majestic Glory, "This is my beloved Son, with whom I am well pleased," we heard this voice borne from heaven, for we were with him on the holy mountain. And we have the prophetic word made more sure.

You will do well to pay attention to this as to a lamp shining in a dark place, until the day dawns and the morning star rises in your hearts. First of all you must understand this, that no prophecy of scripture is a matter of one's own interpretation, because no prophecy ever came by the impulse of man, but men moved by the Holy Spirit spoke from God. (2 Peter 1:17-21)

May we all be Your much loved children, O God, as we strive to do Your will.

DAY OF ORDINARY TIME 216

Prayer is not simply a matter of asking God for what we need, though as children of a loving Father we must never be too proud or too frightened to ask for what we need. But prayer is a dialogue. If God smiles at us in a sudden shaft of sunlight then we must greet Him in return, perhaps with a few words, perhaps just with a smile. If He reveals to us His loving laughter as we make fools of ourselves, we must learn to laugh with Him. This is a hard lesson but a very beautiful one.
— *Prayer for Pilgrims,* Sheila Cassidy (Contemporary)

Do not ignore this one fact, beloved, that with the Lord one day is as a thousand years, and a thousand years as one day. The Lord is not slow about his promise as some count slowness, but is forbearing toward you, not wishing that any should perish, but that all should reach repentance. But the day of the Lord will come like a thief, and then the heavens will pass away with a loud noise, and the elements will be dissolved with fire, and the earth and the works that are upon it will be burned up. Since all these things are thus to be dissolved, what sort of persons ought you to be in lives of holiness and godliness, waiting for and hastening the coming of the day of God. . . . (2 Peter 3:8-12)

Prepare us for Your coming, O Lord.

DAY OF ORDINARY TIME 217

Prayer interprets life by reflecting on it in the context of God.
— *The Experience of Praying,* Sean Caulfield (Contemporary)

This is the message we have heard from him and proclaim to you, that God is light and in him is no darkness at all. If we say we have fellowship with him while we walk in darkness, we lie and do not live according to the truth; but if we walk in the light, as he is in the light, we have fellowship with one another, and the blood of Jesus his Son cleanses us from all sin. If we say we have no sin, we deceive ourselves, and the truth is not in us. If we confess our sins, he is faithful and just, and will forgive our sins and cleanse us from all unrighteousness. If we say we have not sinned, we make him a liar, and his word is not in us. (1 John 1:5-10)

Spirit of Light, flood our hearts with the brightness of Your truth.

DAY OF ORDINARY TIME 218

Contemplation is the essential, fundamental form of Christian prayer. It is meant to be the common prayer of every Christian and the normal development of growth of life in the Spirit. . . . The first step toward understanding contemplation as a form of Christian prayer is to recognize that contemplation as prayer is possible only as the outcome of a contemplative attitude toward life.
— *Forms of Prayer in Christian Spirituality,* Agnes Cunningham
     (Contemporary)

Beloved, I am writing you no new commandment, but an old commandment which you had from the beginning; the old commandment is the word which you have heard. Yet I am writing you a new commandment, which is true in him and in you, because the darkness is passing away and the true light is already shining. He who says he is in the light and hates his brother is in the darkness still. He who loves his brother abides in the light, and in it there is no cause for stumbling. But he who hates his brother is in the darkness and walks in the darkness, and does not know where he is going, because the darkness has blinded his eyes. (1 John 2:7-11)

Teach us to love, O Jesus, as You loved us.

DAY OF ORDINARY TIME 219

Prayer is the continual communication of the self in all the subtleties of one's uniqueness, depth, and mystery, much as one would communicate oneself to an intensely sensitive counselor or, even more commonly, to a genuinely understanding and trustworthy friend.
— *Psychological Dynamics and Religious Living,* Charles A. Curran
     (Contemporary)

I am writing to you, little children, because your sins are forgiven for his sake. I am writing to you, fathers, because you know him who is from the beginning. I am writing to you, young men, because you have overcome the evil one. I write to you, children, because you know the Father. I write to you, fathers, because you know him who is from the beginning. I write to you, young men, because you are strong, and the word of God abides in you, and you have overcome the evil one. (1 John 2:12-14)

In Your written word, O God, may we all find guidance for our life.

DAY OF ORDINARY TIME 220

In Christian terminology the term prayer has come to mean any interior disposition of the soul, any expression of knowledge or love directed toward God, whether or not it is outwardly expressed or articulated in words, attitude or action.
— *Prayer,* Jean Daujat (Contemporary)

It is the last hour; and as you have heard that antichrist is coming, so now many antichrists have come; therefore we know that it is the last hour. They went out from us, but they were not of us; for if they had been of us, they would have continued with us; but they went out, that it might be plain that they all are not of us. But you have been anointed by the Holy One, and you all know. I write to you, not because you do not know the truth, but because you know it, and know that no lie is of the truth. (1 John 2:18-21)

Holy One of God, anoint us with the oil of gladness. May we be filled with a holy joy.

DAY OF ORDINARY TIME 221

Personal prayer is not so much something we do as a response to and an immersion in our experience — a growing awareness of love and forgiveness, the painful loss or forming of relationships, sickness or the vitality of health, celebration or mourning. We must see our experience as more than a series of events or persons, however. It is rather a process in which God transforms us through our very living and being. Prayer is really a way of being before God, before all that is.
— *Solitude and Sacrament,* Katherine M. Dyckman and L. Patrick
      Carroll (Contemporaries)

See what love the Father has given us, that we should be called children of

God; and so we are. The reason why the world does not know us is that it did not know him. Beloved, we are God's children now; it does not yet appear what we shall be, but we know that when he appears we shall be like him, for we shall see him as he is. And every one who thus hopes in him purifies himself as he is pure. (1 John 3:1-3)

Purify me, O God, so that I may be pleasing to You in all ways.

DAY OF ORDINARY TIME 222

Prayer is not to be analyzed like a language. It has none of that form or content, for it receives its content, not from what I have to say, but from the One to whom is is spoken. . . . It becomes prayer by the decision of God to whom it is addressed, but then its nature undergoes a change.
— *Prayer and Modern Man,* Jacques Ellul (Contemporary)

Let no one deceive you. He who does right is righteous, as he is righteous. He who commits sin is of the devil for the devil has sinned from the beginning. The reason the Son of God appeared was to destroy the works of the devil. No one born of God commits sin; for God's nature abides in him, and he cannot sin because he is born of God. By this it may be seen who are the children of God, and who are the children of the devil: whoever does not do right is not of God, nor he who does not love his brother. (1 John 3:7-10)

Help me, O Lord, to keep my eyes fixed on Your face as a child on its parent's face.

DAY OF ORDINARY TIME 223

I do not see prayer primarily as the words that express it, or as the modes it takes, praise, intercession, repentance, but more generally as a conscious attitude of presence and attention before God. . . . Fundamentally all our action and our prayer can both be defined as seeking the face of Christ, in order to reflect him.
— *Prayer at the Heart of Life,* Pierre-Yves Emery (Contemporary)

For this is the message which you have heard from the beginning, that we should love one another, and not be like Cain who was of the evil one and murdered his brother. And why did he murder him? Because his own deeds were evil and his brother's righteous. Do not wonder, brethren, that the world hates you. We know that we have passed out of death into life, because we love the brethren. He who does not love remains in death. (1 John 3:11-14)

Daily You call us, Lord, to love all our sisters and brothers. Help me hear that call today.

DAY OF ORDINARY TIME 224

Praying is paying attention to God's prayer to us. . . . Prayer is not requesting things of God, but receiving what He wants to give you; it is not being heard by God, but hearing God praying to you; it is not requesting God's forgiveness, but opening yourself to His forgiveness; it is not offering yourself to God, but receiving God giving himself to you.
— *Teach Us How to Pray,* Louis Evely (Contemporary)

By this we know love, that he laid down his life for us; and we ought to lay down our lives for the brethren. But if any one has the world's goods and sees his brother in need, yet closes his heart against him, how does God's love abide in him? Little children, let us not love in word or speech but in deed and in truth. (1 John 3:16-18)

Open my heart and my life today, O God, to all whom I will meet.

DAY OF ORDINARY TIME 225

Prayer is quite simple. Essentially, praying is remaining in the Lord "unprotected," with no defenses. . . . Prayer calls for my total presence to the Lord, that He may take possession of me.
— *Praying,* Robert Faricy (Contemporary)

By this we shall know that we are of the truth, and reassure our hearts before him whenever our hearts condemn us; for God is greater than our hearts, and he knows everything. Beloved, if our hearts do not condemn us, we have confidence before God; and we receive from him whatever we ask, because we keep his commandments and do what pleases him. And this is his commandment, that we should believe in the name of his Son Jesus Christ and love one another, just as he has commanded us. All who keep his commandments abide in him, and he in them. And by this we know that he abides in us, by the Spirit which he has given us. (1 John 3:19-24)

Abide with me always, Lord, so that I may truly be one with You.

DAY OF ORDINARY TIME 226

Prayer is essentially a mystery because Christ is a mystery. . . . Prayer is also a work, a discipline. It cannot rest upon mere spontaneity. It does not come easily, just as being a person does not come easily. . . . Prayer means also an entering into timelessness. Prayer is a waiting. It is a hunger; it is love. Prayer is a relatedness, and prayer is a stillness.
— *Prayer Is a Hunger,* Edward Farrell (Contemporary)

Beloved, do not believe every spirit, but test the spirits to see whether they are of God; for many false prophets have gone out into the world. By this you know the Spirit of God: every spirit which confesses that Jesus Christ has come in the flesh is of God, and every spirit which does not confess Jesus is not of God. This is the spirit of antichrist, of which you heard that it was coming, and now it is in the world already. (1 John 4:1-3)

Spirit of Truth, teach us all the truth of God so that we may know and do the will of God.

DAY OF ORDINARY TIME 227

Prayer is the process of mind by which the unknowable finds meaning and becomes a truth; the unseeable takes shape and becomes a thing of beauty; the immeasurable gains substance and becomes a matter of value.
— *Prayer: The Master Key,* James D. Freeman (Contemporary)

Little children, you are of God, and have overcome them; for he who is in you is greater than he who is in the world. They are of the world, therefore what they say is of the world, and the world listens to them. We are of God. Whoever knows God listens to us, and he who is not of God does not listen to us. By this we know the spirit of truth and the spirit of error. (1 John 4:4-6)

Wisdom of God, teach me to listen to Your words always, so that I may speak Your message.

DAY OF ORDINARY TIME 228

We are interested in knowing God. To know God is to commune with Him. Prayer is one way to commune with Him, for prayer is communion.
— *Growing in the Life of Prayer,* Harold Wiley Freer (Contemporary)

Beloved, let us love one another; for love is of God, and he who loves is born of God and knows God. He who does not love does not know God; for God is love. In this the love of God was made manifest among us, that God sent his only Son into the world, so that we might live through him. In this is love, not that we loved God but that he loved us and sent his Son to be the expiation for our sins. (1 John 4:7-10)

Help us to know You, O God, so that we may truly love You.

DAY OF ORDINARY TIME 229

If prayer is, as I believe, not a matter of uttering a few words, even if deeply felt, but of achieving a certain sort of creative awareness, then it is idle to suppose that this can be fitted in, like physical jerks, between dressing and eating breakfast.
— Featured in *London Daily Mail,* Monica Furlong (Contemporary)

Beloved, if God so loved us, we also ought to love one another. No man has ever seen God; if we love one another, God abides in us and his love is perfected in us. By this we know that we abide in him and he in us, because he has given us of his own Spirit. And we have seen and testify that the Father has sent his Son as the Savior of the world. Whoever confesses that Jesus is the Son of God, God abides in him, and he in God. So we know and believe the love God has for us. God is love, and he who abides in love abides in God, and God abides in him. (1 John 4:11-16)

May we confess our deep faith in You, O Jesus, by the way we love others today.

DAY OF ORDINARY TIME 230

Prayer is a complex spiritual experience made up of listening, silence, receptivity, and simplicity before God. It is completed by the praying person's response, words, activity, and fulness in relationship with God.
— *Loving Awareness of God's Presence,* Fabio Giardini
        (Contemporary)

There is no fear in love, but perfect love casts out fear. For fear has to do with punishment, and he who fears is not perfected in love. We love, because he first loved us. If any one says, "I love God," and hates his brother, he is a liar; for he who does not love his brother whom he has seen, cannot love God whom he has not seen. And this commandment we have from him, that he who loves God should love his brother also. (1 John 4:18-21)

Cast fear out of my life, O Spirit of Love, so that I may love You above all.

DAY OF ORDINARY TIME 231

For some time, I have been suggesting that a better approach would be to define prayer as an *opening* of the mind and heart to God. This seems better because the idea of opening stresses receptivity, responsiveness to another. To open to another is to act, but it is to act in such a way that the other remains the dominant partner.
— *Opening to God*, Thomas H. Green (Contemporary)

Every one who believes that Jesus is the Christ is a child of God, and every one who loves the parent loves the child. By this we know that we love the children of God, when we love God and obey his commandments. For this is the love of God, that we keep his commandments. And his commandments are not burdensome. For whatever is born of God overcomes the world; and this is the victory that overcomes the world, our faith. Who is it that overcomes the world but he who believes that Jesus is the Son of God? (1 John 5:1-5)

You alone can make us free, O God. Today help us use our freedom wisely.

DAY OF ORDINARY TIME 232

Prayer is the action drawing a person upward to God and away from self, and the relationship which proceeds from this.
— *The Prayer of the Presence of God,* Dom Augustin Guillerand
        (Contemporary)

I write this to you who believe in the name of the Son of God, that you may know that you have eternal life. And this is the confidence which we have in him, that if we ask anything according to his will he hears us. And if we know that he hears us in whatever we ask, we know that we have obtained the requests made of him. If any one sees his brother committing what is not a mortal sin, he will ask, and God will give him life for those whose sin is not mortal. There is sin which is mortal; I do not say that one is to pray for that. All wrongdoing is sin, but there is sin which is not mortal. (1 John 5:13-17)

If we truly beg You for forgiveness, Lord, You will forgive us out of Your
great love.

DAY OF ORDINARY TIME 233

Faith lives on prayer; indeed faith is, strictly speaking, nothing else but
prayer. From the time we truly begin to have faith, we are already praying,
and when prayer totally stops, faith stops as well.
— *The Holy and the Good,* Bernard Häring (Contemporary)

I rejoiced greatly to find some of your children following the truth, just as
we have been commanded by the Father. And now I beg you, lady, not as
though I were writing you a new commandment, but the one we have had
from the beginning, that we love one another. And this is love, that we follow
his commandments; this is the commandment, as you have heard from the
beginning, that you follow love. (2 John 1:4-6)

Love is Your one desire of all of us, Lord. Teach us the way of Your love.

DAY OF ORDINARY TIME 234

To pray is to try to make ourselves aware of God and in that awareness respond to Him. It is an attempt to raise our minds and hearts to God.
— *Searching for God,* Basil Cardinal Hume (Contemporary)

Look to yourselves, that you may not lose what you have worked for, but
may win a full reward. Any one who goes ahead and does not abide in the
doctrine of Christ does not have God; he who abides in the doctrine has both
the Father and the Son. If any one comes to you and does not bring this doctrine, do not receive him in to the house or give him any greeting; for he who
greets him shares his wicked work. (2 John 1:8-11)

All Your holy teaching, O Jesus, is summed up in our love for one another.

DAY OF ORDINARY TIME 235

To pray is to enter into a relationship with God and to be transformed in
Him. And this relationship is close to the relationships we have with human
beings. . . . It is a "sharing in the divine nature," a "taking of manhood into
God." . . . Prayer is fellowship with God, the healing of a broken relation-

195

ship, but it can only occur in Christ and in His great atoning work of prayer. There is therefore a close connection between prayer and the Cross.
— *True Prayer,* Kenneth Leech (Contemporary)

Beloved, it is a loyal thing you do when you render any service to the brethren, especially to strangers, who have testified to your love before the church. You will do well to send them on their journey as befits God's service. For they have set out for his sake and have accepted nothing from the heathen. So we ought to support such men, that we may be fellow workers in the truth. (3 John 1:5-8)

Hospitality to the stranger is a genuine mark of love. Help us, O God, to be loving neighbors to all.

DAY OF ORDINARY TIME 236

Prayer comes out of the abundance of the heart, as the saying goes in the Gospels: "For a person's words proceed out of what fills his heart." Prayer is a heart that is flowing over with joy, thanksgiving, gratitude and praise. It is the abundance of a heart that is wide awake.
— *Teach Us to Pray,* Andre Louf (Contemporary)

Build yourselves up on your most holy faith; pray in the Holy Spirit; keep yourselves in the love of God; wait for the mercy of our Lord Jesus Christ unto eternal life. And convince some, who doubt; save some, by snatching them out of the fire; on some have mercy with fear, hating even the garment spotted by the flesh. Now to him who is able to keep you from falling and to present you without blemish before the presence of his glory with rejoicing, to the only God, our Savior through Jesus Christ our Lord, be glory, majesty, dominion, and authority, before all time and now and for ever. Amen. (Jude 20-25)

Keep me strong in the faith, Lord, so I may always live in Your presence.

DAY OF ORDINARY TIME 237

Private prayer is a lonely thing, the lonely person may take refuge in prayer, to affirm to himself that his loneliness is not the whole of reality. The lonely person may heal himself a little of the insanity with which his loneliness threatens him, by his contemplation of a universe whose mystery, whose

God, is the denial of loneliness.
— *The Experience of Prayer,* Kevin Maguire (Contemporary)

"When you see the desolating sacrilege spoken of by the prophet Daniel, standing in the holy place (let the reader understand), then let those who are in Judea flee to the mountains; let him who is on the housetop not go down to take what is in his house; and let him who is in the field not turn back to take his mantle. And alas for those who are with child and for those who give suck in those days! Pray that your flight may not be in winter or on a sabbath. For then there will be great tribulation, such as has not been from the beginning of the world until now, no, and never will be." (Matt. 24:15-21)

God of the Universe, all is Yours. I place all my trust in Your loving providence.

DAY OF ORDINARY TIME 238

Prayer is fundamentally a listening to God as He continually communicates His love to us at each moment. We pray when we are attentive to the presence of God, when we lift up our heart and our mind to God's communicating presence.
— *Prayer of the Heart,* George A. Maloney (Contemporary)

"If any one says to you, 'Lo, here is the Christ!' or 'There he is!' do not believe it. For false Christs and false prophets will arise and show great signs and wonders, so as to lead astray, if possible, even the elect. Lo, I have told you beforehand. So, if they say to you, 'Lo, he is in the wilderness,' do not go out; if they say, 'Lo, he is in the inner rooms,' do not believe it. For as the lightning comes from the east and shines as far as the west, so will be the coming of the Son of man. Wherever the body is, there the eagles will be gathered together." (Matt. 24:23-28)

When You come again, O Christ, You will come as judge of all. Help us prepare by leading good lives.

DAY OF ORDINARY TIME 239

There are indeed only two rules of prayer: Pray as the Holy Spirit would have you pray, which is another way of saying, Pray as you best can pray; and the other is, Go on praying.
— *Straight Course to God,* Augustine Morris (Contemporary)

"Immediately after the tribulation of those days the sun will be darkened, and the moon will not give its light, and the stars will fall from heaven, and the powers of the heavens will be shaken; then will appear the sign of the Son of man in heaven, and then all the tribes of the earth will mourn, and they will see the Son of man coming on the clouds of heaven with power and great glory; and he will send out his angels with a loud trumpet call, and they will gather his elect from the four winds, from one end to heaven to the other." (Matt. 24:29-31)

Lord, may we hear Your gentle call to service today. Then the final trumpet call will summon us to glory.

DAY OF ORDINARY TIME 240

When we pray, we affirm the bond of intimacy that exists between ourselves and God. Prayer draws us out of our narrow egos and toward the Divine Other. Everyone who longs for the Divine and seeks to transform his will has to follow the path of prayer.
— *The Journey Homeward,* Susan Muto (Contemporary)

"Watch therefore, for you do not know on what day your Lord is coming. But know this, that if the householder had known in what part of the night the thief was coming, he would have watched and would not have let his house be broken into. Therefore you also must be ready; for the Son of man is coming at an hour you do not expect." (Matt. 24:42-44)

Spirit of Light, teach us to watch patiently every day. Help us to expect Christ daily.

DAY OF ORDINARY TIME 241

Prayer may be defined simply as thinking about God and His will for the soul, in order to do His will. Such thinking leads to conversing with God.
— *The Venture of Prayer,* Hubert Northcott (Contemporary)

"Who then is the faithful and wise servant, whom his master has set over his household, to give them their food at the proper time? Blessed is that servant whom his master when he comes will find so doing. Truly, I say to you, he will set him over all his possessions. But if that wicked servant says to himself, 'My master is delayed,' and begins to beat his fellow servants, and eats and drinks with the drunken, the master of that servant will come on a day when he does not expect him and at an hour he does not know, and will punish him, and put him with the hypocrites; there men will weep and gnash their teeth." (Matt. 24:45-51)

May Your Church, O Christ, face the unknown future with hope and fidelity.

DAY OF ORDINARY TIME 242

Above all, prayer is a way of life which allows you to find a stillness in the midst of the world where you open your hands to God's promises, and find hope for yourself, your fellowman and the whole community in which you live. In prayer, you encounter God in the soft breeze, in the distress and joy of your neighbor and in the loneliness of your own heart.
— *Out of Solitude,* Henri J. M. Nouwen (Contemporary)

"The kingdom of heaven shall be compared to ten maidens who took their lamps and went to meet the bridegroom. Five of them were foolish, and five were wise. For when the foolish took their lamps, they took no oil with them; but the wise took flasks of oil with their lamps." (Matt. 25:1-4)

Make us ready each day, O Christ, for the unexpected. Give us the wisdom to prepare.

DAY OF ORDINARY TIME 243

It is sometimes said that the purpose of prayer is to bring God and man into communion with each other. But this is not achieved just by following the right techniques of prayer. What we can do, however, is to develop an openness in prayer that will make us more aware of the working of God within us. Prayer can help us remove the obstacles that blur our vision of God.
— *Taste and See,* William O. Paulsell (Contemporary)

"As the bridegroom was delayed, they all slumbered and slept. But at midnight there was a cry, 'Behold, the bridegroom! Come out to meet him.' Then all those maidens rose and trimmed their lamps. And the foolish said to the wise, 'Give us some of your oil, for our lamps are going out.' But the wise replied, 'Perhaps there will not be enough for us and for you; go rather to the dealers and buy for yourselves.' " (Matt. 25:5-9)

Bridegroom of our souls, fill us with a deep love for You so that we may always hear Your call to us.

DAY OF ORDINARY TIME 244

Whatever it is that evokes in us the statement or the cry: "I want to pray," we do want and need practical help to respond. And we know that the mere repetition of words, however beautiful, is not going to fill the bill. The cry comes from some deeper, some very deep part of our being, and we need to get in touch with that center and let our prayer arise from there.
— *Centering Prayer,* Basil Pennington (Contemporary)

"And while they went to buy, the bridegroom came, and those who were ready went in with him to the marriage feast; and the door was shut. Afterward the other maidens came also, saying, 'Lord, lord, open to us.' But he replied, 'Truly, I say to you, I do not know you.' Watch therefore, for you know neither the day nor the hour." (Matt. 25:10-13)

Open up our hearts, O God, so that we can welcome Your Son into our hearts and homes today.

DAY OF ORDINARY TIME 245

Prayer is dialogue with Jesus. . . . The important point is that we are invited to meet Jesus, to talk with Him, to love Him, so that we may be completely changed and united in a common endeavor.
— *The Christ Is Alive,* Michel Quoist (Contemporary)

"When the Son of man comes in his glory, and all the angels with him, then he will sit on his glorious throne. Before him will be gathered all the nations, and he will separate them one from another as a shepherd separates the sheep from the goats, and he will place the sheep at his right hand, but the goats at the left." (Matt. 25:31-33)

In my daily life, Lord, help me distinguish between good and bad ways of life. This is my only preparation for Your judgment.

DAY OF ORDINARY TIME 246

There is a lot of self-seeking even in our prayer. We do tend to look for consolation in our prayer, or at least some sign that we are really pleasing God

and getting closer to Him in some way. . . . It is for this reason dryness is painful.
— *Challenges in Prayer,* Basil Pennington (Contemporary)

"The King will say to those at his right hand, 'Come, O blessed of my Father, inherit the kingdom prepared for you from the foundation of the world; for I was hungry and you gave me food, I was thirsty and you gave me drink, I was a stranger and you welcomed me, I was naked and you clothed me, I was sick and you visited me, I was in prison and you came to me.' " (Matt. 25:34-36)

Lord, You will judge us on love. Make my love deep and genuine.

DAY OF ORDINARY TIME 247

Prayer requires nourishment from many sources. Prayer is a spiritual crop. It needs not only the good soil of an open heart, but the seedings of spiritual reading, the rains of grace, the fertilizer of good works, the weeding of self-denial, and the sun of consolation in its seasons. It even needs the drying winds of desolation to keep it from decaying into selfishness.
— *The Pilgrim Contemplative,* Herbert F. Smith (Contemporary)

"The righteous will answer him, 'Lord, when did we see thee hungry and feed thee, or thirsty and give thee drink? And when did we see thee a stranger and welcome thee, or naked and clothe thee? And when did we see thee sick or in prison and visit thee?' And the King will answer them, 'Truly, I say to you, as you did it to one of the least of these my brethren, you did it to me.' " (Matt. 25:37-40)

You call us to hospitality daily, O Jesus. Help me to go out to all I meet.

DAY OF ORDINARY TIME 248

Prayer is a natural, daily, ongoing event . . . it is fellowship with God, communion, if you find that word more real. It is entering into a relationship that God, out of the deep wisdom and love of His heart, desires; it is not nudging His elbow to do for me what I want, it is my utter readiness and humble desire to do what He wants.
— *Christianity Close to Life,* Rita Snowdon (Contemporary)

"He will say to those at his left hand, 'Depart from me, you cursed, into the eternal fire prepared for the devil and his angels; for I was hungry and you gave me no food, I was thirsty and you gave me no drink, I was a stranger and you did not welcome me, naked and you did not clothe me, sick or in prison and you did not visit me.' Then they also will answer, 'Lord, when did we see thee hungry or thirsty or a stranger or naked or sick or in prison, and did not minister to thee?' Then he will answer them, 'Truly, I say to you, as you did it not to one of the least of these, you did it not to me.' And they will go away into eternal punishment, but the righteous into eternal life." (Matt. 25:41-46)

Teach me to love as a child, Lord.

DAY OF ORDINARY TIME 249

Prayer is relationship in life, so the development of contemplative awareness, harmony, a sinking into Being, remains the crux of the matter.
— *Prayer: A New Encounter,* Martin Thornton (Contemporary)

I saw a new heaven and a new earth; for the first heaven and the first earth had passed away, and the sea was no more. And I saw the holy city, new Jerusalem, coming down out of heaven from God, prepared as a bride adorned for her husband; and I heard a loud voice from the throne saying, "Behold, the dwelling of God is with men. He will dwell with them, and they shall be his people, and God himself will be with them; he will wipe away every tear from their eyes, and death shall be no more, neither shall there be mourning nor crying nor pain any more, for the former things have passed away." And he who sat upon the throne said, "Behold, I make all things new." (Revelation 21:1-5)

When the end comes, O Christ, there will be no more sorrow. May we know Your peace forever.

DAY OF ORDINARY TIME 250

Prayer is the Father's will as the way for us to converse and work with Him. . . . By prayer we are united with the Son in His work of intercession to the Father.
— *Our Faith,* Max Thurian (Contemporary)

In the Spirit he carried me away to a great, high mountain, and showed me the holy city Jerusalem coming down out of heaven from God, having the glory of God, its radiance like a most rare jewel, like a jasper, clear as crystal. It had a great, high wall, with twelve gates, and at the gates twelve angels, and on the gates the names of the twelve tribes of the sons of Israel were inscribed; on the east three gates, on the north three gates, on the south three gates, and on the west three gates. And the wall of the city had twelve foundations, and on them the twelve names of the twelve apostles of the Lamb. (Revelation 21:10-14)

We praise You, Lord, and thank You for the treasure of our faith, which comes down to us from the apostles.

DAY OF ORDINARY TIME 251

Prayer is the means by which we find our rest in God and come to that divine oneness of action and will for which we yearn and which will lead us into eternal life.
— *The Life of Prayer,* Mary Clare Vincent (Contemporary)

I saw no temple in the city, for its temple is the Lord God the Almighty and the Lamb. And the city has no need of sun or moon to shine upon it, for the glory of God is its light, and its lamp is the Lamb. By its light shall the nations walk; and the kings of the earth shall bring their glory into it, and its gates shall never be shut by day — and there shall be no night there; they shall bring into it the glory and the honor of the nations. (Revelation 21:22-26)

Spirit of eternal light, enlighten our paths now, so that we may walk forever in Your light.

DAY OF ORDINARY TIME 252

Christian prayer is not constituted by the totality of adoration and gratitude and request offered by all Christians in their individuality but by that which they do together as this or that part of the Catholic Church. Private prayer is a secondary thing. That is not to say that it is not important but simply that it is derivative. It is a continuation of the common prayer of the believing community into the particular life of the individuals who compose it. It is the Church's thanking and offering translated into terms of the individual life each one of us is living.
— *The Use of Praying,* J. Neville Ward (Contemporary)

Then he showed me the river of the water of life, bright as crystal, flowing from the throne of God and of the Lamb through the middle of the street of the city; also, on either side of the river, the tree of life with its twelve kinds of fruit, yielding its fruit each month; and the leaves of the tree were for the healing of the nations. There shall no more be anything accursed, but the throne of God and of the Lamb shall be in it, and his servants shall worship him; they shall see his face, and his name shall be on their foreheads. And night shall be no more; they need no light of lamp or sun, for the Lord God will be their light, and they shall reign for ever and ever. (Revelation 22:1-5)

May Your people praise You for Your everlasting goodness.

DAY OF ORDINARY TIME 253

Real prayer is the uplifting of the soul to a Greater One. It is the opening of the soul to the All-Holy so He can enter and make himself at home.
— *Prayer Without Headaches,* Florence Wedge (Contemporary)

I John am he who heard and saw these things. And when I heard and saw them, I fell down to worship at the feet of the angel who showed them to me; but he said to me, "You must not do that! I am a fellow servant with you and your brethren the prophets, and with those who keep the words of this book. Worship God." And he said to me, "Do not seal up the words of the prophecy of this book, for the time is near. Let the evildoer still do evil, and the filthy still be filthy, and the righteous still do right, and the holy will still be holy." (Revelation 22:8-11)

All praise, honor, and glory to You, O Lord. May all Your people praise You forever.

DAY OF ORDINARY TIME 254

Christian prayer is the highest kind of prayer. It is a person's response to God's revelation of himself. This revelation includes the whole vision of God which the Bible contains, experiences of prophets and psalmists as well as the supreme revelation of God in Christ in the New Testament. The nature of God is the key to prayer. In other words, all our attempts at prayer are our efforts to respond — however imperfectly — to the God who is so gracious that He calls us to worship Him.
— *Prayer,* Olive Wyon (Contemporary)

"Behold, I am coming soon, bringing my recompense, to repay every one for what he has done. I am the Alpha and the Omega, the first and the last, the beginning and the end." Blessed are those who wash their robes, that they may have the right to the tree of life and that they may enter the city by the gates. (Revelation 22:12-14)

O God, You reward all goodness. Share with us the gifts of Your love today.

DAY OF ORDINARY TIME 255

Prayer is a person's instinctive response to the immediate experience of the Other within. It is a phenomenon arising from his compelling need to relate to this being who seeks him out, makes ultimate demands, but also forgives, accepts, and offers help.
— *Rediscovering Prayer,* John Yungblut (Contemporary)

I warn every one who hears the words of the prophecy of this book: if any one adds to them, God will add to him the plagues described in this book, and if any one takes away from the words of the book of this prophecy, God will take away his share in the tree of life and in the holy city, which are described in this book. He who testifies to these things says, "Surely I am coming soon." Amen. Come, Lord Jesus! The grace of the Lord Jesus be with all the saints. Amen. (Revelation 22:18-21)

Come, Lord Jesus, come to take us home with You. Amen.

OTHER BOOKS FOR YOUR READING PLEASURE:

HOMILIES —
> **FOR THE "A" CYCLE** *No. 722, cloth, $14.95*
> **FOR THE "B" CYCLE** *No. 723, cloth, $14.95*

by Rev. John Jay Hughes

Based on the conviction that people are looking for hope and for a meaning to life, these homilies proceed from real-life situations, applying the biblical message and the Church's teaching to the lives of those in the pews

THE SUNDAY READINGS
by Rev. Albert J. Nevins, M.M.

A timely and functional examination of the theme for each Sunday Mass and how the readings relate to that theme. Assists in making the Mass more meaningful. Contains all the readings for all three yearly cycles and feast days. *No. 734, paper, $5.95*

PRAYER BOOK OF THE BIBLE: Reflections on the Old Testament
by Rev. Peter M. J. Stravinskas

Highly devotional book written as a scriptural guide to daily living. Representative passages are used as a daily source of solace and hope. Ideal for a better understanding of the Bible. *No. 606, paper, $4.95*

A LAY PSALTER
by Msgr. John Sheridan

Over 80 complete Psalms with meditations. Foreword by Timothy Cardinal Manning. Perfect as a source of prayer and meditation! *No. 716, paper, $7.50*

THE CHURCH YEAR IN PRAYER
by Rev. Jerome Neufelder

Using the Revised Standard Version, this delightful book combines Scripture, the 2,000-year Christian tradition and a contemporary understanding of prayer in the setting of the liturgical year. Perfect for cultivating personal prayer and the interior life. *No. 729, paper, $7.95*